New Directions in Islamic Thought

New Directions in Islamic Thought

Exploring Reform and Muslim Tradition

Edited by Kari Vogt, Lena Larsen and Christian Moe

I.B. TAURIS
LONDON · NEW YORK

Published in 2009 by I.B.Tauris & Co Ltd
6 Salem Road, London W2 4BU
175 Fifth Avenue, New York NY 10010
www.ibtauris.com

In the United States and Canada distributed by Palgrave Macmillan, a division of St. Martin's Press, 175 Fifth Avenue, New York NY 10010

ISBN 978 1 84511 739 9

A full CIP record for this book is available from the British Library
A full CIP record for this book is available from the Library of Congress
Library of Congress catalog card: available

Typeset in Minion by Stilman Davis
Printed and bound in Great Britain by TJ International Ltd, Padstow, Cornwall

Contents

Credits

An earlier version of Zainah Anwar's chapter appeared under the title "Law-Making in the Name of Islam: Implications for Democratic Governance" in K.S. Nathan and Mohammad Hashim Kamali (eds), *Islam in Southeast Asia: Political, Social and Strategic Challenges for the 21st Century* (Singapore: Institute of Southeast Asian Studies, 2006), pp. 121–34. The updated and revised version is published here with the kind permission of the Institute of Southeast Asian Studies, Singapore (http://bookshop.iseas.edu.sg).

Khaled Abou El Fadl's chapter is adapted from parts of his book *Speaking in God's Name: Islamic Law, Authority and Women* (Oxford: Oneworld, 2001), © Khaled Abou El Fadl 2001.

A note on transliteration

Transliteration of Arabic words in this book follows the example of the *International Journal of Middle East Studies*. We distinguish between technical terms, on the one hand, and names and titles, on the other. Only italicised technical terms are fully transliterated, with diacritics indicating long vowels (*ā, ī, ū*) and emphatic consonants (*ḍ, ḥ, ṣ, ṭ, ẓ*). Names, book titles and similar are capitalised; diacritics are not used, but *ʿayn* and *hamza* are marked. (In the latter category fall words such as Qurʾan, Shiʿi, Sunni and Shariʿa.) The *tāʾ marbūṭa* and initial *hamza* are not transliterated and *ā* is used both with *alif* and *alif maqṣūra*.

Introduction

Kari Vogt, Lena Larsen and Christian Moe

All over the world, Muslims experience tensions between their roles as citizens and their religious affiliation and identity. Urged to respond to contemporary challenges, they often lack the requisite grounding in the Islamic sciences to criticise the tradition with confidence.

This book is concerned with the internal, constructive critiques that seek to address this gap by reformulating Islamic notions in a way consistent with modern understandings of equality, justice and pluralism. They are raised by Muslims with a religious commitment, who take seriously both the tradition they seek to reform and the modern human rights ethic, and who seek to develop coherent and principled justifications for reform. The searching questions they ask of both tradition and modernity, and the often subtle and complex answers they give, do not lend themselves to the easy affirmation of the superiority of a collective identity.

In this, their criticism of the traditional understanding of Islamic norms differs from much of the criticism of Islam that is widespread both in the Muslim world and in the West. Western media and policy circles currently give much attention to critics from a Muslim cultural background who make their often sweeping demands for religious reform from a secular modernist position rather than from a faith commitment. On the public scene of the Muslim world, on the other hand, those who gain prominence as voices of reform are often apologists who reaffirm restrictive religious norms in modern terms of rights and freedoms without caring what those terms entail. The religious reformist thinkers in this book take more complex positions and are therefore exposed to attacks from both sides.

There are many Muslim experts who are already committed to responding to the challenges of pluralist societies, but they are often isolated, lacking access to the main institutions reproducing and disseminating Islamic knowledge, or even the modest resources needed to meet among themselves and publish their findings. As Mehran Kamrava has noted, not only do they lack institutional support, but they are actively resisted, by at least three different forces: 1) religious establishments guarding the orthodoxies on which their own legitimacy rests, 2) state authorities hostile to any talk of democratic freedoms and 3) anti-Islamic voices gaining strength in the West.[1] The current international climate, especially since the tragedy of 11 September 2001, has only exacerbated these problems.

The increasingly strident calls for Islamic reform, then, are not matched by a willingness to listen attentively to reformist voices. As they touch upon sensitive issues, however, the opportunities for them to debate, publish and disseminate ideas are often limited. The longer the growth of these ideas is stunted, the less reformists will be able to make use of future opportunities that may open up when the political climate shifts.

The New Directions project

The project "New Directions in Islamic Thought and Practice" offered Muslim reform thinkers a forum where they could present and discuss their ideas and develop strategies for further action, according to their own agenda, in a broad intra-religious dialogue across traditions and disciplines. It was backed by the Oslo Coalition on Freedom of Religion or Belief, a coalition of experts and representatives from religious and other life-stance communities, academia, NGOs, international organisations and civil society. Based at the University of Oslo and funded by the Norwegian government, the Oslo Coalition carries out a number of projects to promote freedom of religion or belief worldwide.[2]

The project brought together some of the leading voices of Islamic reformism in some of the most pluralistic and dynamic institutions of Islamic thought during three international workshops in Yogyakarta, Indonesia (2004); Sarajevo, Bosnia-Herzegovina (2005); and Istanbul, Turkey (2007). It proved possible to have free, frank and friendly exchanges of views. We are grateful to the people and institutions who were our hosts and partners in this enterprise: Dr Amin Abdullah,

Dean of the State Islamic University (UIN) Sunan Kalijaga, Yogyakarta; Dr Enes Karić, Dean of the Faculty of Islamic Studies, Sarajevo; Dr M. Akif Aydın, director of the Center for Islamic Studies (ISAM), Istanbul; and their hard-working staff members, who went out of their way to make everything go smoothly. Our particular thanks go to Dr Ziba Mir-Hosseini (London) and Dr Fikret Karčić (University of Sarajevo), who formed the core of our international advisory group of Muslim scholars, helped to create a platform of ideas for the project, find partner institutions and identify speakers who should be invited, and kept our workshop sessions on track and the argument lively.

Most of this book has evolved out of thoughts originally presented and discussed in Yogyakarta, Sarajevo or Istanbul. It was often in the course of these discussions, as much as in the formal papers given, that issues were raised and emphases emerged that pointed to "new directions in Islamic thought". We were therefore compelled to solicit additional essays addressing these questions in greater depth specifically for this book. This added to the pressure of selection from the nearly forty workshop papers, not all of which could find their way into this volume. Our chosen focus has been on those contributions that we felt spoke most directly to present reformist concerns from an activist as well as an academic point of view. Responding to our wish to take stock of developments in reformist thought, many scholars offered fine retrospectives of developments in the Islamic disciplines, but we have included only those contributions that went on to draw normative conclusions pointing to ways forward.

The new reformist thinkers

Islamic thought has undergone periodic revivals and reformulations, encountering and assimilating the ideas of other cultures and traditions as it spread across the world. A movement of reform seeking to come to terms with the specific challenges of modernity and Western hegemony dates back at least to the early nineteenth century. The questions raised and approaches proposed by this first wave of modern reformers are still with us.

The contemporary reformist thought represented in this book, however, in our view represents a new wave, one that is responding to the new intellectual and political climate of the post-colonial second half of the twentieth century. Our workshop series showed it to bring new arguments to the debate, to cover a wide intellectual range and to establish itself as part of Muslim tradition.

As an intellectual enterprise, the current wave of Islamic reformism is many-stranded rather than a single trend or doctrine. Various methodologies are being tried out. The approaches represented in this book include: the identification of general objectives of the Shariʿa as a source and criterion of particular norms, the un-reading of patriarchal interpretations of the Qur'an, distinctions between the universal and the context-specific parts of the scriptural message, and the criticism of the extra-religious assumptions relied on by religious jurisprudence, such as theories of sexuality and natural gender differences.

These various approaches in the new reformist thought are informed by recent advances in the social and human sciences. Old texts are approached with a new hermeneutics that acknowledges the situated nature of interpretation and that favours the re-reading of Muslim intellectual heritage in its full breadth, rather than a positivist return to the sources. The research tools of modern sociology and anthropology are used to confront the idealist assumptions of traditional Islamic jurisprudence with the social realities under which Muslim men and women live.

Potentials and prospects

Contemporary reformism is a global discourse without one geographical centre. Many of the leading reformist thinkers, though, are based in Western countries, whether as exiles, as migrants in the global knowledge economy, or as native citizens. Here, the reformists' institutional opportunities – for academic posts, conferencing and publishing – are greater, and the key constraints – authoritarian states and religious establishments – are absent or weaker, while the new challenges faced by Muslims living as minorities in secular democracies place a premium on new ideas. A vibrant community of reformist scholars has sprung up in universities across North America. After 9/11, though, the environment has grown more hostile and security measures taken by Western governments for protection against Islamic radicals have also made problems for reformists.

Though they are published by Western university presses, the appeal of the new reformists should not be dismissed as being limited to a liberal Western non-Muslim audience. Our workshop in Indonesia, in particular, opened our eyes to how eagerly the works of our contributors and workshop speakers are read, translated, circulated and debated by an Islamic academic culture interested in cutting-edge ideas. Nor is it confined to the ivory tower. Muslim women's organisations, such as Sisters in Islam and Women Living Under Muslim Laws, search the scholarly reformist literature for arguments they can use in their struggle for gender justice on the ground.

This raises two points that we feel should be borne in mind when considering the future prospects for Islamic reform. Whether this reformist discourse will manage to establish itself and extend its influence, and perhaps even in time become the predominant interpretation of Islam, will depend on a number of social, political and economic factors, including the currently dire international relations between the West and the Muslim world. But, in this equation, there is one very simple, basic and permanent factor that is easily overlooked.

Our first point is that fifty per cent of the world's Muslims are women. The vast variation in cultural background, social situation, religious commitment and political outlook among Muslim women worldwide militates against generalisations. But women do have shared needs for transcending the traditional framework in order to realise their full equality before the law, whatever specific forms those needs take for women from different backgrounds and walks of life. This makes for a vast social base from which constituencies for reform can be built. As Muslim women increasingly enter higher education, the professions and politics, moreover, it seems inevitable that they will also play an increasing part in the production of Islamic knowledge. Certainly, the "women's question" will remain a central object of reformist concern. We find it likely that women's demands for change will also increasingly become a driving force for the adoption of reformist ideas.

Second, the contemporary discourse is grounded in the social activism that many of the new reformist thinkers, as public religious intellectuals, combine with their role as academics and, sometimes, religious leaders. Some work with grassroots organisations engaged in struggles for social justice, e.g. against gender or racial discrimination, or they develop their ideas in dialogue with such movements, which offer platforms and channels for reformist thought to reach broader segments of society. Despite attempts to dismiss or isolate them, then, reformist thinkers, both women and men, have in fact had a social impact over the past decades. This holds out hope that the new directions they stake out for Islamic thought today will be part and parcel of tomorrow's Islamic tradition.

Part One

The Changeable and the Unchangeable

1 The changeable and the unchangeable

Abdolkarim Soroush

The changeable and unchangeable in Islamic thought and practice is a topic with its own reformist lineage. About 45 years ago, there were articles written by a very prominent Muslim philosopher in Iran, namely Ayatollah ʿAllama Tabataba'i, the celebrated author of the *Tafsir al-Mizan*. The articles bore the title, "The Changeable and Unchangeable in Islamic Thought". ʿAllama Tabataba'i was a persistent reader of Rashid Rida, and those who have read his *Tafsir* will realise that to a very great extent he was under Rida's influence and had an eye on his arguments. Sometimes, perhaps most of the time, he opposed him, disliked his ideas and criticised him, but, nevertheless, he was always mindful of the arguments put forward by Rashid Rida. The idea of *al-thābit wa al-mutaḥawwil* or *al-thābit wa al-mutaghayyir*, the changeable and the unchangeable, can be found in Rida's writings.

I do not think any of our past prominent thinkers, such as al-Ghazali, Fakhr al-Din al-Razi, Nasir al-Din Tusi, and so on, have used the same categorisation, whether in the domain of *fiqh* (jurisprudence), or in philosophy, or elsewhere. I am not saying that they were negligent or ignorant of it, or that the idea of *ijtihād* (exerting one's utmost efforts to find the truth) was absent. To be sure, the notions of *mujtahid* and *ijtihād* were well known to everybody, both to the layman and the learned.

However, this very division or classification of Islamic thought in theory, or Islamic teachings in practice, into *al-thābit wa al-mutaḥawwil* is a very modern classification. This modern classification, of course, means that we, as Muslims, have encountered and faced some modern challenges and problems that have induced us to introduce this idea and this categorisation of the changing and unchanging.

The essential and the non-essential

Something in traditional *fiqh* which does comes very close to the idea of the unchangeable, of course, is the idea of *al-ḍarūrī*. The jurists divided *al-aḥkām*, the regulations, into two, the *ḍarūrī* and the non-*ḍarūrī*, the essential and the non-essential. There has always been debate and controversy about the instances of this *ḍarūrī*, the essential and the non-essential. Everybody agreed on the fact that there are essentials and non-essentials, in principle, but as to the application of the principle, i.e. determining what the essentials and the non-essentials are, there has always been a huge controversy both in the Shiʿi branch of Islam and the Sunni branch of Islam, to the extent that the idea has come under doubt. I mean to say that the words essential and non-essential have come to be somewhat loosely used, because everybody knows that it depends on individual taste or individual argument, rather than on a general, universal consensus.

The distinction between thought and practice is important here, because there are essentials in the domain of thought, and there are essentials in the domain of practice. For example, everybody says that prayer (*ṣalāh*) is essential, in the sense that it is one of the pillars of Islamic practice, so is the alms tax (*zakāh*) for example, and many other things. Essentials in the realm of thought and principles include: belief in the unity of God and belief in the prophethood of the Prophet Muhammad.

Then again, we are not very sure what falls under these essentials. The whole idea of apostasy hinges on this: If you reject one of the essentials, you are an apostate. Whether you will be considered an apostate, then, depends on what is to be counted as an essential and, since that is subject to great controversy, there will accordingly be further dispute and disagreement over the idea of apostasy. That is why it is not that simple to accuse somebody of being an apostate, i.e. of refusing their belief and rejecting Islam.

It may come as a surprise to learn that Ayatollah Khomeini – in his writings, debates and lectures in Qom as a Grand Marjaʿ, even before he became the leader of the Islamic Revolution – came very close to the idea that even rejecting the hereafter would not make you an apostate. He suggests it is sufficient that you believe in the unity of God and in the prophethood of the Prophet; if you so believe, you are a Muslim, even if you do not believe that there is a next life. Khomeini did not consider belief in an afterlife an essential.

I think both Muslims and non-Muslims would agree on the importance of the belief in the world after death, in the next life, in the punishment of God, in heaven and hell. It is everywhere in the Qur'an: you find more than a thousand verses in the Qur'an about life after death. Nevertheless, a Grand Mufti like Khomeini held this view. He did not hide it, but presented it in his books and let it be published, even after he became the Leader. It is clear that the idea of essentials varies from one *faqīh* to another, from one scholar to another, so there is no universal agreement on what is to be counted.

As to the essentials in practice, one may believe that pillars of Islam such as *ṣalāh*, prayer, *zakāh*, alms tax, etc., are all essentials and so, perhaps, is *ḥijāb* (the veil), for example. But according to Khomeini, who is very explicit on this point, someone today could say: "Yes, the Prophet has commanded us to say our prayers, to pay our *zakāh* and so on, but all these belong to his age, and we are not under this command any longer, and we are not the addressee of the sayings of the Prophet in this time." Even so, that person would be a perfect Muslim. He is not denying or rejecting any essentials, because he is endorsing the belief that the prophethood of Muhammad is intact and that he has ordered his followers to pray and pay *zakāh*. He is only saying that there are conditions attached to these matters and that now there may be new conditions.

I am only relating the ideas of Ayatollah Khomeini. I am sure that, if I were to make these claims, I would be accused of apostasy, but since the claims have the backing of a Grand Mufti, one will perhaps give it a second thought.

The discussion so far may all seem very theoretical, but a very clear and vivid historical example is the *jumʿa* (the Friday prayers). The Friday prayer is not prescribed in a *ḥadīth*, but in the Qur'an – everybody knows it: "… When the call is proclaimed to prayer on Friday, hasten earnestly to the Remembrance of Allah, and leave off business …" (62:9).

Now, the Shiʿites actually abandoned and cancelled this *jumʿa* prayer for twelve centuries. Even though it was in the Qur'an, even though everybody knew that the Prophet himself held the Friday prayers, and that the *khulafāʾ* (caliphs) held Friday prayers, the Shiʿites did not do it at all. It was not because they did not think that it was Islamic, and it was not because they did not think that it was an essential part of Islam. After all, the Shiʿi *fuqahāʾ* (jurists) were pious *ʿulimāʾ* (scholars), but they thought and argued that there are conditions for holding Friday prayers. For twelve centuries after the Twelfth Imam, they held that those conditions were not, and could not, be fulfilled. They thought that the Friday prayers should be held by the Islamic state, and, if there was no Islamic state, there would be no Friday prayer whatsoever. I am not saying that this argument was right, nor that it was wrong – I am only recalling a very important piece of the history of *fiqh* in Islam.

So, there are essentials and non-essentials, changeables and unchangeables, but exactly what those changeables and unchangeables are, is at the mercy of the *faqīh*, and not in a loose sense of the words: it depends on the arguments and conditions one puts forward and on the principles one goes along with. *Jumʿa* prayer offers a very vivid example, and there are other examples.

There are now jurists in Iran, grand jurists, who think that religious penalties, such as cutting off the hand of the thief, should not be applied at all. Some of these kinds of brutal physical punishment are in the Qurʾan and some are in the *ḥadīth*. Cutting off the hands of thieves is in the Qurʾan, not in a *ḥadīth*, and the text is very strong. Stoning is not in the Qurʾan, but of course, it is present in the *ḥadīth* and in the practice of Muslims. Nevertheless there are *fuqahāʾ* in Iran now, and there have been some in the past, who think that these punishments should not be applied: like the Friday prayer, their application depends on the state, and since we do not have an Islamic state in the sense that a Prophet or an Imam is the head of the state, all this should be cancelled and abandoned. This is not a reformist idea, it is held by the traditional jurists. They have their own arguments, distinguishing the essential from what is not essential.

So, though we share the idea of the *ḍarūrī* and the non-*ḍarūrī*, one should be very careful and be aware that the instances are very varied. They vary from one *faqīh* to another, each of whom has his own argument.

The ambiguous and the non-ambiguous

These were some examples of the archaeology, so to speak, of the problem of the changeable and unchangeable. To consolidate my argument, one important point to which I would like to draw your attention is this: we have the classification of the *āyāt* (verses) of the Qurʾan into *muḥkamāt* and *mutashābahāt*. It is found in the Qurʾan itself: "He it is Who has sent down to thee the Book: In it are verses *muḥkamāt*; they are the foundation of the Book: others are *mutashābahāt*" (3:7).

A very loose translation of these terms, on which we might provisionally agree, is the ambiguous and the non-ambiguous. The non-ambiguous verses (*muḥkamāt*) are the foundation or central part of the book – literally, the Mother of the Book (*umm al-kitāb*). The ambiguous verses (*mutashābahāt)*, the ones that are not *muḥkamāt*, form the rest of the book. There have been many interpretations of which verses are the *muḥkamāt* and which the *mutashābahāt*. Strangely enough, this verse, which is supposedly one of the non-ambiguous ones, has received many different interpretations. Tabataba'i said that "this verse is no doubt among the *muḥkamāt*." But why and how can we say that? That is his view about the interpretation of this verse, but there are at least twenty other views. This surprising fact is very telling and we have to draw a lesson from it.

This too has a clear bearing on the point at hand here. We all agree that there are *muḥkamāt*, to be sure, and there are *mutashābahāt*, but which verses are which, exactly? That, again, is at the mercy of the interpretation of the commentators of the Qur'an. Ever since the first commentators, like al-Tabari, down to the present age, one will see that there have been many differences and disagreements among them. Some people have said that the verses about God and His attributes are *mutashābahāt*. Some people have said that only the verses about the religious rituals are *muḥkamāt*. Some said that only the letters at the beginning of some suras are *mutashābahāt*, the rest are *muḥkamāt*, and so on and so forth. As with the essentials and the non-essentials, again we have a classification into two kinds of verses. In principle we all agree on the classification, but when it comes to its application in practice, we disagree – it depends on the individual commentator or interpreter.

One lesson or implication I would like to draw from this is that, ontologically speaking, there are no *muḥkamāt* and *mutashābahāt*. There is nothing ambiguous or non-ambiguous, changeable or unchangeable, as things *per se*. The distinction is epistemological or hermeneutical, that is to say, for each one of us some things are changeable and some are non-changeable, some *āyāt* are *muḥkamāt* and some are *mutashābahāt*. To put it another way, it is in the process and in the context of interpretation that *muḥkamāt* and *mutashābahāt* are distinguished from each other, that the changeable and unchangeable actually emerges. It is not already given. We cannot say that God has revealed some ambiguous verses to his Prophet and some non-ambiguous ones. That is not the case. In the process of interpretation, that is, for us, some verses emerge as ambiguous ones and some as non-ambiguous. For me as an individual, some verses are ambiguous and some non-ambiguous; another person would draw the line between them differently. It is exactly the same as with the changeable and unchangeable.

The metaphorical and the literal

Another example, which is again important in the process of interpretation, is the distinction between the metaphorical and the non-metaphorical. To be sure, there was a small group of commentators in Islamic history who thought that God only speaks literally and does not use metaphors. Indeed, they thought that it would be a shortcoming on the part of God if he took refuge in metaphorical pictures, because He does not need to, being all-powerful and able to use language in whatever way he wants in order to convey his message. However, that was only a small group. The rest of the commentators, as far as I know, all agree that there are allegorical and metaphorical discourses in the Qur'an as well as literal ones.

Again, in principle we agree that there are metaphors. For example, in the context of the next life, the Qur'an speaks of "a Day that will make children hoary-headed" (73:17). They say that this is a metaphorical way of saying what a hard day it will be, that people will suffer such a hardship that small children become like old men. There are many other instances of metaphorical expressions in the Qur'an, and it is no wonder that we find them there. The Qur'an is after all very poetic; the Qur'an is a higher poetry, one might say.

But again, what exactly are those verses in which metaphors have been used, and what are the verses that we have to take only in their literal meaning? Is there a fixed group or class of verses which are to be interpreted literally and a fixed class of verses which are to be interpreted metaphorically? Again, ontologically speaking, there is no such thing: the question is epistemological or hermeneutical. The distinction is something that emerges in the process and in the context of interpretation.

The ocean of interpretation

By interpreting, a metaphorical interpretation or a literal interpretation is created. In the process of interpretation you distinguish the essential and the non-essential, the *muḥkamāt* and the *mutashābahāt*. It is by interpreting that you create the changeable and the unchangeable. The whole history of *fiqh* and the whole history of Qur'anic interpretation demonstrates this fact: there has been no fixed set of changeables and unchangeables, no fixed set of *muḥkamāt* and *mutashābahāt*.

The principle that I have followed as my main thesis in Islamic and Qur'anic interpretation, and which I have elaborated extensively in my books, can be summed up in a very simple sentence: Islam is nothing but a series of interpretations of Islam.

Likewise, Christianity is nothing but a series of interpretations of Christianity, and so on and so forth. For the same reason and by the same token, in the Bible, there are *muḥkamāt* and *mutashābahāt*; in Rumi, a mystic poet, there are *muḥkamāt* and *mutashābahāt*. These are texts, after all, and you have to interpret them. The very act of interpretation produces *muḥkamāt* and *mutashābahāt*, literal and metaphorical interpretations.

The nature of interpretation is that it is ongoing, that it changes. It cannot be arrested. It is not up to any particular body. One will find this to be the case wherever there is a set of fixed principles and a class of interpreters, but when I say that everything is contingent on interpretation, this does not necessarily mean that interpretations will diverge. Sometimes they converge. In the case of the five daily prayers, for example, all the interpretations actually do draw together.

Therefore, when we talk about interpretations, it does not mean that sooner or later, we will come up with bizarre ideas about the prayers or about *zakāh*. It does not mean a chaotic process. It is not by any means chaotic, because the texts, the principles, the methodology and the consensus of the community of scholars, all underlie the process of interpretation. There is a tradition of interpretation because there is a convergence of interpretation.

It also does not mean that there are no true and false interpretations. You can argue that your own interpretation is true, and that mine is false. We can have this argument on the individual level but, sociologically, science is a collective enterprise. It is not about my personal ideas, or anybody else's personal ideas, but the ideas of the community of believers. In the community of believers, everyone puts forward his own ideas, interpretations and theories. Looking at the community and the tradition in history, we see that some interpretations have been more resistant to criticism and refutation. These ideas are now prevalent and form orthodoxy. There are principles and methodologies underlying the process of interpretation, then, and there is a convergence of interpretations, and there is a collective enterprise that forms an orthodoxy. None of this annuls the idea of interpretation. Understanding is dependent on interpretation, just as all colours depend on light.

So we are immersed in an ocean of interpretations. If you put forward another interpretation, you are immersing yourself more and more into that ocean. Let us not talk about the text. Let us talk about the interpretation of the text, for that is what we gain from the text. The interpretation is what is available to us, not the text itself.

We agree on the categories, but let us not be dogmatic about their application, because the application of the essential and non-essential, the changeable and unchangeable, has been a matter of dispute and disagreement among Muslims. But there is one absolute essential and one unchangeable. That is the *Kitāb* (book) and the *Sunna*. In order to be a Muslim, you always have to refer to the *Kitāb* and the *Sunna*. The prophethood of the Prophet, and the *Kitāb*, and the *Sunna*: these are the unchangeable, the essential. As to the rest, they are always subject to interpretation.

2 "Hold(ing) fast by the best in the precepts" – The Qur'an and method

Asma Barlas

To speak of the changeable and unchangeable in Islamic thought or practice is to speak of the universal and the particular, since what is unchangeable in religious contexts is generally the universal, while what is particular passes away. To delineate the two, one must consider the relationship between revelation and history, and thus between sacred and secular time.[1]

I will begin, then, by speaking about these relationships, but only in passing, both because this is such a brief essay and also because the Qur'an as divine discourse (the unchangeable, or universal) already incorporates within it the reality of the Qur'an as text, by which I mean, following Paul Ricoeur,[2] a discourse fixed by writing and interpreted by us in time and space (the changeable, or particular). Thus, even though divine discourse and its interpretations are not the same, the Qur'an unsettles neat binaries between the changeable and unchangeable, between the universal and particular, and between sacred and secular time, obliging us to rethink the relationships between them in a more complex manner.

Although I will attempt to do that here, it will only be in the context of my argument that the Qur'an itself enables continually evolving thought and practice as long as we read it in contextually appropriate ways. My real purpose is to suggest such a method for reading it and, in so doing, to demonstrate the centrality of an anti-patriarchal Qur'anic hermeneutics to a praxis of liberation.

The changeable and the unchangeable

As a Muslim, I believe – indeed, must believe – that revelation is unchangeable in the sense that it is enduring and universal, but what endures only acquires meaning within some vector of time and not outside it, and even the universal manifests itself in time. Sacred and secular time may not be synchronic, as the Qur'an makes clear, but time is nevertheless an identifiable marker of our relationship to God.[3] Thus, revelation occurs in the context of an unfolding human history, and it is partly this quality that makes it both universal and particular. It is particular because it addresses us in the immediacy of our lives, and it is universal because it remains relevant to each of those moments in our lives throughout time.

Indeed, one could argue that what makes revelation universal is its timeliness (relevance to history) and not its timelessness (ahistoricity); and, going further, that because it occurs in time, revelation is itself open to historicisation.[4]

This principle applies also to the Qur'an inasmuch as one cannot "proceed to the abidingness of the Qur'an, in word and meaning [without proceeding] from its historical ground and circumstance".[5] In other words, we cannot recontextualise the Qur'an – make it relevant to all historical contexts, hence universal – without first contextualising or historicising it. And yet there is a paradoxical tendency among Muslims, which is to recognise the historical contexts of Qur'anic *āyāt* (verses) but to dehistoricise the Qur'an, because of their conviction that what renders the Qur'an sacred is its ahistoricity rather than its transhistoricity. In part, this belief stems from the mistaken view that historicising the Qur'an's contexts also means historicising its contents.[6]

This incoherent position has engendered a lasting problem in Qur'anic exegesis: the tendency to universalise particular Qur'anic injunctions, a practice that has had specially injurious consequences for women, as Amina Wadud[7] has argued.

Ironically, the same Muslims who deny the relevance of history to (re)reading the Qur'an also draw on history to defend readings of the Qur'an by the first Muslim community because of its proximity in historical time to the Prophet. Thus it is in the name of sacred history that the thought and practice of the first Muslims is declared paradigmatic and unchangeable, and it is temporal distance from this community, and from an arbitrarily closed canon, that defines what is changeable or innovative (*bid'a*), hence non-normative, in religious thought.

Time is thus used to demarcate the changeable and the unchangeable and the enterprise of history is employed to defend the Qur'an's sacredness. This simultaneous denial and embrace of historicity is used to argue against change. As I have argued in another context,[8] it is also used to defend a Qur'anic exegesis that dates from medieval times and tends to be patriarchal.

There is a second sense in which I, as a Muslim, believe – indeed, must believe – that the Qur'an is unchangeable, and this is in the sense that it is unalterable. But what is unalterable is only so in the sense that it cannot be undone. Thus, divine discourse is unalterable because it has already been expressed through a speech act of the Prophet;[9] it is not unchangeable in the sense that its meanings are fixed or monosemic. No speech act, or text, has only one set of meanings, and certainly not a discourse as rich and complex as revelation, as the Qur'an itself affirms.[10]

Yet, there is another paradoxical tendency among Muslims, which is to admit the inexhaustibility of revelation, but to insist that only one reading of the Qur'an is authentic. And this reading, as I have just noted, has patriarchalised our understanding of Islam by declaring God to be partial to men and to male authority over women. I have challenged the patriarchal[11] epistemology of such readings elsewhere; here, I will offer only an indirect critique by defining an alternative method to read the Qur'an that does not reduce it to a partisan text.

Approaching the Qur'an

This method, which I derive from the Qur'an's own hermeneutics, rests on four principles relating to theology, methodology, ethics and authority. I will clarify them only very briefly here.

The theological principle states that since our understanding of God's word can not be independent of our understanding of God, we must seek the hermeneutic keys for reading the Qur'an in the nature of divine self-disclosure.[12] The three aspects of God's self-disclosure that I have explored in my own work are God's Unity (*Tawḥīd*), Justice (defined negatively as not doing *ẓulm* to anyone by transgressing against their rights),[13] and Unrepresentability. Each of these principles, militates against a patriarchalised view of God as well as theories of male privilege that suggest affinities between Islam and patriarchy.

The doctrine of *Tawḥīd* maintains that God's rule brooks no intermediaries, much less other rulers. Inasmuch as men set themselves up as intermediaries, rulers, or guardians over women, I believe they also violate an essential tenet of *Tawḥīd*. Similarly, the exclusion of *ẓulm* from divine self-definition serves as an argument against patriarchies which habitually transgress against women's rights, thus doing *ẓulm* to them. As such, we can only project patriarchy into the Qur'an at the cost of ascribing *ẓulm* to God. The Qur'an's prohibition against representing

God, on the other hand, undercuts the homo-social heresy that a masculinised God has a special affinity with men.

This is, of course, a simplified version of my argument and my point is merely to show that basing our readings of the Qur'an on a theologically sound view of God opens up infinite, and infinitely liberating, ways of encountering scripture.

A second component of an anti-patriarchal hermeneutics is a methodological one, and it derives from the Qur'an's injunctions to privilege its foundational *āyāt* over the allegorical and to read it as a whole. The emphasis on holism is crucial given the severity of the Qur'an's own warning against dividing it into "arbitrary parts" or making it "into shreds" (15:89–93), that is, reading it selectively or piecemeal.

Read as a whole and with attention to its foundational *āyāt*, the Qur'an provides no basis for claiming that men are ontologically superior to women, even if by a single degree, or are guardians over women, or can beat disobedient wives, or marry at will, contrary to popular readings of the so-called misogynistic verses that hinge on forcing single meanings onto single words or phrases.[14]

The third component of this method is an ethical one and it derives from two Qur'anic verses: one in which God instructs Moses to "enjoin Thy people to hold fast by the best in the precepts" (7:145); and another which says that "Those who listen to the Word and follow the best [meaning] in it … are the ones whom God has guided, and … endued with understanding" (39:18).

The Qur'an itself, then, establishes that not all its readings may be appropriate and it places on its readers the moral responsibility of judging between their contextual legitimacy by selecting only the best, which it leaves to us to define. In addition to demonstrating that revelation is inherently polysemic (of many meanings), the concept of "the best" also suggests the need for continual reinterpretation, given that our ideas of what is the best are historically contingent, hence liable to change.

Emphasising the best also shows that hermeneutic and existential questions are connected, since, to be able to choose between readings, one must minimally have the freedom to engage in open and rational debate, which is impossible in anti-democratic and repressive societies and communities.

The last aspect of the hermeneutics I am describing impinges on the notion of authority, specifically on who is authorised to interpret scripture. Historically, of course, only male scholars and socially sanctioned interpretive communities have interpreted the Qur'an. However, the text itself calls on each one of us to use our own intellect and reasoning, *ʿaql* and *ʿilm*, to decipher its *āyāt*. Significantly, in the Qur'an, *ʿaql* and *ʿilm* are not a function of literacy, much less of scholarship and, indeed, it is unambiguous in stating that it came also for the unlettered Bedouin in the desert (another sense in which it is universal).

In effect, the authority to interpret the Qur'an derives from the Qur'an itself, not from public sanction, or reason, or existing structures of interpretive authority among Muslims. In fact, the structure of Muslim authority and public reason have effectively closed off the Qur'an to fully half the *umma* (community), the women. The irony of this only emerges when one recalls the tradition that the Qur'an became the only scripture to address women (33:35) after Umm Salama dared to ask why it was not addressing them as it was still being revealed to the Prophet. The unchangeable changed to embrace the concerns of a woman!

I have always viewed this as a teaching moment in a divine pedagogy[15] that, meant to provide a lasting lesson to the *umma* by opening up the space for Umm Salama's question – I assume God gave her the grace to ask it. Indeed, it offers several lessons, some of which I have drawn out elsewhere.[16] To these I will add some new ones here, by way of a conclusion.

Unending lessons

The lessons I want to stress are pertinent to the issues I have discussed in this essay, which began as an engagement with philosophical issues and seems to be ending up as a homily.

For one thing, the timeliness of Umm Salama's question renders it timeless since her particular concern, why the Qur'an was not addressing women, has become a universal one for Muslim women today as the Qur'an appears to remain silent on many issues of pressing concern to us. I believe this is because throughout our history, women have been kept from asking questions of it, much less from interrogating it in the spirit of Umm Salama. Instead, a class of self-appointed, male intermediaries has inserted itself between the Qur'an and women, buttressed by public reason and communal authority. However, as Umm Salama's example shows, if women do not directly engage the scripture, they also cannot expect it to be responsive to our needs.

Second, God's responsiveness to her confirms that questioning the scripture as a woman is a divinely sanctioned right. I make this point because the same *umma* that venerates Umm Salama also denigrates women's readings of the Qur'an on the pretext that they are a Western form of feminism grafted onto Islam that incites gender warfare. But, the first woman to interrogate the Qur'an was neither engaged in a gender war, nor was she a Westerner or a feminist; nor, indeed, was she a scholar, but the Prophet did not therefore silence her.

To me, the lessons are clear: men cannot claim the Qur'an as their own, because the Qur'an has been opened to women for all times and only women can answer for their understanding of it on the Day of Dīn. Nor can only scholars have the right to interpret the Qur'an, because it came also for the unschooled. Nor indeed can public reason become the sole basis for defining Islam, because public reason has proven to be misogynistic, patriarchal and resistant to change. Rather, each believer must struggle to understand scripture themselves by means of whatever grace has been given them by God; this is their vocation as Muslims.

These are also the lessons that, I believe, should guide our explorations of the changeable and unchangeable. The Qur'an tells us that everything will perish but the face of God (28:88, 55:26–7). Hence that is the only unchangeable in Islamic thought and practice – all else is changeable and will pass, whether we will it to or not. This certainty should liberate us from a "fear of freedom"[17] and allow us to embrace a universe of unthought possibilities.

3 Law and ethics in Islam – The role of the *maqāṣid*

Mohammad Hashim Kamali

It is due to their relevance to real-life issues of vital concern to people's welfare that the *maqāṣid* (goals and purposes of Shariʿa) have become the focus of attention in recent decades, as is attested by numerous scholarly works, books and conferences that have concentrated on developing this important, yet somewhat neglected, chapter of the Shariʿa. The five essential goals of Shariʿa are life, intellect, religion, property and family, and the commitment to protect them; this shows clearly that the *maqāṣid* are concerned with priorities of the first order in almost any legal tradition, including the Shariʿa. The *maqāṣid* provide the judge and jurist with tools to validate measures they may take to protect the underlying values of the law. This is a different approach from the methodology of legal reasoning that is offered by the science of the sources of law, the *uṣūl al-fiqh*, which encourages legal reasoning and *ijtihād* through the application of certain methodologies. The latter approach can be indirect and fairly distant to one's purpose. In its long history of development, the methodology of *uṣūl al-fiqh* has also become somewhat burdened with technicality and literalism, as I shall explain in the following pages.

The fresh focus on *maqāṣid* is due also to a general awareness that the methodologies of *uṣūl al-fiqh* and *ijtihād* are on the whole predicated on medieval social values, retrospective and slow to relate effectively to the modern processes of adjudication and law making. To speak of *ijmāʿ* (general consensus), *qiyās* (analogical reasoning) and *istiḥsān* (juristic preference), for instance, involves engaging in a great deal of technicality and fulfilling a series of difficult conditions. The *maqāṣid* are inherently dynamic by comparison and capable of evolution in tandem with the changing conditions of society.

And lastly, the *maqāṣid* also resonate more strongly with the advancement of essential human rights. The Muslim world is currently witnessing growing support for international human rights law and the *maqāṣid* are seen to be offering a preferable approach to that of the *uṣūl* methodologies in that respect.

In his articulation of the theory of *maqāṣid* in the fourteenth-century Andalus, al-Shatibi (d. 1388) was motivated by his vision of unity in the face of the ever-widening scope of disagreement among Muslim schools and jurists, and set himself the task to bring them closer by focusing on the broader objectives and principles of Shariʿa. Al-Shatibi believed that the prevalently unitarian impulse of Shariʿa was being diluted by excessive scholastic and sectarian disagreements.[1]

Through the development of his theory of *maqāṣid*, al-Shatibi strove to achieve two major objectives, one ethical and the other legal. His ethical purpose was to sensitise the individual to the meaning and purpose of Shariʿa, so that he might become a self-motivated person who would internalise the purposes of the law and become a willing carrier of its values. Al-Shatibi's second purpose was to promote unity in the *corpus juris* of the Shariʿa, so that the jurist and practitioner might be guided by an integrated vision of its goals and purposes.[2]

Al-Shatibi successfully articulated his pioneering work, but it took much longer than he had hoped to bring about the desired unity in the corpus of Shariʿa. This unity remained tenuous and became even more so with the collapse of the Ottoman caliphate and the division of the *umma* into a multiplicity of nation-states, each with constitutions and laws of their own. The *maqāṣid al-sharīʿa* thus remained a marginalised prospect until the mid-twentieth century, when they gained a fresh momentum. The *maqāṣid* were seen once again to be instrumental in bringing internal coherence to the *corpus juris* of Islamic law and reducing disagreement not only between the established schools of law, but also between the more recent traditionalist and revivalist tendencies that the Muslim world has experienced even beyond the confines of law and jurisprudence.

It is naturally important that the law and legal reason are informed by a sense of direction and a purpose they seek to realise. It is also meaningful for the law enforcement agencies, the litigants and the judge, to have a clear vision of the interests and objectives they seek to serve. People often know the *ḥukm* (injunction) of the Shariʿa without knowing its *ḥikma* (wisdom and purpose, synonymous with *maqṣad*, sing. of *maqāṣid*). It was knowledge of the *ḥikma* and the insight it conveyed, as Rashid Rida (d. 1935) rightly noted, that enabled the Companions of the Prophet to act as jurists and judges in remote territories and cultural settings and still have the ability to respond to the people's needs.[3]

'Ubayd Allah Sindhi (d. 1944) observed that the law was not eternal, but the goal and wisdom embodied in it created in man the ability to think and to change himself in accordance with his inner motivation and insight. Life needs for its purposes that there be both a code of law and an awareness of the goals and purposes it pursues. If the code of law and its purposes go hand in hand, social harmony and better enforcement can be realised.[4] The *ḥikma* and the *maqṣad* thus pave the way for a progressive *fiqh*. However, when the *fiqh* is isolated from its goals, its ability to improve understanding is diminished.

Definition of maqāṣid

Classical texts on *uṣūl al-fiqh* do not provide a clear definition of *maqāṣid*, nor do they provide a methodology for their identification. Even al-Shatibi, who gave the *maqāṣid* a new profile, did not attempt to define them, although he did address the identification of *maqāṣid*. 'Allal al-Fasi (d. 1974) defined the *maqāṣid* as "the goals and purposes of Shari'a and the hidden wisdom (*al-asrār*) the Lawgiver has considered in the enactment of all of its rulings".[5] This is a sound definition except for the use of *al-asrār* which characterises the *maqāṣid* as secrets, whereas the Shari'a and its *maqāṣid* are premised on openness and accessibility, even though some of its rules and purposes may require verification and may be less than self-evident. The definition thus raises the question whether all the *maqāṣid* consist of *asrār*! Ibn 'Ashur (d. 1973) has given a more detailed but complex definition of *maqāṣid*. Here I will only discuss his comments on the requirements of a *maqṣad*. For a concept to qualify as a *maqṣad* it must be firm and permanent (*thābit*, *min ghayr zawāl*), as well as evident (*ẓāhir*), general (*'āmm*) and exclusive (*ṭard*).[6] A *maqṣad* must apply, in other words, to all that it can apply to, without constraints of time and circumstance. A hidden concept that is not provable by evidence, or one that is prone to convergence and confusion with other concepts would not qualify. A *maqṣad* should also be constant in that it is not liable to change in time and place and it should be distinctive, self-contained and exclusive.

Ahmad al-Raysuni similarly defined the *maqāṣid* as "goals and objectives for whose realisation the Shari'a has been enacted for the benefit of [God's] servants".[7] Another reviewer, 'Iwad al-Qarni, has modified this definition to say that the *maqāṣid* of Shari'a are goals and objectives that the Shari'a seeks to realise for the people's benefit in this world and the next.[8] The *maqāṣid* of Shari'a, in other words, include the benefits of 'people' (*al-khalq*) generally instead of 'servants' (*al-'ibād*), which might imply only the Muslims, and are concerned with the people's benefits in this life and the next.

This definition is in line, it seems, with Ibn Taymiyya's (d. 1328) definition of the *maqāṣid*, although he may not have articulated it as such. His commentator, Khalid al-Daris, wrote that Ibn Taymiyya saw the *maqāṣid* as "goals, both general and specific, intended by the Lawgiver for the benefits of His servants in their religious and temporal affairs".[9] The *maqāṣid* thus vary in their scope and subject matter in that they can be either general or specific and may promote people's benefits (*maṣāliḥ*) in this world or the next, but they apply to humanity at large and not only to faith communities or followers of the revealed religions.

History of maqāṣid

Historically the *maqāṣid* represent a belated development in the juristic legacy of the leading schools (*madhāhib*). Even to this day, many a reputable textbook of *uṣūl al-fiqh* does not include the *maqāṣid* in its usual coverage of topics. This is due partly to the nature of the subject, which is concerned with the philosophy and purpose of the law rather than the specific formulations of its text. The Qur'an has not always declared the goals and purposes of its laws, and Muslim jurists were reluctant to articulate them for fear of indulgence in speculation. Although the *maqāṣid* are obviously relevant to juristic reconstruction and *ijtihād*, they have not received due attention in the conventional expositions of the theory of *ijtihād*. It was not until the time of al-Ghazali (d. 1111) and then al-Shatibi that significant developments were made in the formulation of the theory of *maqāṣid*.

The basic outlook that was advocated by the notion of *maqāṣid* was not denied by the leading schools, yet it remained on the fringes of juristic thought. Except for the Zahiri school, which maintained that the *maqāṣid* are only known when they are identified and declared by the clear text, the majority did not confine the *maqāṣid* to the clear text, but held that they could be found either in the clear text or in the rationale and effective cause (*'illa*) of the text. To understand the cause and rationale of a legal text was thus thought to be another way of seeing its goal and purpose, for the majority understood the Shari'a to be rational and goal oriented, with its rules generally founded in identifiable causes. A mere conformity to rules that went against the purpose and outlook of Shari'a was, therefore, considered unacceptable.[10] Thus we note differences of orientation among the leading schools toward the *maqāṣid*: some were more open to it than others, but elaboration of the goals and objectives of the Shari'a was generally not encouraged.

The term *maqāṣid* was initially used in the writings of Abu 'Abd Allah al-Tirmidhi al-Hakim (d. 932) and recurrent references to it appeared in the works of Imam al-Haramayn al-Juwayni (d. 1085), who was probably the first to classify the *maqāṣid* into the three categories of essential, complementary and desirable (*ḍarūriyyāt*, *ḥājiyyāt*, *taḥsīniyyāt*), which has gained general acceptance ever since. Al-Juwayni noted that the Prophet's Companions showed a high level of awareness of the objectives of the Shariʿa and added that "one who did not ponder over the *maqāṣid* of the commands and prohibitions did so at one's peril and was likely to lack insight into the Shariʿa".[11] Al-Juwayni's ideas were developed further by his pupil, Abu Hamid al-Ghazali, who was generally critical of *maṣlaḥa* (public interest) as a proof of law, but validated it if it promoted the *maqāṣid* of Shariʿa. As for the *maqāṣid* themselves, al-Ghazali wrote categorically that the Shariʿa pursued five objectives, namely those of religion, life, intellect, property and lineage.[12]

A number of prominent writers continued to contribute to the *maqāṣid*. Fakhr al-Din al-Razi (d. 1208), the author of *al-Mahsul*, and Sayf al-Din al-Amidi (d. 1233), the author of *al-Ihkam*, identified the *maqāṣid* as criteria of preference (*al-tarjīḥ*) among conflicting analogies and they elaborated an internal order of priorities among the various classes of *maqāṣid*. Amidi also confined the essential *maqāṣid* to only five. Incidental references were made to *maqāṣid* in the context of the effective cause (*ʿilla*) of *ḥukm* in the construction of analogy (*qiyās*). The Maliki jurist, Shihab al-Din al-Qarafi (d. 1285) added a sixth to the existing list, namely the protection of honour (*al-ʿirḍ*), and this was endorsed by Taj al-Din ʿAbd al-Wahhab Ibn al-Subki (d. 1370) and later by Muhammad Ibn ʿAli al-Shawkani (d. 1834).

The list of five values was evidently based on a reading of the relevant parts of the Qurʾan on prescribed penalties (*ḥudūd*). The value that each of these penalties sought to vindicate and defend was consequently identified as an essential value. The latest addition (i.e. *al-ʿirḍ*) was initially thought to have been covered under lineage (*al-nasl*, also *al-nasab*), but al-Qarafi explained that the Shariʿa had enacted a separate punishment for slanderous accusation (*al-qadhf*) which justified the addition.[13] ʿIzz al-Din ʿAbd al-Salam al-Sulami's (d. 1262) renowned work, *Qawaʿid al-Ahkam*, was in his own characterisation a work on *maqāṣid al-aḥkām* (purposes of injunctions) and addressed the various aspects of *maqāṣid* especially in relationship to *ʿilla* and *maṣlaḥa* in greater detail. Thus he wrote at the outset of his work that the greatest of all the objectives of the Qurʾan was to facilitate benefits (*maṣāliḥ*) and the means that secure them, and that the realisation of benefits also included the prevention of evil.[14]

Ibn Taymiyya was probably the first to depart from the notion of confining the *maqāṣid* to a specified number and added, to the existing list of *maqāṣid*, such themes as fulfilment of contracts; preservation of the ties of kinship; honouring the rights of one's neighbour, in so far as the affairs of this world are concerned; and love of God, sincerity, trustworthiness and moral purity, in relationship to the hereafter.[15] Ibn Taymiyya thus revised the scope of *maqāṣid* from a designated list into an open-ended order of values and his approach is now generally accepted by contemporary commentators, including Muhammad ʿAbid al-Jabiri, Ahmad al-Raysuni, Yusuf al-Qaradawi and others.[16] Al-Qaradawi has further extended the list of *maqāṣid* to include social welfare support (*al-ṭakāful*), freedom, human dignity and human fraternity among the higher objectives of Shari'a.[17] Jamal al-Din 'Atiyya further expanded the range and identified 24 *maqāṣid* which he then classified under four headings: *maqāṣid* that are of concern to the individual, to the family, to the *umma* and to humanity at large.[18]

It would appear from this analysis that the *maqāṣid* remain open to further enhancement which will depend, to some extent, on the priorities of every age. I propose to add protection of the fundamental rights and liberties, economic development, research and development in technology and science, as well as peaceful coexistence among nations to the structure of *maqāṣid*, as they are crucially important and can find support, for the most part, in the Qur'an and Sunna.

Identification of maqāṣid

As already indicated, Muslim jurists have differed in their approach to the identification of *maqāṣid*. The first approach to be noted is the textualist approach, which confines the identification of *maqāṣid* to the clear text, to the commands and prohibitions, which are the carriers of *maqāṣid*. The *maqāṣid*, according to this view, have no separate existence outside the framework of clear injunctions. They can be found provided that a command is explicit and primary (*taṣrīḥī*, *ibtidā'ī*) and it conveys the objective of the Lawgiver in the affirmative sense. A subsidiary command that explains another or is in some way attached to it will not qualify as *ibtidā'ī* and a text that is ambiguous will not be *taṣrīḥī*. Prohibitions are indicative of the *maqāṣid* in the negative sense in that the purpose of a prohibitive injunction is to suppress and avert the evil that the text in question has contemplated.[19] Al-Shatibi spoke affirmatively of the need to observe the explicit injunctions, but then he added that adherence to the obvious text should not be so rigid as to alienate the rationale and purpose of the text from its words and sentences. Rigidity of this kind, Shatibi added, was itself contrary to the objectives (*maqāṣid*) of the Lawgiver and would be tantamount to neglecting the clear text itself. When the text, whether a command or prohibition, is read in conjunction with its objective and rationale, this is a firm approach, one which bears greater harmony with the intentions of the Lawgiver.[20]

Ever since al-Shafi'i (d. 820), who is regarded as the chief architect of *uṣūl al-fiqh*, *ijtihād* had remained rooted in the interpretation of words and sentences of the text, and beyond the text it was basically confined to analogical reasoning (*qiyās*). The former approach was text-bound and literalist, and the latter was tied to the correct identification of the effective cause. The methodology of *qiyās* was also increasingly subjected to technical conditions and requirements. This was the *uṣūlī* approach to *ijtihād*. The *maqāṣid* approach which was projected by al-Shatibi sought to free *ijtihād* from the strictures of literalism and *qiyās*. To construct *qiyās*, one needs to identify an original case, and a new case, and then a precise effective cause, and each of these steps must fulfil a long list of requirements, which are incidentally all a juristic construct that partakes in speculative thought. This approach is, moreover, not necessarily focused directly on the purpose of the Lawgiver and the people's interest, or *maṣlaḥa*. The two approaches, of the text and of the *ʿilla*, also essentially combined into one, as the *ʿilla* is extracted from the text, but since the text most often does not explicitly declare its *ʿilla*, the jurist extracts it through a close analysis of the meaning of words, whether literal or figurative, general or specific (*ḥaqīqī, majāzī, ʿāmm, khāṣṣ*) and so forth. To look, for example, at the Qurʾanic text on the prohibition of wine drinking (5:90), the jurist had to determine the precise meaning of *khamr* (wine) in the linguistic usage of the Arabs that prevailed at the time. For *khamr* referred to the type of wine that was extracted from grapes. Whether the meaning of that expression could be extended to other substances and varieties of wine was a question to be decided! The jurist had to also look into the precise import of the Qurʾanic expression "*faʾjtanibuhu*" that prohibited wine drinking as to whether it conveyed a strict ban or a mere reprehension and educational advice. For the Qurʾan is replete with commands and prohibitions that convey different meanings in terms of their precise juridical value. Questions also arose as to whether the prohibition of *khamr* was an absolute ruling of permanent validity, or meant only to address a circumstantial mischief of the Arab society of the time. Providing credible answers to such questions could hardly be devoid of speculation and doubt. Similar doubts also arose in the determination of the effective cause (*ʿilla*) of the prohibition, which in this case is intoxication of the kind that overwhelms the intellect and rational judgement. This may be a definitive *ʿilla* in the case of *khamr*, but not so when it is applied to the milder varieties of intoxicants, such as *nabīdh* (an extract of dates known at the time); and not when considering whether drinking a small amount of wine that did not intoxicate was equally prohibited! Then, for each new variety of intoxicant, one had to start a fresh series of investigations, and the process was bound to become altogether issue-laden and speculative.

Then there is the *maqāṣid*-oriented approach to the development of Shariʿa, which is premised on the realisation of benefit (*maṣlaḥa*) and prevention of mischief (*mafsada*). This takes for granted the rationality of the laws of Shariʿa, assuming that *maṣlaḥa* is the one grand *ʿilla* of all the laws of Shariʿa that applies universally to all relevant cases. From this basic premise all that the jurist needs to ascertain is the presence of *maṣlaḥa* and what is known as *ḥikma* (rationale, wisdom) in every new case and new ruling. *Ḥikma* is the *maṣlaḥa*-oriented name for *ʿilla*. *ʿIlla*, in the terminology of *uṣūl*, is an attribute that obtains in the subject matter of a ruling (*ḥukm*), and it is an indicator of the presence and continued validity of that ruling. Intoxication is thus an attribute of wine (*khamr*) and its presence is indicative of prohibition. In a similar vein, interest or unwarranted increase (*ribā*) is the attribute of a usurious sale and the cause of its prohibition. Similarly, travelling and sickness constitute the *ʿilla* for breaking the fast in the fasting month of Ramadan. As for the *ḥikma*, it is the reason, motive and rationale of the ruling, which is either to realise a benefit or to prevent a mischief and harm. Hence the *ḥikma* of the prohibition of liquor is prevention of harm that materialises from loss of the faculty of reason; the *ḥikma* of the prohibition of *ribā* is to prevent exploitation and the *ḥikma* of breaking fast in Ramadan for the sick and the traveller is prevention of hardship and harm.

The jurist is thus engaged in evaluative thinking, instead of determining the meaning of words, the scope of their application, etc. This rationalist engagement, it may be added here, can draw much support from the causes and occasions of revelation (*asbāb al-nuzūl*) which elucidate the original intent and context of the law. *Asbāb al-nuzūl* is yet another important theme to which the *uṣūl* jurists have paid little attention, as it was relegated to a subsidiary role in relationship to interpretation, analogy and *ijtihād*. In his writings on the hermeneutics of the Qur'an and *ḥadīth*, the late Fazlur Rahman has elaborated the crucial importance of *asbāb al-nuzūl* in devising fresh approaches to the understanding of the text. Muhammad ʿAbid al-Jabiri has similarly underlined the importance of *asbāb al-nuzūl* for the *maqāṣid*.[21] Besides, most of the injunctions of Shariʿa are easily understood, as Shatibi has reminded us, and their objectives can be known and ascertained from the reading of the clear text. Shatibi has similarly concluded that whatever is complementary to the *maqāṣid* and in the service thereof is also a part of the *maqāṣid*. The question then arises: We know that the *maqāṣid* are known from clear injunctions, but can they also be known from a general reading of the text by way of induction? Shatibi has given an original response to this question.

Induction (*istiqrāʾ*) to Shatibi is one of the most important methods of identifying the *maqāṣid*. There may be various textual references to a subject, none of which may be in the nature of a decisive injunction. Yet their collective weight is such that it leaves little doubt as to the meaning that is obtained from them. A decisive conclusion may, in other words, be arrived at from a plurality of speculative expressions. Shatibi illustrates this by saying that nowhere in the Qur'an is there a specific declaration to the effect that the Shariʿa has been enacted for the benefit of the people. Yet this is a definitive conclusion which is drawn from the collective reading of a variety of textual proclamations.[22] The inductive method, according to al-Shatibi, raised the credibility of one's conclusions from odd incidents to the level of broad and definitive (*qaṭʿī*) principles. Yet al-Ghazali wrote that the Companions were, on the whole, inclined to pursue the meanings and purposes (*al-maʿānī*) of the laws of Shariʿa, but in doing so, they were content with a strong probability and did not make certainty (*yaqīn*) a specific requirement in every case.[23]

The typical classification of *maqāṣid* into the three categories of essential, complementary and desirable (*ḍarūrī, ḥājī, taḥsīnī*), and the conclusion that the Lawgiver has intended to protect these are based, once again, on induction, as there is no specific declaration on them in the textual sources. On a similar note, the ruling of the Shariʿa that the validity of an act of devotion (*ʿibāda*) cannot be established by means of *ijtihād* is an inductive conclusion which is drawn from the detailed evidence on the subject, there being no specific injunction on it. It is also the same inductive method which has led the *ʿulamāʾ* to the conclusion that protection of the five values of faith, life, intellect, property and lineage is of primary importance to the Shariʿa – there being no textual ruling to specify any category or number of values in that order.

Shatibi's inductive method is not confined to the identification of objectives and values but also extends to commands and prohibitions, which may either be obtained from the clear text, or from a collective reading of a number of textual proclamations that may occur in a variety of contexts.[24] Shatibi then goes a step further, to say that the inductive conclusions and positions that are so established are the general premises and objectives of Shariʿa and thus have a higher order of importance than the specific rules. It thus becomes evident that induction is the principal method of reasoning and proof to which Shatibi resorted in his theory of the *maqāṣid*, and that he thereby made an original contribution to this theme.

Classification of maqāṣid

We have already discussed the classification of *maqāṣid* into the three types of essential, complementary and desirable. The first of these categories, namely *ḍarūriyyāt*, subsumes the five *maqāṣid* of life, intellect, religion, property and lineage. Questions arise over their scope and the order in which they appear. It is suggested that the number and scope of *ḍarūriyyāt* should be revised so as to respond to the socio-cultural realities of modern life. The essential *maqāṣid* should thus include such other values as social justice, fundamental rights, freedom and equality. The classical order of the five *maqāṣid* that begins with the protection of religion, followed by the protection of life and then of intellect, should also be reversed. For it is only logical that the list should begin with life, which is the starting point and carrier of all values, to be followed by intellect (*ʿaql*), which is also the criterion of understanding. Then should come religion, which promotes spirituality and moral values.[25] The priority of life over the religious duties can actually be seen in the detailed *fiqh* rules which readily grant concession on, or postpone, religious duties in life-threatening situations. For example, when someone sees another drowning whom he can save, but by doing so he is likely to miss the time of the prayer (*ṣalāh*), priority must be given to saving life – this is in accordance with the Qurʾanic declaration on the value of life: "one who gives life to one person, it would be as if he gives life to the whole of mankind" (5:32). A question also arises over the limited scope of the *fiqh* discourse concerning *ʿaql*. For the conventional *maqāṣid*-related discourse on *ʿaql* hardly reaches beyond the typical examples given of the ban on alcohol and other intoxicants! Challenging new issues that need attention include such themes as secularism, religion and science, reason and revelation, and the like, which call for fresh responses on the role of *ʿaql*.

In addition to the familiar triple classification just reviewed, *maqāṣid* have been further classified into the general purposes (*al-maqāṣid al-ʿāmma*) and particular purposes (*al-maqāṣid al-khāṣṣa*). The general goals are those that characterise Islam and its Shariʿa overall, and they are on the whole broad and comprehensive. Prevention of harm (*ḍarar*) is a general goal of Shariʿa and applies to all areas and subjects. Particular goals are theme-specific and relate to specific subjects. Examples of the particular goals are those that pertain to e.g. family matters, financial transactions, labour relations, witnessing and adjudication, and the like.

Another binary classification of the *maqāṣid* is their division into definitive goals (*al-maqāṣid al-qaṭʿiyyah*) and speculative goals (*al-maqāṣid al-ẓanniyyah*). The former consist of goals that are supported by clear evidence in the Qurʾan and Sunna, such as the protection of the life and property of individuals, the administration of justice, the right to financial support among close relatives, and the like. The speculative goals fall below that rank and may be subject to disagreement. To say, for example, that knowledge of *uṣūl al-fiqh* is one of the *maqāṣid* may well fall under the category of *ʿaql*, yet it is not a matter of certainty and may have to be placed under the category of speculative *maqāṣid*. Similarly to say that even the smallest amount of wine is just as forbidden as a larger amount is a doubtful position simply because it may not intoxicate, which is the effective cause of the prohibition at issue.

Al-Shatibi has also classified the *maqāṣid* into the aims and purposes of the Lawgiver (*maqāṣid al-shāriʿ*) and the human aims and purposes (*maqāṣid al-mukallaf*). To say that securing human welfare and benefit is God's illustrious purpose behind the laws of Shariʿa illustrates the former, whereas seeking employment in order to earn a living, for example, illustrates the latter class of *maqāṣid*.[26]

Maqāṣid have also been classified into the primary objectives (*al-maqāṣid al-aṣliyyah*) and subsidiary objectives (*al-maqāṣid al-tabiʿiyyah*). The former refer to the primary and normative goals that the Lawgiver, or a human agent, has originally intended and they constitute the basic purposes of the laws of Shariʿa in the evaluation of human acts and conduct. For example, the primary purpose of knowledge (*ʿilm*) and education is to know God and the proper manner of worshipping Him, and also to explore and understand His creation. Similarly the primary goal of marriage is procreation, and the primary purpose of attending lectures is to increase one's knowledge.

The secondary goals are those which complement and support the primary ones. The secondary purpose of marriage, for example, is friendship and sexual satisfaction. The secondary purposes of seeking knowledge can be obtaining academic qualification, personal accomplishment and refinement of one's speech and conduct.[27] It is important therefore to observe the consistency of the secondary goals with the primary goals, as severing the link between them could amount to unacceptable distortion. When marriage is used, for example, only as a means of sexual gratification without any loyalty and commitment, the purpose of marriage is distorted. Similarly, a ritual prayer that is performed merely for ostentation is not valid. This may be said generally of the laws of Shariʿa and their valid objectives: the laws of Shariʿa must not be isolated from their proper purposes. For example, recourse to legal stratagems (*ḥiyal*) inconsistent with the purposes of the law would distort the Shariʿa, and such stratagems must be avoided. Thus when someone makes a gift of his assets to another at the end of the year and receives back the same shortly after, and the exercise is merely intended to avoid the obligatory *zakāh* tax, his stratagem will not absolve him of the *zakāh*. We do not wish to engage with the subject of stratagems, on which the schools and jurists are not in agreement, but merely to say that when an ingenious device or method is used for a beneficial purpose, without corrupt intentions, it is no longer a trick, or *ḥīla*, but a form of *ijtihād*.[28]

Maqāṣid that relate to *ḍarūriyyāt* may be regarded as definitive (*qaṭʿī*). Those which are identified by induction (*istiqrāʾ*) from the clear injunctions (*nuṣūṣ*) may also be added to this category. As for *maqāṣid* that cannot be included in either of these two categories, they may still be seen as definitive if there is general consensus or clear legislation in their support. Additional *maqāṣid* that are identified outside this range may be classified as speculative (*ẓannī*), unless and until they are elevated to the rank of the definitive through general consensus or legislation. In the event of a clash between these *maqāṣid*, the definitive *maqāṣid* will take priority over the speculative. An order of priority in the traditional ordering is also suggested among the definitive *maqāṣid* in favour of those which preserve life and faith over the other three; protection of the intellect comes next, followed by property and lineage. A similar order of priority applies between the essential *maqāṣid*, those which are deemed complementary, and those which fall under the desirable.

The "accomplishers" (*mukammilāt*, sing. *mukammil*) is a category additional to the foregoing classifications of the *maqāṣid*, which can be appended to any one or more of its various headings as may be deemed appropriate. The *mukammilāt* are not a separate category as such, as they are concerned mainly with the ways and means that help to realise, as best as possible, the intended subject matter of the goal(s) to which they are attached, be it the essential, the complimentary or the desirable. The accomplishers may have been identified in the text either of the Qur'an or the *ḥadīth*, failing which they may be identified by recourse to rationality and *ijtihād*.

To illustrate an accomplisher of the essential or *ḍarūrī*, we note that the Qur'an enjoins that a future obligation (*dayn*) or a mortgage (*rahn*) should be documented and reduced into writing (2:283). Documentation in this case is not a goal in itself, but a means toward the protection and preservation of property (*māl*), which is one of the essential *maqāṣid*. Then, by way of analogy, the same requirement is extended to all contracts involving exchange of values, which should also be documented so as to protect them against disputation and doubt *ex post facto*. To illustrate the accomplisher of a complementary goal (*mukammil al-ḥājī*), we may refer to contractual options (*al-khiyārāt*) that can be stipulated, on the authority of *ḥadīth*, in a contract of sale: upon concluding a sale, for instance, the purchaser may stipulate an option that he will ratify the deal in three days or so. The permissibility of sale is a complementary (*ḥājī*) interest and the provision of an option merely serves to ensure that the sale meets its desired purpose, i.e. that it is free of fraud, misrepresentation and ignorance. To illustrate the accomplisher of a desirable goal, we may refer to all legitimate measures taken in order to keep the marketplace clear of trade in unclean and harmful substances, or which ensure that the passageways in the marketplace are not overcrowded.[29]

It is a condition of the accomplisher or *mukammil*, however, that it does not exceed or overrule the initial goal and purpose which it seeks to accomplish. To take our previous example of sale and option again, the purpose of the option as a *mukammil* is to prevent uncertainty and ignorance (i.e. *gharar*) in the sale at issue, but if one were to exaggerate the *mukammil* and demand total exclusion of all uncertainty and *gharar*, it would be difficult to achieve and might even obstruct the sale altogether. A slight amount of uncertainty is unavoidable and usually tolerated in many transactions, including sale. To give another example, the existence of the counter-values in a contract of exchange is desirable, yet if this were to be demanded in a contract of lease (*ijāra*), it would nullify the contract as only one of the two sides of the contract is usually present in *ijāra*, not both. To demand the *mukammil* of sale also in *ijāra* – for this latter is also a variety of sale – would thus exceed the characteristics of this contract and may even obstruct it altogether.[30]

Salient maqāṣid: overview of the Qur'an and Sunna

The textual sources of Islam place ethics at the centre of their order of values, so much so that, when discussing the three divisions of Shariʿa into theology (*kalām*, *ʿaqā'id*), ethics (*akhlāq*) and practical rules (*fiqh*), Muslim jurists consider ethics as the infrastructure of Islam and *fiqh* as a means of realising ethics. The *fiqh* rules, especially in the sphere of civil transactions (*muʿāmalāt*), may change with changing conditions, but the *akhlāq* as well as devotional matters (*ʿibādāt*) are basically unchangeable – although there is some recognition of the role of custom (*ʿurf*) as a criterion of legal and ethical judgement that may have a bearing on ethics, and custom is liable to change.

Unlike man-made laws which are usually confined to a bare exposition of commands and prohibitions, the Qur'an typically expresses the goals and purposes of its laws, the benefits of adherence to them, and the harm that can be expected from non-compliance in this world and the hereafter. The Qur'an uses a variety of expressions: at times, it may convey definitive injunctions, at others it may employ the persuasive language of education and guidance. This is sometimes done through illustrations, parables and historical examples of bygone nations and their prophets.

In almost all of these, the purpose is to sensitise the individual to a set of moral and legal values that secure human welfare and justice. The Qur'an also puts a high premium on reason, personal responsibility and truth. The salient Qur'anic principle of promotion of good and prevention of evil (*amr bi al-maʿrūf wa nahy ʿan al-munkar*) constitutes the ultimate purpose of a great deal of its commands and prohibitions. Compassion (*raḥma*) is singled out as the most important purpose of the Prophethood of Muhammad (21:107), and also as a salient purpose of the Qur'an, which describes itself as "Guidance and Mercy" (10:57). *Raḥma* and its derivatives are mentioned in 315 places in the Holy Book, which undoubtedly makes it one of the major themes and objectives of Islam. *Raḥma* is most clearly manifested in the realisation of *maṣlaḥa*, which the *ʿulamā'* have generally considered to be the all-pervasive objective of the Shariʿa. *Maṣlaḥa* is to all intents and purposes synonymous with *raḥma*.

ʿAdl or *qisṭ* (justice) is also a manifestation of God's mercy. It is an important attribute of the individual character and a principal objective of the Shariʿa in its own right. The Qur'an accentuates the centrality of justice when it states: "We sent our Messengers and revealed through them the Book and the Balance so that justice may be established amongst mankind" (57:25). Justice is thus identified as the final goal of the revealed scriptures, the prophets and the evidence they brought with them, indeed of all that is most sacred in the order of values known to Islam. Justice is the subject of 53 verses in the Qur'an and its opposite, *ẓulm* (injustice), occurs on over 300 occasions. The Qur'an seeks to establish justice as an integral part of the Muslim personality, and justice in its legal sense aims at attaining an equilibrium between rights and obligations. The three types of justice that receive attention in the Qur'an and *ḥadīth* include corrective justice, distributive justice, as well as political justice in the sphere, for example, of selection and appointment of officials.[31]

Tahdhīb al-fard (educating the individual) is also an important objective of the Shariʿa. In an order of priority, it may even be placed before *maṣlaḥa* and *ʿadl*. For the latter are both essentially community-oriented values that acquire much of their meaning in the context of social relations, whereas the former seeks to make each individual a trustworthy agent and carrier of these values that benefit himself and the community. Indeed, the overall purpose of a great number of stipulations of the Shariʿa, especially in the spheres of *ʿibāda* (ritual worship) and *akhlāq* (moral teachings), is to train the individual to acquire the virtues of *taqwā* (God-consciousness), and thus, to aid the fulfilment of the totality of divine guidance.[32]

Three renowned twentieth-century authors have differed somewhat on the Qur'anic order of values. Whereas Izutsu highlighted submission (*islām*) and calm self-control (*ḥilm*) as the overriding themes of the Qur'an,[33] Daud Rahbar accorded that status to justice and demonstrated how the other themes were subordinate to justice.[34] Fazlur Rahman implicitly rejected Rahbar's thesis by showing how God's mercy creates, informs and animates the universe, and identified mercy as the most prominent in the Qur'anic order of values.[35] George Hourani's "Ethical Presuppositions of the Qur'an"[36] convincingly demonstrated that ethical value stands on a different plane and has an objective reality in the Qur'an, which he identifies as the chief source of ethical knowledge. Hourani identifies ethical value, which also subsumes *ḥilm*, justice and mercy, as the running theme and draws the conclusion that the quest for moral excellence is the governing principle of much wider significance in Islam.

The spiritual model of the Muslim community is Abraham, whose submission to the Lord exemplified the essence of Islam (16:120–1). In 2:127–9, upon raising the foundations of the Kaʿba along with his son Ishmael, Abraham prayed: "O, our Lord, make us to be submissive to Thee, and of our posterity a community submissive to Thee (*umma muslima*) …." A community submissive to the Lord was what Muhammad as Prophet was gathering together. The Qur'an also stresses the universality of the Abrahamic ethic by asking, "And who desires other than the Abrahamic ethic (*milla Ibrāhīm*) except the one who depreciates himself?" (2:130)

Submission to God entailed a radical break with the customary attitudes of the Arabs, who were a proud and passionate people, but the duty of submission that was demanded entailed a total reform of the self. Pre-Islamic Arabs wavered in basic dichotomies between *jahl* (ignorance) on the one hand and *ḥilm* and *ṣabr* (patience, perseverance) on the other, between hot-blooded impetuosity and calm self-control. The *jāhil* (ignorant) was hostile and blindly jealous of his honour and the *kāfir* (unbeliever) was wrapped up in himself, and devoted to less than ultimate issues.[37] Abraham was a *ḥalīm* person, self-controlled, moderate, and also generous (9:114, 11:75). *Ḥilm* and *ṣabr* complement one another and feature in over 90 verses in the Qur'an. *Ṣabr* implies patience in the face of adversity, control of anger and an essential optimism. The faithful should advise one another to "be truthful and be patient" (103:3). Patience and forgiveness "are indeed the greatest achievements (*inna dhalika min ʿazm al-umūr*)" (42:43). Those who internalise these qualities are the rightly guided leaders and God will reward them beyond measure (2:1567, 39:10).

The five essential *maqāṣid* (*ḍarūriyyāt*), namely life, intellect, religion, property and lineage, are all informed by a moral purpose. To protect and promote religion means maintenance of its three principal pillars (*arkān*), that is, monotheism (*tawḥīd*), the truth of prophethood and belief in the hereafter, all of which postulate a sense of accountability on the part of the believer. *Tawḥīd* also plays a unifying role, binding the community together and constituting the source of its equality. A society in which no other attribute except devotion to God and moral rectitude (*taqwā*) can qualify one individual's superiority over the other (49:13) is founded in the essential equality of its members. Belief in the omnipotence of God also promotes moral autonomy and freedom from bondage to all other powers. The ritual prayer (*salāh*), the obligatory charity of *zakāh*, fasting and the *ḥajj*, which are the pillars of Islam, are all designed to promote self-discipline, help the needy and sensitise the faithful against indulgence in a hedonistic lifestyle. The *ḥajj* is a visible exercise in equality and in broadening the individual's outlook to the wider interests of humanity beyond local and national boundaries.

The whole idea of *maqāṣid* is probably taken from the renowned *ḥadīth-cum-*legal maxim to the effect that "human affairs (are judged) by reference to their objectives" (*al-umūr bi-maqāṣidaha*). It is similarly pronounced in another *ḥadīth* that "acts are judged by their intentions" (*innama al-aʿmal bi'l-niyyāt*). Intention is inextricably linked with *maqṣad* and purpose in that a verified intention, or *niyya*, is invariably purposeful and aims at a certain consequence. With reference to transactions and contracts, it is provided in a legal maxim that "credibility in contracts is attached to meaning (and purpose) not to words and structures" (*al-ʿibratu fi al-ʿuhūd li al-maʿānī lā li al-alfāẓ wa al-mabānin*).

The Qur'an and Sunna thus attend to goals and purposes much more than to forms and procedures. The kind of literalism and preoccupation with language that the *uṣūl al-fiqh* is known for stands at odds with this aspect of the Qur'an and Sunna. It is only natural to say, as Ibn ʿAshur pointed out, "In their dealings with one another, people usually follow purposes and meanings more than anything else when they enter contracts and agreements, when they borrow, when giving gifts and when they demand their rights of one another."[38]

Fiqh, uṣūl al-fiqh and the maqāṣid

It is often said that the *maqāṣid* are definitive (*qaṭʿī*), whereas much of the *uṣūl al-fiqh* is based on *ijtihād* and is on the whole speculative or *ẓannī*. This was apparently one of the reasons that prompted al-Shatibi to advance his theory of the *maqāṣid*: he thought the objectives of law and religion must be definitive, but the *uṣūl al-fiqh* fell short of that, and the result was excessive diversity and disagreement in Islamic legal thought. Al-Shatibi's evaluation of the *maqāṣid* as being definitive was based on the analysis that they refer on the whole to the universals (*kulliyyāt*) of Shariʿa.[39] We have some reservations over al-Shatibi's assessment on this, especially in the face of the binary classification of the *maqāṣid* into definitive and speculative (*qaṭʿī, ẓannī*) categories, as we have already discussed. All one can say perhaps is that the *maqāṣid* aspire to greater assurance and certainty compared to *uṣūl al-fiqh*. Besides, the *maqāṣid* are mainly identified through our reading of the Qur'an and *ḥadīth*, and we know that the text in these sources is not always definitive. It would also be an overstatement to classify the whole of *uṣūl al-fiqh* as *ẓannī* and speculative.

Uṣūl al-fiqh is primarily concerned with inference (*istinbāṭ*) and extraction of rules (*aḥkām*) from the textual dispensations of Qur'an and *ḥadīth*, but the *maqāṣid* are not involved in textual analysis as such. Whereas the methodology of legal reasoning in *uṣūl al-fiqh* tends to encourage disagreement (*ikhtilāf*), the *maqāṣid* are designed to encourage unity of purpose over essentials. We know that the conventional *fiqh* tends to be atomistic and issue-oriented, and has most likely influenced the *uṣūl* in the same direction. This is because the *fiqh* has chronologically preceded the *uṣūl al-fiqh*, and the latter has to some extent inherited the atomistic tendency of the former.[40]

The *uṣūl al-fiqh* and its inferential methods basically stood on two pillars, namely the Arabic language, and the goals and purposes of Shariʿa. The *ʿulamā'* of *uṣūl* almost exclusively concentrated on text and language, often at the expense of the goals and purposes. Then came the decline of *uṣūl al-fiqh* around the fifth/eleventh century, when the discipline almost came to a halt with the so-called "closing of the door of *ijtihād*", and remained deficient with regard to the *maqāṣid*. There was no significant change in that situation for another three centuries until the emergence of al-Shatibi.

Furthermore, the *uṣūl al-fiqh* premises and doctrines were influenced by the values of the medieval society in which they originated. The focus in those days was on private matters and personal status issues, which became the principal occupation of *fiqh*, and in turn also of *uṣūl al-fiqh*. Both of these disciplines focused on private law, thus paying scant attention to public law and governance. The tenacious hold in the subsequent centuries of indiscriminate imitation (*taqlīd*) and its backward-looking scholarship further exacerbated the situation and undermined the capacity of both the *uṣūl al-fiqh* and the *maqāṣid* to keep pace with the changing social conditions.[41]

Appraisal of maqāṣid

The relative strength or weakness of the various *maqāṣid* in relationship to one another is a subject on which the *maqāṣid* literature is still at its early stages of development. For the rulings of Shariʿa found in the Qurʾan, Sunna and juristic *ijtihād* are not always evaluated in accordance with the juristic conceptualisation of the *maqāṣid* nor with any particular order in which they have been classified. The question, for instance, as to which are the primary purposes (*maqāṣid aṣliyya*) as opposed to those that may be classified as subsidiary goals (*maqāṣid farʿiyya*), has not been adequately explored. This can also be said with regard to distinguishing between the means and the ends, as a *maqṣad* can sometimes become a means (*dharīʿa*) to another *maqṣad*. Therefore Ibn ʿAshur said that, except for some occasional references made to them by ʿIzz al-Din ʿAbd al-Salam al-Sulami in his *Qawaʿid al-Ahkam* and Shihab al-Din al-Qarafi in his *Kitab al-Furuq*, these subjects largely remained undeveloped.[42] Early contributions to this subject are basically confined to one classification of themes into the renowned five or six headings of the essential goals (*ḍarūriyyāt*), whereas the other two categories of complementary goals (*ḥājiyyāt*) and embellishments (*taḥsīniyyāt*) are not thematically identified. This triple classification refers to the intrinsic merit and relative value of the *maqāṣid* involved. Questions may also arise as to where, for example, personal freedom or equality can be placed in this classification. Perhaps one could say that this triple classification is inappropriate for these subjects, and that one may consider the binary classification of primary and subsidiary (*aṣliyya* and *farʿiyya*) to be more suitable for them. It is also possible, indeed likely, that equality and freedom could be placed under both necessary and primary *maqāṣid* (*ḍarūrī*, *aṣlī*), and would as such stretch across categories. Supposing we have found suitable answers to these questions, a range of other questions may arise as to how one might class the sub-varieties of freedom, such as freedom of religion, freedom of movement and freedom of expression. Protection of lineage and its purity is an essential goal (*ḍarūrī*), which would possibly suggest that the permissibility of marriage, which is a means toward that goal, is also an essential. A question may also arise as to the value one attaches to the permissibility of divorce. Some of these questions can perhaps be addressed through resorting to the category of the accomplishers (*mukammilāt*) as previously discussed, and others by reference to the legal maxim "What is indispensable for the attainment of a *wājib* also becomes a *wājib*." Yet our quest for developing a more comprehensive methodology for the identification of *maqāṣid* must continue, which is why we explore further answers to this question: Are there additional guidelines?

The intrinsic merit indicator has obviously been used in the renowned classification of *ḍarūrī/ḥājī/taḥsīnī*, but there are other indicators that can also be used to help identify the correct order and placement of the various rules and goals of Shariʿa – in the areas of commands and prohibitions, rights and duties, and even some of the unregulated aspects of conduct – under one or the other of the *maqāṣid* categories. These indicators may be summarised as follows:

1) The presence or absence of a text in the Qur'an and *ḥadīth*, the precedent of the Companions and their general consensus (*ijmāʿ*) provide important indicators on both the identification and relative appraisal of the *maqāṣid*. In the presence of a text, the clarity or otherwise of that text – whether it is definitive or speculative (*qaṭʿī, ẓannī*), clear and self-explained (*muḥkam, mufassar*) or ambiguous and obscure (*mujmal, mutashābih*),[43] and so forth – would help determine the grade and class of the ruling in question and its possible placement under a relevant class of the *maqāṣid*.

2) Another indicator to help with the appraisal of *maqāṣid* is by reference to the benefit (*maṣlaḥa*) they realise or the mischief (*mafsada*) they are likely to prevent. This would involve a rational evaluation of the possible benefits and harms in the light of prevailing social conditions. One may need to ascertain whether the benefit in question is a comprehensive and general (*kullī*) one that concerns the largest number of people and relates to a vital aspect of life, or whether it is a partial benefit (*juz'ī*) that lacks those attributes. To promote justice is a general and a vital benefit, and so is consultation (*shūra*) in governance, but certain varieties of transactions such as a lump-sum sale (*bayʿ al-juzāf*) or even an interest-free loan (*qarḍ ḥasan*) may not include the largest number nor the most vital interests of the people. Yet when one seeks to ascertain the goal and purpose of Shariʿa in the validation of a *ḥukm*, the benefit that *ḥukm* serves, or the mischief it prevents is not always known from the knowledge of the *ḥukm* itself, but need to be verified through reflection, inquiry and *ijtihād*.[44]

3) In a similar vein, the existing *fiqh* literature and fatwa collections on the renowned scale of five values (*al-aḥkām al-khamsa*)[45] could help in the identification and relative appraisal of the *maqāṣid*. Additional information of interest can be found under the binary *fiqh* classification of transgressions into the major and minor sins (*al-kabā'ir wa'l-ṣaghā'ir*), and indeed in the literature relating to the pillars and essentials of Islam, the *arkān al-khamsa*,

that are grounded in the clear text. It will be noted that many of the foregoing categories consist essentially of ethical categories such as the recommended, the reprehensible, the permissible, the minor sins and the like.

4) Another way of evaluating the *maqāṣid*, as already noted, is by reference to punishments the Shariʿa may have provided for a certain conduct. Such punishments may indicate a certain value and purpose. In this vein, as already noted, the prescribed penalties of *ḥudūd* were used by the early writers on *maqāṣid*. But even among the *ḥudūd* offences, there are some, such as slanderous accusation (*qadhf*) and wine drinking (*shurb*), that carry lesser punishments. This would suggest that the values protected by them belong to the second order of *maqāṣid* (i.e. *ḥājiyyāt*). With regard to *shurb*, one may add further that it is actually a *taʿzīr* offence that calls for a discretionary punishment, but has somehow been included in the *ḥudūd* even though the Qur'an does not specify a punishment for it.[46]

5) The Shariʿa rulings (*aḥkām*) can also be evaluated, and the *maqāṣid* they pursue verified, by reference to the strength or weakness of a promise of reward or a warning (*al-waʿd wa al-waʿīd*) that the text may contain. For while a promise of reward may only have an educational value, if made in an emphatic language it may well be suggestive of a *maqṣad*, whether an essential one or one that may command a lower order of priority, depending on the text which carries it and one's overall reading of the Qur'an and *ḥadīth*.[47] For example, the Qur'an promises a great reward for being good to one's parents, and there is an equally emphatic warning for those who annoy them. The Prophet has also severely warned those who attribute deliberate lies to him. The immediate purpose in both cases is self-evident and may be evaluated as falling under the essential goals of protecting family values and religion, respectively. Compare these with the promise of reward for one who supports his wife and family above the basic essentials of life, or one who provides food for animals and birds. The *maqṣad* in the former is to promote family affection and loyalty, a complementary *maqṣad* perhaps; and in the latter compassion to animals, which may fall under the category of *taḥsīniyyāt*.

The last objective, namely compassion to animals, tends to acquire a higher profile in some *ḥadīth* texts, one of which warns of a severe punishment for a woman who had reportedly starved her cat by tying her to a pole until she died, or a promise of great reward (of entry to paradise) for a man who had saved the life of a dog that was dying from thirst in the desert. There are numerous *ḥadīth* texts which promise a great reward for apparently small acts of merit pertaining to *ʿibādāt*, such as recital of a certain verse at a certain time, or for so many times. The goal and purpose that such promises pursue are often detectable in the context. The weight attached to such acts is sometimes symbolic, not necessarily focusing on the acts in question but the principles they visualise, which may be mercy and compassion, or the merit attached to the remembrance of God. The expressions are in some cases figurative, intended to make an impact or provide education and guidance. It has even been said that they may not necessarily invoke the reward and punishment in question.[48]

It is understood from the foregoing examples that a goal and purpose of a lower order may exceptionally take a higher profile in stressful and life-threatening situations, in which case one would need to ascertain the immediacy of the *maqṣad* in question within its surrounding circumstances, and say, for instance, in the matter of saving the life of a dying animal, that the *taḥsīnī* is elevated to the rank of *ḍarūrī*. This does not change our basic position, however, that clemency to animals generally fall under the category of *taḥsīniyyāt*.

6) The value of a *ḥukm* and the goal pursued by it can also be ascertained by reference to its repetition and recurrence in the Qur'an and *ḥadīth*. References to justice, compassion (*raḥma*) and patience (*ṣabr*), for example, are abundant in the text, as already noted. The same can perhaps be said of charity beyond the obligatory *zakāh*, and helping the poor, which occur frequently in the Qur'an and *ḥadīth*. One may add here the proviso, however, that repetition in the sphere of obligatory duties (*wājib* and *ḥarām*) is relatively less important than it is in the sphere of ethical values such as *mandūb* and *makrūh* (recommended and reprehensible). For when a *wājib* or a *ḥarām* is conveyed in a clear and categorical text, further repetition may not necessarily add anything to it, although the Hanafis do take notice of the factor of repetition, side by side with textual clarity, even with reference to the *wājib* and *ḥarām*. Thus they raise the *wājib* into an emphatic duty (*farḍ*) and *makrūh* (reprehensible) to the level of *makrūh taḥrimī* (reprehensible closer to *ḥarām*), as opposed to *makrūh tanzīhī* (*makrūh* for purity), which is closer to permissible or *mubāḥ*.[49] Repetition, then, tends to play a relatively more important role in the context of ethics than it does with regard to clear legal injunctions.

Maqāṣid and gender justice

We now pose the question of how the *maqāṣid* can be used in support, for instance, of gender justice and the advancement of a regime of equality of rights between men and women. Our response to this question begins in the first place by looking at the textual evidence in the Qur'an and *ḥadīth* to see if equality (*musāwā*) can be identified as a purpose and *maqṣad* of the Shari'a. This would entail a search for supporting evidence in these sources.

When we have completed this step, the question may arise whether the texts identified in support of equality are explicit and normative (*taṣrīḥī, ibtidā'ī*), whether they can clearly establish a value point in the first place, and whether they can do so without recourse to interpretation – or whether, to the contrary, they lack clarity, relate only indirectly to our purpose, or relate in some ways but have a different focus, in which case they may fail to strengthen our case.

Should we be able, on the positive side, to find more than one clear text in the Qur'an and *ḥadīth* that endorse and substantiate the purpose sought, that would further strengthen the result of our inquiry. When these steps are successfully taken and they all deliver affirmative results on gender equality, we may conclude and identify it as a goal and purpose (*maqṣad*) of the Shari'a that is supported by unequivocal evidence.

It is also possible that the textual evidence so located addresses a particular situation that is circumstantial and time-bound, in which case we may or may not be able to use it. If the text also contains elements that may derogate from or negatively influence the underlying value we are verifying, that too is likely to weaken our case. But we may need to resort to interpretation, especially in situations where we have a large number of quotations from the Qur'an and *ḥadīth*. In that eventuality, recourse may be had to the rules of interpretation to resolve an apparent conflict or divergence in the totality of the evidence. Our attempt at interpretation may also involve a degree of reliance on the general knowledge of the relevant principles of Shari'a, so that we remain in context and avoid engaging in literalism or taking unwarranted liberties with the use of evidence.

It would require lengthy detail to discuss all the relevant evidence in the Qur'an and *ḥadīth* on gender equality and justice. All one can say, perhaps, is that there are about 12 verses in the Qur'an[50] that need to be quoted in the first place, and about half that number that may be used in our attempt to interpret some passages of the former category. The *ḥadīth* represent an even larger picture, and a great number of passages need to be discussed and analysed. The evidence that we have in both sources also contains divergent elements that tend to weaken the case for equality, but which need to be interpreted in the light of the overall evidence and general knowledge of the Shari'a. The values of modern society and approved social custom (*'urf*) would also have a bearing on our interpretation. I have discussed most of the key evidence in the sources in my previous publications, and have reached the conclusion that the Qur'an and *ḥadīth* are supportive of gender equality in almost all areas of concern, with the exception, perhaps, of the distribution of shares in inheritance, which have been specified in the Qur'an.[51] It has, however, been explained that a woman is supported by her male relatives prior to marriage, and by her husband thereafter, hence the difference that the man is, in most cases, but not always, entitled to a share double that of the woman in the same degree of relationship to their deceased relative. This might also mean that when a woman is not supported by any of her relatives, she may, through recourse to juristic preference (*istiḥsān*), be entitled to an equal share in inheritance.

Textual evidence in the Qur'an and *ḥadīth* is clear on the equality of men and women in creation, in their essential dignity, their moral responsibility, their spiritual attainments and their equality in the eyes of God. They are also equal in their entitlement to education, to employment and earnings for the work they do, and also with respect to participation in government and in the conduct of *ḥisba* (promotion of good and prevention of evil). A woman can be a full *mujtahid* and a judge of the Shari'a Court. Although the Hanafi school is more supportive of this latter position than the other three Sunni schools, twentieth-century Muslim scholarship has almost reached a consensus on women's eligibility to all judicial positions. Women are also fully qualified to own and dispose of property, and to manage their own financial affairs both before and after marriage. These are among the conclusions that jurists and commentators have drawn from the textual evidence. There are also verses on polygamy and divorce that have been given novel interpretations by twentieth-century Muslim scholarship, making both subject to a court order, and no longer a unilateral privilege, as it were, of the husband. Many Muslim countries have adopted these positions and introduced new laws as a result.[52]

The text thus addresses particular areas of gender equality, but in the meantime establishes a main purpose and direction that may be followed when addressing other instances of inequality, and new questions that may arise with the change in the socio-economic conditions of society. Once gender equality is identified as a valid *maqṣad*, it would dispose of the need to look for authority on every issue of concern. Equality can, in other words, be pursued as an overall objective of law-making, adjudication and *ijtihād* in all areas and walks of life, within the broader moral and ethical guidelines of Islam.[53]

Conclusion

The *maqāṣid* have on the whole remained weak and theoretical and have not had much of an impact on fatwa, adjudication and *ijtihād*. The writers of *fiqh* manuals thus continued to address individual issues and drew conclusions that sometimes stood at odds with the goals and purposes of the law. Muslim writers also wrote profusely on *fiqh* and *uṣūl al-fiqh*, but next to nothing on the *maqāṣid*. The neglect of *maqāṣid* was, however, unjustified, simply because of the dynamic character of the subject, which closely relates to the living experiences of people. Worse still, this neglect continued even after al-Shatibi's innovative contribution. The Shari'a was subsequently confronted by the colonial onslaught which split the Islamic heritage into unfamiliar dualities. Shari'a law was thus isolated from modern law, the Shari'a courts from civil courts, and modern education from religious education. The *maqāṣid* were too weak then, as they are to this day, to provide a recourse which could stem the tide of divisiveness. Yet at this stage, it was not only the *maqāṣid* but also the Shari'a as a whole, that were neglected and marginalised.

We know that the Shari'a was marginalised during colonial rule. What we are saying now is that if there is an interest, as there undoubtedly is, in the revival of Shari'a, then the *maqāṣid* would provide a useful tool toward that end. Yet one ought to be aware of one's limitations, in order to avoid repeating past mistakes. One would not want to be simplistic about the role the *maqāṣid* can play or expect that the recourse to *maqāṣid* could easily set aside and overcome all disagreement and unify the extremely diverse realities and interests of the world's Muslims in the twenty-first century. Such an expectation would qualify as what Sherman Jackson has called "false universalism", "for it suggests a belief in the possibility and propriety of subsuming the massive diversity of the modern Muslim community under a single, concrete articulation of the *maqāṣid al-Sharī'a*".[54]

Jackson's critique is not out of place, when seen in the light of the present state of the discipline and what I have specified of its weaknesses. The *maqāṣid* would need to be developed, nuanced and refined before they can play their proper role in bringing the Shari'a closer to the living realities of Muslims today. The *maqāṣid* are also not entirely separate from the rest of the Shari'a and can only play a positive role when enriched by the cumulative knowledge and resources of the wider heritage. But the discourse is developing and we see that a great deal of scholarly attention is being paid to the *maqāṣid*, especially in recent decades. This is because the *maqāṣid* are seen to have the potential of responding positively to the contemporary needs and realities of Muslims.

The *maqāṣid* as a discipline of Shari'a studies is still in its evolutionary phase and it is most likely to remain an open chapter that will continue evolving over time. When we identify *maṣlaḥa*, human dignity or justice as goals and objectives of Shari'a, they are all capable of continual enrichment in tandem with the progress of society and civilisation. Whereas the *uṣūl al-fiqh* is rich in methodology, the *maqāṣid* tend to be wanting of methodological refinement. Methodological accuracy would help develop a higher degree of assurance over the identification of *maqāṣid*, and the dynamics of how they interact with one another. The *maqāṣid* are likely to become an engaging theme of contemporary Islamic jurisprudence, and to be enriched by the scholarly interest and contributions of researchers at a more accelerated pace than before.

4 Human rights and intellectual Islam

Mohsen Kadivar

The substance of this chapter originally appeared, in a different form, as a two-part article published in Iran in 2003.[1] *In the first part of the article, there is a survey of six areas of conflict between historical Islam and human rights norms: 1) inequality between Muslims and non-Muslims, 2) inequality between men and women, 3) inequality between slaves and free human beings, 4) inequality between commoners and jurists in public affairs, 5) freedom of conscience and religion versus punishments for apostasy, and 6) extra-judicial punishments, violent punishments and torture. It demonstrates in detail how numerous precepts of Islamic jurisprudence (fiqh) conflict with international human rights norms, specifically in Twelver Shiʿi fiqh and the contemporary law of Iran, but* mutatis mutandis *in the Sunni schools as well. The second part, which follows here in a slightly abridged form, discusses the scope and methodologies for resolving these conflicts.*

That a few occasional and rare verdicts should conflict with human rights is not a problem, but that traditional Islam's well-known views or unanimous and consensual verdicts should conflict with human rights is seriously problematic.[2] The question of conflict between the notion of human rights and traditional Islam goes much deeper than the realm of opinions. The conflict is not confined to the verdicts of theologians and experts on Islamic law; it is a question of conflict between Scripture, i.e. some verses, as well as many Narratives, and the notion of human rights.

Muslims who allow the notion of human rights into their consciousness should be aware of the epistemic mayhem and the deep conflicts that they will have to cope with when this new guest steps into the abode of their minds. "Human rights" is a notion that is based on particular epistemological and philosophical underpinnings and presuppositions, and particular views about human beings. Human rights cannot be accepted without accepting these underpinnings and premises. A law that attaches precedence to religion and beliefs over the humanness of human beings, or attaches precedence to people's maleness or femaleness over their humanness, or recognises the ownership of slaves, has, first, defined the cosmos and human beings in a particular way and, then, accepted propositions about distinctions in rights on the basis of this conception of human beings and the cosmos. Deducing such rulings would undoubtedly have been impossible without an epistemological cohesion of this kind. One of the epistemological principles that pertain when we deal with different laws or with different propositions is the principle of avoiding contradictions. The human mind is unable to accept two wholly contradictory or conflicting propositions at one and the same time. Hence, it goes without saying that the notion of human rights cannot be combined with laws that are based on underpinnings and premises (and, consequently, results and conclusions) that are in conflict with and contrary to human rights.

Traditional Islam, too, as an epistemic constellation, is a particular system of rights with its own underpinnings and premises. This constellation includes Scripture and the Tradition of the Prophet, the technical opinions of experts on Islam (such as the fatwas issued by *fuqahā'*, the verdicts of experts on Islamic ethics and theological propositions) and the practices of experts on the Shariʿa, the faithful and Muslims over the course of history. Traditional Islam holds first, that conflict with the notion of human rights is certain in all three of these areas and secondly, that, precisely because of this, the notion of human rights is incorrect and unacceptable. It is possible to agree with and accept the first proposition with some amendments. That is to say, I believe that there is a great deal in the practices of Muslims and experts on the Shariʿa over the course of history, and even today, that conflicts with human rights; that, secondly, the verdicts and fatwas of religious experts contain many propositions that conflict with human rights; that, thirdly, there are points in the Verses of the Holy Qur'an and the Traditions attributed to the Prophet and the Shiʿi Imams that conflict with human rights – less in the Verses and more in the Narratives. Moreover, the conflict between traditional Islam and human rights is not minor and superficial; it is serious and deep-rooted. Accepting and preferring either one of the two sides of the conflict has important corollaries and consequences that ought not to be disregarded.

Theoretical underpinnings of the conflict between historical Islam and human rights

In historical Islam, human beings are not the focal point of the discussion; the focal point is God, and the Shariʿa revolves around the axis of religion and divine duties. The preoccupation of traditional Islam is to identify and respect these duties, which are known as Shariʿa precepts. In dealing with the corollaries and phenomena of the modern age, such as human rights, democracy, civil society, etc., historical Islam has offered a general, unchanging response: if these affairs really play a part in true human felicity and are intrinsically correct and valid, they have, without a doubt, been taken into account in advance and in full in Muslims' divine duties and Shariʿa precepts; and if they do not play a part in true human felicity, they are condemned to invalidity. All that is necessary has been taken into account in God's eloquent wisdom, including people's true rights.

In view of the growing acceptance of the notion of human rights in Islamic societies, Islamic experts have opted for two courses: on the one hand, they try – as much as possible – to reduce the prominence of those religious precepts that conflict with human rights, and try to justify them in some way. On the other hand, they try to find and highlight the points in Islamic texts that corroborate human rights, and their overall aim is to remove Islam from the firing line of human rights-based criticism.

To be fair, we would have to say that such stipulated "true human rights" are different from the internationally accepted notion of "human rights". Traditional Islam's conflict with the notion of human rights has been established on the basis of an *a posteriori* investigation; that is, the precepts of traditional Islam were compared to the articles of the Universal Declaration of Human Rights and other international conventions, and the result of the investigation was that there are at least six areas of conflict.[3] I think it is unlikely that the adherents of historical Islam can deny this conflict. In order to extricate themselves from this conundrum, they suggest the idea of "true human rights" from an *a priori* perspective. I think that, if we explore and draw out the "theory of true human rights", then the epistemic underpinnings and the theories about religion and human beings that underlie historical Islam will become clear: true human rights are a part of the intrinsic interests that have been fully taken into account by All-Knowing God in the formulation of Shariʿa precepts. These rights are unchanging; they do not vary over time, in the different stages of the advancing life of humanity and in different locations. The creator of these rights is the Creator of human beings. Performing one's duties and Shariʿa precepts is the surest way of abiding by human beings' true rights.

Now, the question arises: How do we identify human beings' true rights? The only valid way is to refer to God's revelation, i.e., to see what the Lawgiver has presented in Scripture or in the Tradition of the Prophet (peace be upon him). So, the trustworthy method of learning about true human rights is text-based and narration-based. From the Shiʿi perspective, consensus is not an independent source: it is a way of proving tradition. Reason, too, as a discoverer of Shariʿa precepts can take us from one Shariʿa precept to a second Shariʿa precept that is a corollary of the first precept. This kind of proof is known as non-self-justifying reasoning, and it is incontestably accepted.

The fundamental problem lies in the possibility of discovering human beings' true rights using human reason, without the assistance of the Shariʿa, revelation and narration. Can human beings recognise their own true rights? The acceptance of rational good and bad by the Muʿtazilites and the Shiʿis could have paved the way to an affirmative answer. On this basis, reason is capable of independent understanding regarding the goodness of justice and the badness of injustice, and whatever reason rules, the Shariʿa will also rule. Hence, whatever reason finds just should also be religiously obligatory, and whatever reason finds unjust should be religiously prohibited. This rational approach has not found much reflection in *fiqh*. As Sayyid Mohammad Baqir al-Sadr (1935–80) wrote at the beginning of *Al-Fatawa al-Waziha*, you can deduce a full course of demonstrative *fiqh* (Islamic jurisprudence), without needing to seek recourse in the rulings of reason a single time. Why? Because it is effectively impossible for human reason to achieve an all-embracing grasp of the hidden harms and benefits of minor matters. The rulings of reason are either certain and definite, or presumptive. A certain and definite understanding of the essential harms and benefits of matters, including true human rights, is impossible. A presumptive and non-definite understanding is futile and unreliable. Hence, it is not possible to discover true human rights with human reason; the only way to ascertain these rights is to refer to the Shariʿa and to the narrations of Scripture – there is no other way.

In traditional Islam "true human rights" are reduced to Shariʿa precepts or human beings' religious duties. What these true rights might be is an intrinsic matter inscribed on an immutable scroll beyond the reach of human reason and understanding. But divine duties and Shariʿa precepts are within reach through the narrated accounts. "True human rights" do not lend themselves to discussion, but Shariʿa precepts can be discussed, at least among experts on religion. On this basis, let us abandon the idea of speaking about true human rights, and concentrate on the question of Shariʿa precepts. It is clear that Shariʿa duties and religious precepts differ depending on one's religion, creed, gender, freedom or slavery, and even on whether one is a *faqīh* or not. Of course, from the traditional perspective, these differences do not by any means amount to discrimination; quite the reverse, they are the very essence of justice. That is to say, every precept relates to the essential merit of its beneficiary. Since God is just and wise, every single Shariʿa precept is unquestionably just and wise.

For our purposes, traditional Islam's most important underlying principle, in terms of epistemology and theories about religion and human beings, is the limited scope of human reason or the human mind. The human mind is incapable of understanding human beings' true rights. The innate incapacity and congenital fallibility of the human mind in assessing what is more and what is less important to human life is the foundation and source of the other principles of this historical thought system. Among these other principles, which are based on the fallibility of reason, is the idea that the human mind is seriously limited in its capacity to have an all-embracing grasp of what does or does not constitute justice. The logical implication of this principle is that justice and injustice can only be identified in practice through the sacred words of the Lawgiver. When the human mind is incapable of recognising whether a ruling is just or not, justice is perforce that which the Lawgiver identifies as just, and injustice is, likewise, that which the Lawgiver identifies as unjust. In other words, traditional Islam has, in practice, accepted the approach of the Ashʿarites. The second principle that follows from the mind's fallibility is the inability to legislate for this-worldly life. The faulty human mind is not qualified to make laws. In view of human beings' inability to have an all-embracing grasp of true human needs and true human felicity, and because human beings are swayed by their appetites and carnal desires, human laws lead to social feuds and conflict. In order to establish peace and calm, the only place to turn is to the laws of God, i.e. the Shariʿa, and the divine Lawgiver, i.e. God. The importance attached to this principle is evident from the fact that an argument for the necessity of prophethood has been based on it, and the argument has been cited by many Islamic theologians and even by some Muslim philosophers. Thirdly, in view of the fact that Shariʿa precepts have been formulated by All-Knowing God and human laws are products of fallible and limited human minds, it is self-evident that divine duties and Shariʿa precepts are superior to human laws (including the conventions on human rights). This superiority is on such a scale that there is never any need to put it to the test, because the human mind's innate fallibility disqualifies it as an arbiter in this field, and the superiority is a necessary consequence of the acceptance of God's eloquent wisdom.

One of historical Islam's other underlying principles in terms of its theories of knowledge and religion is that it is possible to formulate unchanging laws, laws that do not need to vary, regardless of the many changes in human life, from the simple conditions of life many centuries ago to the complicated conditions of life today. This is because laws that are based on hidden, intrinsic harms and interests exist and apply regardless of time and place. Likewise, most of the Shariʿa precepts that exist in the Tradition of the Prophet and the Infallible Imams, as reflected in the respected field of *fiqh*, are considered to be unchanging, eternal precepts. This belief has two logical consequences: first, the field of *fiqh* is of the first order of importance among the Islamic fields of learning, to the point where the works produced by Muslim scholars in the field of *fiqh* outnumber the works that they have produced in other Islamic fields, such as ethics, theology, annotation, history, philosophy and mysticism, and *fuqahā'* have been accorded more esteem and importance. Secondly, more importance has been attached to the narration- and Shariʿa-based fields than to the rational and empirical fields.

In traditional Islam, human beings have no intrinsic nobility and dignity, although they are of potentially noble fabric. The closer human beings move to the axis of dignity and nobility, the greater is their status: the further away they move from this divine axis, the lower their ranking. Hence human beings can range from being God's friends and the closest to God of God's creatures, to being even more lowly than four-legged animals and the most abject of creatures. Human beings' status depends on their closeness or otherwise to divine virtues and perfection. On this basis, human beings' true rights depend on their standing in terms of faith and religion. Hence, speaking of human rights and equal rights for all, man or woman, Muslim or non-Muslim, free or slave, is meaningless and unjust.

In this constellation, the world has to be understood in the light of the hereafter. Good decisions in this world have to be based on consideration for the afterlife, and human beings must not devote and confine themselves to this-worldly considerations. The important thing is to ensure felicity in the hereafter, and this-worldly life matters to the extent that it serves the afterlife. So, it is not surprising that this-worldly affairs are of secondary importance.

The above discussion was a brief analysis of historical Islam's underpinnings in terms of its theories of knowledge, religion, human nature and the cosmos. Now, let us compare these underpinnings to the principles that underpin the notion of human rights. This notion is based on a belief in the relative competence of the human mind or human reason to understand needs, interests and harms. Self-justifying critical reason is the foundation of modernity, and the notion of human rights is one of its products. From this perspective, human minds are capable of identifying and formulating human rights. Collective human reason undertakes this identification and formulation, and it does not consider its achievement to be definitive and immutable. It is, in fact, prepared to complete and amend its precepts as humanity gains new experiences. Human rights conventions are a product of the latest experiences of the collective reason of contemporary human beings. Such reason holds that if these principles of human rights are respected, all human beings will enjoy greater peace and justice. This thought system maintains that human reason is capable of discovering what does, and what does not, constitute justice and that collective human reason can assess the justice or injustice of human relations and laws. On this basis, human beings are capable of formulating just laws for governing their societies and their environments. Human rights conventions are examples of international laws created by the collective reason of contemporary human beings.

In view of the variety of religions and creeds in human societies and in view of the fact that they all have allocated particular rights to their followers, the notion of human rights – while respecting all religions and creeds and recognising their place in people's private lives – is neutral on religion and creed in the public sphere; in other words, human rights have been formulated for human beings *qua* human beings, before they believe in any particular religion and creed. Thus, individuals' religions or creeds do not alter their rights in any way and the principles of human rights are not based on any particular religion or rite.

It is important to note that the notion of human rights has been formulated on the basis of an *a posteriori* approach. In other words, it is based on human experiences and a practical comparison of various approaches to ensure that this approach is the best one. The notion of human rights is not based on any hidden mysteries that are beyond human comprehension. Hence, it can easily prove its superiority over rival approaches and demonstrate its success in practice. When human rights are respected, individuals have the opportunity to pursue their lives as they see fit, freely and autonomously. Whether they live as believers or atheists is for them, not others, to decide; but the notion of human rights is neither atheistic nor monotheistic.

A comparison of the underpinnings of historical Islam and those of human rights conventions reveals that the difference between these two systems is deep and fundamental. Accepting either one entails a rejection of the other, unless one chooses to believe in both in a superficial way by shutting one's eyes to their conflicting roots and implications.

Notion of human rights preferable to historical Islam's position

What are we to do in the face of the deep and fundamental disparity between historical Islam and the notion of human rights? Which one of the two should we accept? What should we do with the other one? This is a normative problem. There is no easy answer. Before attempting an answer, let me make some preliminary points.

First, one side of the conflict is historical Islam or traditional Islam, not Islam in the absolute sense. Historical Islam is a particular conception of the religion of God. Criticising it or, possibly, rejecting it, does not entail criticism or rejection of Islam. One can be a Muslim and believe in the singleness of God, the truth of Judgement Day and the Mission of Muhammad Ibn ʿAbd Allah (peace be upon him), but have a different reading of Islam from the historical and traditional reading. Hence, we must approach the normative decision freely, fair-mindedly and as unbiased investigators, not as dogmatists nor in a partisan and unthinking way.

The second preliminary point is that, in view of the discussion in the previous section, the conflict can be viewed as a conflict of narrated words versus reason (*naql wa ʿaql*). Historical or traditional Islam relies on narrated accounts, and the human rights system relies on reason. Viewing the conflict as one of narrated accounts versus reason is much more realistic than viewing it as revelation versus reason, or religion versus reason.

Thirdly, it seems that in judging between the two sides of this conflict, an *a priori* investigation is inappropriate since the conflict has arisen precisely because of the utilisation of an *a posteriori* approach. That is to say, numerous religious precepts and duties have been declared to be in breach of human rights norms and, so, resorting to an *a priori* method would not be convincing. In other words, in making the judgement, it is not appropriate to rely on the speaker's standing and to say that, since the words were spoken by God or the Prophet, there is no need to prove the validity of the words. The *a posteriori* approach demands that we compare two claims on their own merits in order to establish which is correct and which is not. In the contemporary world, Shariʿa precepts have to be defended on the grounds that they are rational and more just and better than comparable solutions.

The fourth point is that the human rights system belongs to the modern age and did not exist in pre-modern times. Historical Islam, too, is being discussed in the modern age; in pre-modern times, the traditional reading of Islam did not face a problem known as conflict with the notion of human rights. In other words, this is a new problem that belongs to the modern age, and it cannot be extended to pre-modern times. Historical Islam dealt successfully and honourably with the problems that arose in pre-modern times.

And the last point is that this conflict is one of the subdivisions of the debate between tradition and modernity. Here, historical Islam represents tradition, and the notion of human rights represents modernity.

Now, let us attempt to judge between historical Islam and the notion of human rights. In order to proceed as carefully as possible, let us judge each of the six areas of conflict in turn. Regarding the first area, i.e. inequality of rights between Muslims and non-Muslims, traditional Islam's position is not defensible in the contemporary world. Religion and creed must not lead to legal discrimination. Believing in a true religion and doing good deeds will be rewarded in the hereafter based on the judgement of All-Knowing God. But in this world, equal rights for all and non-discrimination on the basis of religion and creed is closer to justice. In a world populated by the followers of different religions and creeds, each of which considers itself in the right and all others in the wrong and accords special rights to its own followers, the fairest way is to reject all these special rights and not to involve religious beliefs in human rights. If God has put the blessings of nature at everyone's disposal without any distinction or discrimination, why should we not proceed on the same basis? What rational argument could possibly justify discrimination on the basis of religion and faith? In conditions of equality, people can turn to and accept a religion with greater sincerity, without their decision being tainted by fleeting, this-worldly motivations. If we decide to judge rationally historical Islam's religious arguments in favour of different rights for Muslims and non-Muslims, and for orthodox believers and followers of other Islamic sects – rather than to accept them unquestioningly because we are devout and because we feel we must judge words on the basis of who has spoken them – then, we cannot doubt that equal rights for all is closer to truth and justice than discrimination on religious grounds.

Regarding the second area, i.e. inequality of rights between men and women, there is no reason to attach precedence to gender over humanness. Why should physiological and biological differences give rise to differences in rights? If racial differences cannot give rise to differences in rights, why should gender differences do so? That women should always be treated as underlings and men always treated as superiors lacks any rational justification. The criterion of superiority in the hereafter is piety, not gender and, in this world, opportunities and resources should be made available for healthy competition. Women are not inferior to men in terms of rationality, the ability to learn and occupational skills, nor are they inferior to men in the political, economic and cultural fields. In sum, equal rights for all, regardless of gender, is in keeping with common sense, whereas giving women fewer rights than men goes against fairness, justice and reason.

Regarding the third area, i.e. different rights for free people and slaves, far from there being reasons for this kind of discrimination, there are reasons against it. While it is impossible to do away with multiple religions and more than one gender among human beings, slavery is something that can be eliminated, and it no longer exists in its traditional form today. Common sense, justice and fairness cannot abide the existence of slavery and, *a fortiori*, cannot tolerate discrimination between slaves and non-slaves. There can be no doubt about the correctness of the human rights position of doing away with slavery and ruling out discriminatory rights in this respect.

Regarding the fourth area, i.e. inequality between *fuqahā'* (Islamic jurists) and commoners in the sphere of public affairs, contrary to the previous three areas, there are differences of opinion on this issue within traditional Islam, and this form of discrimination is not accepted as a self-evident necessity among religious experts. The critics believe that there is no valid religious evidence in support of it, that it cannot be supported by any rational argument and, most importantly, that there are arguments against it. Why should the public sphere and the political arena be entrusted to *fuqahā'*, and their views be given precedence over those of the public? Why should *fuqahā'* and clerics have special rights to key posts and in drawing up society's overall policies? What argument is there in support of *fiqh*-based politics as against science- or reason-based politics? It is patently clear that democracy is preferable to absolute rule or rule by a *faqīh* or a cleric.

Regarding the fifth area, i.e. freedom of opinion and religion and the punishment of apostasy, freedom of opinion and religion is a prerequisite of equal rights for all and the rejection of discrimination on the basis of religion. Freedom of opinion and religion, freedom to express one's beliefs, freedom to perform religious acts and ceremonies, freedom not to perform religious acts, freedom to change one's religion and opinion, and freedom to propagate one's religion and opinion all fall within this framework. Reason supports freedom of religion and does not abide this-worldly punishments for changing one's religion. Rejecting or restricting freedom of religion and laying down punishments for apostasy, including execution or jail with hard labour, makes traditional Islam appear irrational and weak. The way to safeguard believers' faith is to strengthen their religious knowledge, not to deprive them of freedom of religion and opinion. There can be no doubt that the human rights position in support of freedom of opinion and religion is rationally preferable. I have proved this in a separate article.[4]

As to the sixth area, i.e. extra-judicial punishments, violent punishments and torture, today, human reason does not accept that people can be punished and even executed without a trial in a competent court and without the right of defence for the accused. In punishing offenders, the main aim – more than the actual physical punishment or execution or the general form of the punishments – is to uproot offences and to warn the public not to commit offences. Violent punishments have in many instances lost their effectiveness in this respect. Today's world prohibits the use of torture for extracting information or breaking a prisoner's resistance. If penal precepts in traditional Islam are not considered to be essential to devoutness, the notion of human rights must be given precedence in the three above-mentioned areas of penal law.

Hence, in all six areas, i.e. equal rights for all and the rejection of discrimination on the basis of religion, gender, slavery and religious expertise, as well as on freedom of religion and thought and the rejection of extra-judicial and violent punishments and torture, the position of human rights conventions is more defensible, more rational, more just and preferable, and the precepts of historical Islam on these issues are not acceptable in our time.

Historical Islam's solutions for resolving the conflict

Is traditional Islam capable of extricating itself from this quandary? Is it possible to resolve this conflict on the basis of the criteria of traditional *fiqh* and the methods used for formulating opinions (*ijtihād*), i.e. the formulation of opinions on secondary principles? The answer is negative. Traditional Islam has compulsory criteria and standards that cannot be cast aside without departing from the whole framework. Adhering to the criteria and standards leaves the conflict unresolved.

First, the religious evidence cited in support of some of these problematic precepts consists of Verses from the holy Qur'an. Traditional Islam maintains that these Verses yield unchanging and absolute precepts (not conditional on time and place), which are never abrogated. Taking these Verses at face value, we would, in all fairness, have no choice but to accept unequal rights for Muslims and non-Muslims, and for men and women, in many instances, unequal rights for free people and slaves; and the administration of violent punishments. A traditionalist *faqīh* has no choice but to submit to Shariʿa precepts that conflict with human rights.

Secondly, the religious evidence cited in support of nearly all the Shariʿa that conflict with human rights consists of the Narratives recounting the words and deeds of the Prophet and the Shiʿi Imams. Many of these Narratives are well-documented, reliable and perfectly valid on the basis of the accepted criteria of *fiqh*. The clear sense and purport of the relevant Narratives lead to the precepts that are considered to be in violation of human rights today. Traditional Islam believes that these valid Narratives convey to us unchanging and permanent precepts, and that "whatever was considered permissible by Muhammad will be permissible until Judgement Day and whatever was considered prohibited by Muhammad will be prohibited until Judgement Day". In some minor instances, there are also well-known opposing opinions, which are also based on some Narratives; e.g. concerning the age when girls become adults. However, opposing opinions on many of the relevant precepts lack any kind of corroboration in the Narratives. Even if generalities are cited in support, the problem remains that there is contrary evidence in the form of some Verses and reliable Narratives. With these sources and within this framework, a traditionalist *faqīh* cannot stray very far from the existing opinions and fatwas.

Thirdly, many of the Shariʿa precepts that contravene human rights are consensual. Opposing opinions are rare on many of these precepts and there is unanimity over them. The majority of the opinions in favour of the precepts are well known. Most importantly, some of the precepts that conflict with human rights are considered to be essential elements of *fiqh* or essential elements of religion. In traditional *fiqh*, precepts of this kind are unchangeable. How can it be possible to resolve the conflict with human rights while abiding by these criteria?

Fourthly, if the precepts relating to social transactions, like the worship-related precepts, are based on hidden interests or benefits, independent reason will be incapable of comprehending these interests. Hence, a traditionalist *faqīh* cannot not use the ruling of reason in favour of human rights in this arena, because, as far as he is concerned, independent reason cannot rule on these instances. What greater prohibition can there be against the rational approach than the words and deeds of the Lawgiver, which are exemplified in the Verses and the reliable Narratives that underpin the precepts? It is also impossible to ascertain for certain what justice would demand in such cases, just as reason is unable to comprehend the criteria underlying the precepts, unless they have been clearly stated by the Lawgiver.

Certainly, minor, superficial amendments are possible. For example, some precepts that are closer to human rights on women's affairs can be included in the marriage contract – as long as they do not invalidate the contract altogether. For example, the wife may be allowed to act in the husband's stead with the delegated right of initiating a divorce. A second possible way of bringing about amendments is by resorting to the principle of "distress and hardship". By proving distress and hardship, the wife can obtain a divorce without the husband's consent. Using the notion of "not bringing Islam into disrepute" is a third way of instigating amendments. For example, a sentence of stoning is occasionally not carried out, on the grounds that it would bring Islam into disrepute. On occasion, some religious punishments, especially flogging, are not carried out in public, on the same grounds. The fourth way, at least concerning the fifth and sixth areas of conflict (among the Shiʿa), would be to halt the implementation of religious punishments during the absence of the twelfth Infallible Imam. With the halting of these punishments, these areas of conflict would be resolved. However, it is obvious that these kinds of solutions cannot take us very far. The majority of the Shariʿa precepts that conflict with human rights do not lend themselves to amendment through the inclusion of conditions in a marriage contract or by appealing to the principle of "distress and hardship". Using the notion of "not bringing Islam into disrepute" is also very difficult. Claiming to understand hidden interests and harms would entail abandoning the criteria of traditional Islam. If reliance on these kinds of secondary axioms and notions turns into a routine procedure, and if they are applied more frequently than the original precepts, it will imply that there is something wrong with the formulation of the original precepts, otherwise there would be no need for so many opt-out clauses.

Although traditional *fiqh* holds that precepts can be divided into unchanging precepts and changing precepts, it also maintains that the precepts that are discussed in the field of *fiqh* are all unchanging precepts. In fact, the problem that traditional *fiqh* is facing today, i.e. disparity with the notion of human rights, falls squarely in the realm of the precepts that traditional Islam considers unchanging. Hence, the division of precepts into the two categories of unchanging and changing does not solve the problem.

One of the people who correctly recognised the inability of traditional *fiqh* and traditional methods to solve contemporary problems, and strove to use the element of interests or expediency – and the demands of time and place – to amend the situation, was the late Ayatollah Khomeini. He was of the view that the level of debate in seminaries and the framework of theory in which they work could not solve the problem. When there was protest over his new fatwa that made it permissible to play chess, he retorted: "Based on your reading of the Traditions and Narratives, modern civilisation has to be razed to the ground and people have to live in huts or remain in the desert for ever." Ayatollah Khomeini found the solution he was looking for in the absolute authority or guardianship of the state over *fiqh*. Based on his view, an Islamic state can prevent anything – whether worship-related or otherwise – that contravenes the interests of Islam, for as long as it does so. He explicitly said that the Islamic state was authorised to eliminate some precepts, such as precepts on the share crop system and sleeping partner investors. Ayatollah Khomeini believed that Shari'a precepts were mediate and accidental goals (rather than final and essential ones), instruments and tools for running the state and spreading justice. On this basis, the ruling *faqīh* (Islamic jurist) can annul all the Shari'a precepts that are not suited to the time and place or do not fulfil the interests of the state for as long as this is the case, and can also formulate new precepts that fulfil the interests of the state or are demanded by the time and place.

Now, let us imagine that a state is established in line with Ayatollah Khomeini's theory, and that it considers it to be in the interests of the state that human rights should be respected, or holds that respect for human rights is demanded by the current time and place. Would such a state be able to prevent the implementation of precepts that are contrary to human rights? Without a doubt, it would.

Expediency-based *fiqh* and allowing state-decreed precepts is more effective than the previous four solutions we looked at, because it can block all Shari'a precepts, worship-related or otherwise, as long as they are contrary to the interests of the state. Moreover, the state can formulate new precepts whenever it considers this to be in the interests of the state. So, if the ruling *faqīh* or his appointees consider it to be in the interest of the state to respect human rights, they can annul any Shari'a precept, i.e. precepts that traditional Islam views as "unchanging precepts", and even precepts that are considered to be essential elements of religion or essential elements of *fiqh*, if they conflict with human rights. Without a doubt, this innovation would resolve the conflict between traditional Islam and human rights.

However, this venerated solution has several problems. The most important problem is that it departs from the framework of traditional Islam and the accepted methods of formulating opinions. Many traditionalist *fuqahā'* believe that there is no valid evidence in the Shari'a in support of the theory of the guardianship of the *faqīh*. The absolute authority/guardianship of the state over *fiqh* only has the endorsement of its progenitor and some of his students; it is not accepted among traditionalist *fuqahā'*. Traditional *fiqh* is very cautious and – unlike Ayatollah Khomeini – is neither of the view that interests or expediency can be clearly ascertained, nor that precepts based on interests or expediency can take precedence over all Shari'a precepts, especially the worship-related ones. This point is not a problem in and of itself. If the expediency-based solution or the idea of state *fiqh* is right, it should be accepted, whether within the framework of traditional *fiqh* or outside of it, but the solution offered by expediency-based *fiqh* cannot be viewed as traditional Islam's answer to the problem. Resorting to the state's interests means abandoning the criteria of traditional Islam in order to resolve its conflict with human rights.

Be that as it may, expediency-based *fiqh* will not solve the problem either. First, obtaining state precepts or expediency-based precepts is only an intermittent and temporary solution, since the unchanging Shariʿa precepts will continue to be religiously valid; an unchanging precept will only be annulled (at the level of practice, not at the level of religious validity) by the ruling *faqīh* or his appointees if they ascertain that it is in the state's interests to do so – and only for as long as this is the case – and believers will have a duty to act on the state precept instead while it is valid. As soon as the state no longer considers the expedient precept valid, it will be annulled, and believers will revert to compliance with the former, unchanging precept. State precepts are not a permanent solution to the conflict with human rights. They are more like a painkiller that temporarily alleviates the conflict without curing it.

Secondly, expediency-based *fiqh* will put *fiqh* under the control of the state and political power. The absolute power of the guardian state over *fiqh* will make Shariʿa precepts subject to state expediency and political power, and condemn them to endless changes in line with the vagaries of state interests. Moreover, a state that believes that it is in its interest to abide by human rights would have rejected in advance any special rights for *fuqahāʾ* and clerics in the public sphere and in politics. In other words, ascertaining such interests would lead to the disqualification of the guardian state itself. Can we imagine a state that would be prepared to inform the people in all sincerity that it should not have the rights that it has? The notion of human rights is fundamentally incompatible with the theory of expediency-based *fiqh* and an absolute, appointed, guardian state run by *fuqahāʾ*.

Thirdly, even if we disregard the above-mentioned problems, if the number of state precepts keeps growing in such a way that society's interests seem to lie in the temporary annulment of the majority of Shariʿa precepts, and if these interests persist over a number of years and decades, would these two facts not suggest that we had made some fundamental errors in deducing the unchanging Shariʿa precepts in the first place? Otherwise, why would we need constant opt-out clauses and endless patchwork?

Although Ayatollah Khomeini's idea is open to serious criticism, his courage in criticising traditional *fiqh*, whilst remaining appreciative of it, is laudable, as is his acknowledgement of the fact that the accepted methods of formulating opinions in *fiqh* were ineffective when it came to dealing with the problems of the modern world.

Historical Islam – and traditional *fiqh* in particular – cannot extricate itself from this impasse without reassessing its methods and underpinnings. It seems that formulating opinions (*ijtihād*) on secondary religious principles (*furūʿ*) has reached the end of its historical life. The ineffectiveness, in our times, of traditional *fiqh* and its methods (i.e. formulating opinions on secondary principles) must not prevent us from being grateful to it for the services it has rendered in the past. New methods all owe a debt of gratitude to their predecessors. Moreover, the traditional method of deducing precepts is still valid for worship-related issues such as the ritual prayers, fasting and *ḥajj*, because reason cannot enter the realm of worship, and there is no conflict with human rights in this realm.

International and national efforts to combine traditional Islam and human rights

At the international level, over the past quarter of a century, six declarations and draft declarations on Islam and human rights have been issued by the Islamic Council for Europe (1980, 1981), the Kuwait Conference (of the International Commission of Jurists and the Union of Arab Lawyers, 1980) and the Organisation of the Islamic Conference (Mecca, 1979; Ta'if, 1981). The most recent and most official Islamic declaration of human rights was issued at the Nineteenth Islamic Conference of Foreign Ministers in Cairo in 1990 – based on a draft prepared in Tehran – under the title "The Cairo Declaration on Human Rights in Islam". Apart from these declarations, which are at most a delineation of the common view of human rights among Muslims, Islamic countries have not managed to approve any binding convention, treaty or covenant in this respect. Be that as it may, these mere declarations are still cause for hope. We must see them as an indication that Islamic communities recognise the need to consider human rights. These declarations have endeavoured to highlight those points in international human rights conventions that are in keeping with traditional Islam, to extract corroboration from scattered bits of Islamic teachings and to prove that Islam was the forerunner of respect for human rights. The novel points in the Cairo Declaration, in comparison with international human rights conventions, include the recognition of the right to struggle against colonialism as "one of the most evil forms of enslavement" (Article 11) and the recognition of everyone's "right to live in a clean environment, away from vice and moral corruption, an environment that would foster his self-development; and it is incumbent upon the state and society in general to afford that right" (Article 17). The Cairo Declaration represents a big stride in terms of prohibiting discrimination between slaves and free people, and prohibiting slavery itself. Article 11 states: "Human beings are born free, and no one has the right to enslave, humiliate, oppress or exploit them, and there can be no subjugation but to God the Most-High."

The Cairo Declaration and the other declarations were completely unsuccessful in dealing with the other five areas of conflict between traditional Islam and the notion of human rights, and confined themselves to general phrases, ambiguity, brevity or silence, effectively confirming the conflict. For example, Article 10 of the Cairo Declaration states: "Islam is the religion of unspoiled nature. It is prohibited to exercise any form of compulsion on man or to exploit his poverty or ignorance in order to convert him to another religion or to atheism." What about exercising compulsion to make someone remain a Muslim? Is that allowed? At any rate, this declaration, in the mould of traditional Islam, has not recognised freedom of religion, and has formally recognised the right to discrimination on the basis of religion. That is to say, unlike international human rights conventions, which are neutral on religion, the Cairo Declaration is bound by and committed to Islam. On the question of gender discrimination, the Cairo Declaration has been unable to go further than saying that "woman is equal to man in human dignity, and has rights to enjoy as well as duties to perform; she has her own civil entity and financial independence, and the right to retain her name and lineage" (Article 6). Article 24 states: "All the rights and freedoms stipulated in this Declaration are subject to the Islamic Shariʿa."

The Cairo Declaration is the height of traditional Islam's efforts in the realm of human rights, and it has failed to resolve these five areas of conflict. The declaration is discriminatory in terms of, first, religious rights and religious intolerance, secondly, gender discrimination, thirdly, discriminatory rights in the public sphere (of course the declaration is silent on the question of special rights for *fuqahāʾ*, and has confined itself to speaking about everyone's "right to assume public office in accordance with the provisions of the Shariʿa"), fourthly, failure to recognise the right to freedom of opinion and religion and fifthly, implicit recognition of degrading, violent and extra-judicial punishments.

The Constitution of the Islamic Republic of Iran is the height of traditional Shiʿi Islam's efforts in the realm of human rights. The Constitution has officially recognised discrimination between Muslims and non-Muslims, and Shiʿis and Sunnis, in Articles 12, 13 and 14. Discrimination between men and women has been subtly included in the form of Articles 20 and 21. The question of slavery has been passed over in silence, although Article 4 lays the groundwork for recourse to all the Shariʿa of traditional Islam. The Islamic Republic's Constitution has explicitly recognised discrimination between *fuqahāʾ* and commoners in the public sphere in Articles 5, 57, 109 and 110, and it is a standard-bearer in this respect. Although Articles 23 and 24 give recognition to freedom of opinion, freedom of religion – including the right to change religion, publicise one's own religion and so on – is out of the question, in view of the fact that it has been said in Article 4 that the Shariʿa absolutely governs all the articles of the Constitution and all other laws and regulations. Article 38 has explicitly banned all forms of torture and Article 36 has ruled out extra-judicial punishments and stated that "only competent courts are entitled to pass a sentence and execute it." Hence, the situation is better in the sixth area of conflict, i.e. punishments, than in the other areas. Torture and extra-judicial punishments have been prohibited, while violent and degrading punishments have been passed over in silence, although Article 4 effectively leaves the door open to the application of such punishments. Among the laws of the Islamic Republic of Iran, the Islamic Penal Law is considered to be the most problematic in terms of violating the norms of human rights.

The conduct of the Guardian Council (which vets legislation for compliance with the Constitution and the Shariʿa) shows that the council's approach is further away from respect for human rights than that of the the constituent assembly that drew up the Constitution in 1979.

On the basis of traditional Islam, it is impossible to advance any further in terms of human rights than the Cairo Declaration and the Constitution of the Islamic Republic of Iran. Examining these two documents testifies to the disparity between traditional Islam and human rights norms. Unless *fuqahā*ʾ are allowed to formulate opinions (*ijtihād*) on primary religious principles (*uṣūl*) and unless there is a fundamental transformation in their way of thinking, the conflict between Islamic countries' laws and the notion of human rights is irresolvable in these areas.

Abuse of human rights and its causes

The opponents of the notion of human rights usually raise a number of objections. One is that human rights are said to be a political tool that is used by the US or the European Union to exert pressure on developing countries, especially Islamic ones, whereas human rights violations by their allies, especially Israel, are overlooked. Another objection is that human rights are said to be in keeping with Western societies and their way of life. It is said that accepting them would mean surrendering to the West: we Muslims do not need the paraphernalia of the infidels' world. Is there anything wrong with our religion, that we have to try to make up for it by using the handiwork of infidels and the enemies of Islam?

There are a number of answers to these objections. On the whole, it is regrettable that these kinds of superficial objections are raised in the name of religion, making it seem as if faith and religion are in conflict with the notion of human rights. In response to the first objection, it has to be said that human rights norms are violated more frequently in developing countries than in developed countries, although developed countries are not very sensitive to human rights violations in other countries. If their interests conflict with respect for human rights in developing countries, they never hesitate to act on the basis of their interests. The notion of human rights is a necessary condition of a healthy world; it is not a sufficient condition. Respect for human rights requires binding mechanisms. We never said that one swallow would make a spring, and that believing in human rights would solve all the problems of contemporary humanity. We made a much more modest claim: respect for human rights norms will solve some of the problems of contemporary human beings.

Moreover, nothing is immune to abuse. Has religion not been abused in numerous ways over the course of history? Have tyrannical states not used religion, which is a source of compassion, as a tool for cruelty and for consolidating and justifying their power? The notion of human rights, too, can be abused, but such abuses by no means detract from the desirability of religion and human rights.

In response to the second objection, it has to be said that human rights, in and of itself, is either right or wrong. Geography does not play a part in its rightness or wrongness. The fact that an idea originates in the East does not make it more right, nor does the fact that an idea originates in the West make it wrong. None of the articles of the Universal Declaration of Human Rights or the two international covenants on civil, political, economic, social and cultural rights were designed solely with Western societies in mind. Human rights should be defended not because they originate in the West but because they are right, rational and in keeping with justice and fairness.

Over the course of history, similar objections have been raised against logic and philosophy. It was once said that anyone who applied logic was a heretic. Centuries had to pass before it became clear that there was no connection between formal logic and polytheism or monotheism. For centuries, philosophy was rejected as "infidels' spittle" because it originated in Greece, but it is clear today that no system of thought, even religious learning, can answer its critics without being explained rationally. Accepting the notion of human rights is not surrendering to the West; it is surrendering to reason and justice. Religion is the answer to particular human needs, not the answer to everything that human beings need. There were times when religion was expected to solve medical problems too. But today no one expects medical prescriptions from religion. If we do not expect religion to have the answers to questions about physics or chemistry, why should we expect it to have the answers to questions relating to economics, politics or law? We should expect religion to answer our religious needs. A detailed treatment of this subject must be left for some other occasion. At any rate, resisting the notion of human rights in the name of religion inflicts one of the biggest blows on religiosity and religious faith, and it provides an excellent pretext to people who are opposed to religion.

Intellectual Islam's solution to the conflict between traditional Islam and human rights

Now, after all the descriptions, analyses and judgements, it is time to offer a solution. What is the solution to the conflict between historical Islam and the notion of human rights? In accepting the notion of human rights, what "Islam" do religious intellectuals offer as a replacement for traditional Islam? What does "intellectual Islam" consist of? What are its characteristics?

Since the time when Muslims had to take a stance on modernity and its trappings, including human rights and democracy – and once it had become clear that traditional Islam's answers were not appropriate – they have witnessed the birth and development of a new movement, which is not unique to either Sunnis or Shiʿis, nor to either Iran or the Arab countries, nor to either the Middle East or the Far East. There have been different – but in a sense common – efforts among all Muslim elites to present a new image of Islam and to offer a new reading of Scripture and the Tradition of Muhammad. This movement is known as intellectual Islam or Islamic modernism. Whilst remaining committed to the eternal message of God's revelation, it believes that, in historical Islam, the sacred message has been mixed with the customs and conventions of the age when revelation was made, that all of traditional Islam's problems in the modern age emanate from the customary part of traditional Islam, and that the sacred message can still be defended with great pride. The main duty of insightful religious experts and *ʿulamāʾ* is to extract the sacred message again and to push aside the sediment of time-bound customs. Hence, this solution is not confined to resolving the conflict between traditional Islam and human rights; it will also resolve other conflicts, such as those of reason, science and democracy, with traditional Islam.

Islam's teachings can be divided into four parts: first, matters of faith and belief, i.e. faith in Almighty God, faith in the hereafter, Judgement Day and the afterlife, and faith in the Seal of the Prophets Muhammad Ibn ʿAbd Allah (peace be upon him) and his mission. Secondly, matters of morality: i.e. purifying the self and equipping oneself with moral values and virtues in line with the most important aim of the Prophet's mission. Thirdly, matters relating to worship: i.e. prayer, fasting, *ḥajj* and alms, as the most important manifestations of servitude and submission to God. Fourthly, non-worship-related Shariʿa precepts, which are known as the *fiqh* of social transactions and include precepts relating to civil law, commercial law, penal law, public and private international law, fundamental rights, and precepts relating to victuals and drinks.

More than 98 per cent of the Verses of the holy Qurʾan concern the first three parts: i.e. matters of faith, morality and worship, and only about 2 per cent have been devoted to the *fiqh* of social transactions. Although the proportion of non-worship-related precepts is much higher among the Narratives than among the Verses, they form only about 10 per cent of the Narratives. But, in traditional Islam, the fourth part, i.e. the *fiqh* of social transactions, has gained indescribable importance, to the point where it has overshadowed the parts of religion that relate to faith, morality and worship. In the worship-related precepts, too, their *fiqh*-based form and shape has cast a shadow over the other dimensions of this quintessential component of religion. By contrast, the main defining characteristic of the modern reading of Islam is that the focus of attention is on matters of faith, morality and worship as the main body of God's religion, in the sense that these three matters are given greater depth, regain the significance attached to them in the Qur'an and flourish as the main mark of religiosity. The main difference between the modern reading and the traditional reading is over the fourth part; i.e. the *fiqh* of social transactions. Modernist Islam does not deny the need for Islamic law and jurisprudence (Shariʿa and *fiqh*), but it is a critic of historical Islamic law and traditional jurisprudence, and it disagrees with the stances adopted by *fuqahāʾ* the past on numerous precepts. Hence, it presents a new *fiqh*. Although this new *fiqh* has a common stance with traditional *fiqh* on some precepts, it has serious differences with it on some other precepts, including the Shariʿa precepts that conflict with human rights. In terms of overall volume, the new *fiqh* is smaller than traditional *fiqh*, and on the criteria underpinning its methods for formulating opinions, it differs from the principles of traditional *fiqh*.

Each and every (non-worship-related) Shariʿa precept had three particular characteristics in the age of revelation: 1) It was deemed to be rational by the conventions of the time. 2) It was deemed to be just by the conventions of the time. 3) In comparison with the precepts stipulated by other religions and rites, it was deemed to be a better solution. In the light of these three characteristics, all these precepts were progressive solutions in the age of revelation, and laid the groundwork for a successful religious system. Collective human reason did not have better solutions at the time, and rational conduct endorsed these precepts and did not consider any of them to be unjust, violent, degrading or irrational.

In other words, all Shariʿa precepts were formulated by the wise Lawgiver in accordance with the best interests of the worshippers. The interest of the human species (*maṣāliḥ al-nawʿiyya*) formed the basis of the formulation of Shariʿa commands and harms to the species formed the basis of Shariʿa prohibitions. It is impossible to find a precept that was formulated without the consideration of species interests or harms. One of the most important marks of species interests is justice. Hence, Shariʿa precepts have been formulated in accordance with justice and fairness, and the conventions of the age of revelation totally sensed this justice and fairness.

A Shariʿa precept will only remain valid as long as it fulfils these species interests. On this basis, there are two types of precepts: the first type are precepts that are permanently linked to species interests or harms; in other words, they will always retain the same quality, and this quality will not vary in different times and places. Precepts such as the obligation of being fair, the obligation of thanking the Benefactor, the prohibition on injustice and betrayal, the obligation of respecting a trust and honouring a pledge, the prohibition on lying, and so on, will always remain unchanged. The second type of precepts are those whose quality of goodness or badness may change. Most of the Shari'a precepts relating to social transactions are of this second type. In other words, in some times and places, they are in keeping with people's best interests and, while this is the case, they are valid. There is no doubt about the existence of these two types of Shari'a precepts; this is a division that has been recognised in many books on theology and the principles of *fiqh*. The conflict between Shari'a precepts and the notion of human rights which we have been discussing never occurs among the first type of precepts; in other words, none of the Shari'a precepts that are permanently linked to interests or harms, conflict with human rights. The conflict relates to the second type of Shari'a precepts.

At the level of the "in itself", the first type of Shari'a precepts is created for all eternity, but the wise Lawgiver – knowing better than anyone the potential of actions and circumstances and the way they vary over time and place – makes the second type of precept conditional on the continuation of the circumstances, and temporary in this sense. In other words, the precepts concerning actions that may be beneficial in some circumstances and harmful in others have not been formulated by God as permanent and unchanging precepts; from the start, they were made conditional on the continuation of the relevant circumstances.

However, at the level of the "for us", virtually all Shari'a precepts (i.e. precepts of the second type) are presented in an absolute and permanent form and without any conditions attached. There was a specific advantage to not stipulating a time frame for Shari'a precepts that were, in fact, temporary and conditional on the circumstances: it was unnecessary to stipulate that a precept was temporary long before the relevant circumstances had expired, since it is easier for people to act on a permanent precept than on a temporary, conditional one. Since the circumstances in the original time period and the circumstances in the subsequent era differ, if the Lawgiver had formulated precepts on the basis of the subsequent time frame, they would not have been in keeping with best interests in the original time. But if the Lawgiver were to formulate precepts for the original period and not allow them to be abrogated in the subsequent time – when they would no longer be in keeping with people's best interests – it would mean that the Lawgiver would be demanding something from people that was against their best interests, something that is unthinkable. Hence, concerning these kinds of actions which may be appropriate or inappropriate in different circumstances, there is no option but to formulate temporary precepts. Actions of this kind do not lend themselves to being governed by permanent precepts. If the goodness or badness of an action depends on impermanent circumstances, the only solution is to formulate temporary precepts, which in themselves are only valid as long as they continue to be in line with people's best interests. Since at the level of the "for us", it is always better to present precepts in an absolute and unconditional form, nearly all precepts have been issued in this way, without the stipulation of expiry conditions in terms of time and place. But as Shaykh al-Ta'ifa Tusi (d. 1068), the great rationalist *faqīh*, said: faced with Shari'a precepts, the pious have to be confident that these commands and prohibitions pertain for only as long as they "continue to be in their best interests". In other words, all Shari'a precepts (of the second type) are in fact conditional and temporary: they pertain only as long as the circumstances that make them in keeping with people's best interests persist.

Most of the commands and prohibitions and the precepts that we find in the holy Qur'an and in the Traditions are of the second type. That is to say, although the language of the evidence is absolute and non-conditional, in reality and in themselves, they are conditional on, and bound by, the continuation of the underlying best interest and are set to expire when that interest expires. The fact that a Shari'a precept is based on the Qur'an does not mean that it is a permanent precept which rests on permanent interests. Many of the Shari'a precepts that rest on variable interests are also based on the Qur'an. In fact, the idea of one precept being abrogated or superseded by another is one of the most important topics of discussion in Qur'anic studies, theology and the principles of *fiqh*. Abrogation means discarding a Shari'a precept by virtue of the fact that its term has expired.

The main prerequisite for abrogation is that the abrogated precept must be of the second type; i.e. precepts that are not associated with permanent interests or permanent harms, but with interests or harms that may change with variations in time and place. Hence, abrogation does not apply to the first type of precept, but it does apply to the second type and has in fact occurred in the past. It goes without saying that the abrogation of a precept that is based on the Qur'an means the abrogation of the precept without the abrogation of the recitation. In other words, whilst accepting that the abrogated Verse has been revealed to the Prophet by God, and will forever be a part of the Qur'an and included in recitations and in the discussion of the miraculousness and eloquence of the Qur'an, the relevant precept is abrogated and superseded by another Verse. In other words, the first Verse presented a temporary and conditional precept and, although phrased in an absolute language, we realise, with the revelation of the second Verse, that the precept has reached the end of its term and is no longer in our best interests, and that our duty in practice is to abide by the second Verse (i.e. the abrogating Verse). In the words of Imam 'Ali (peace be upon him) anyone who cannot distinguish between an abrogated precept and an abrogating precept is condemned to perdition and will lead others to perdition.

At any rate, the realm of abrogation is one of the essential elements of the field of exegesis. Among the most important instances of abrogation in the Qur'an are the abrogation of the Najawi Verse (58:12) by 58:13; the abrogation of the number of warriors (8:65) by 8:66; the precept on widows (2:240) by 2:234; the precept on the punishment for lewd acts in 4:15–16, the precept on inheriting on the basis of faith in 8:72 by 33:6; and the changing of the *qibla* from Jerusalem to the Holy Mosque (2:142–50). Referring to the existing books on Qur'anic studies and studying the abrogated and abrogating Verses will leave no doubt that even Shariʿa precepts that are based on the Qur'an and multiple Traditions can still be abrogated, and that this has indeed occurred in specific instances. A Shariʿa precept that has been based on a single Tradition may also be subject to abrogation.

The essence of the discussion lies in the answer to the following question. The fact that the abrogation of Verses, multiple Traditions and single Traditions is a possibility and has actually occurred is not disputed. The dispute is over what can serve as an abrogator. The proof and argument of the abrogator cannot be weaker than that of the abrogated. The abrogator of a Verse has to be another Verse or a multiple Tradition (a multiply attested account of the Prophet's words and deeds). The abrogator of a multiple Tradition can be a Verse or another multiple Tradition. A presumed single Tradition is not qualified to abrogate a Verse or a multiple Tradition. Now it must be asked, is the proof and argument of definite reason qualified to abrogate a Shariʿa precept?

The question can be rephrased as follows: What is to be done when there is conflict between a narrated proof and a rational proof? If the rational proof is definite, it can serve as a yardstick for reassessing the manifest meaning of the narrated proof. In other words, the narrated proof is interpreted in the light of the rational proof or, to put it more precisely, the rational proof is favoured over the narrated proof. This is the unanimous view of those Islamic experts who believe God must act justly (*ʿulamāʾ ʿadliyya*), whether Muʿtazilites or Shiʿites. The corollary of this dignified position is that narration-based Shariʿa precepts can be abrogated by the rulings of definite reason. The position of Islamic experts who view reason as one of the four legitimate proofs in connection with the Shariʿa effectively means that a narration-based Shariʿa precept can be abrogated by a reason-based Shariʿa precept. If all the Shariʿa precepts of the second type (precepts that are based on interests that can vary over time and place) are in fact conditional on the continuation of the relevant interests and, therefore, temporary, and, if reason can somehow rule definitively that the relevant interests have expired, the relevant Shariʿa precept is clearly abrogated by the ruling of reason. Once reason has so ruled, the former Shariʿa precept no longer constitutes an actual duty. If reason is qualified to discover Shariʿa precepts, it is undoubtedly also qualified to discover when a Shariʿa precept has reached the end of its term. The idea that the ruling of reason can serve as an abrogator simply means that reason is capable of imposing time limits on Shariʿa precepts.

It would seem that traditional thinking on theology, the principles of *fiqh* and Qur'anic exegesis does not have any problems with the various stages of this argument, apart from holding to the following point: if reason ever comes to such an understanding, its conclusion is binding, but definite reason has not come to such an understanding that we might base ourselves on it. In fact, the dispute with these traditionalist scholars will be over the minor premises, not the major premises. In other words, the disagreement with them is not over principles but over actual, concrete instances (when reason may be said to be certain about something). Whatever stance we take in this dispute, the result will have deep consequences. If we investigate the root causes of this problem, we find that until about two centuries ago, no conflict was observed between narration-based arguments and reason-based arguments. Moreover, *fuqahā'* used to find the answers they were seeking to the problems of their time in their understanding of Scripture and Tradition, so they had no need to refer to reason-based arguments. Even the understanding of the rationalists, who believed that reason also had binding force, did not differ substantially from that of the traditionalists. For example, a glance at the views of al-Ghazali (d. 1111), an Ash'arite, Ibn Abi al-Hadid (d. 1258), a Mu'tazilite, Shaykh Yusuf al-Bahrani (d. 1772), a traditionalist, and Sahib Jawahir (Shaykh Muhammad Hasan al-Najafi, d. 1850), a rationalist, would reveal how small a part was played by reason in the derivation of Shari'a precepts.

The distinguishing feature of the modern age is the blossoming of reason. Critical reason does not recognise any red lines and has begun questioning everything, even things that were unquestionable in the past. Contemporary human beings have grasped many things that were shrouded in mystery in the past. This does not mean that modern human beings know everything and that nothing remains unknown to them; on the contrary, as the scope of their knowledge has increased, so has their recognition of the extent and depth of their ignorance. They ask courageous questions and offer modest answers. No religious scholars can consider themselves independent of new rational studies, such as the methods of analysing meaning, methods of interpreting texts (hermeneutics), the philosophy of religion, modern theology, the sociology of religion, the psychology of religion, the methodology of history, philosophy, law, ethics, etc. Objections and criticism cannot be foreclosed by simply saying that all the social transactions precepts are in the service of God and closed for discussion, or by appealing to hidden interests and harms. Contemporary human beings are certain that owning slaves is unjust, irrational and reprehensible. They do not consider just and rational discrimination on the basis of religion or gender. They consider it unfair and irrational that *fuqahā'* and clerics should have special rights in the public sphere. They declare any limitation on freedom of religion to be a constriction of innate human rights. They find violent punishments intolerable. When reason comprehends and recognises a ruling, it is binding, essentially binding. Contemporary human beings do not doubt their powers of comprehension in these matters. If there are people who have not yet attained this level of comprehension, they have no right to dismiss the comprehension of others and the rational conventions of our day.

The rationality of contemporary Muslims is not in line with – and actually conflicts with – the narration-based proof of some of traditional Islam's Shariʿa precepts. Reason is strong enough today to serve as a yardstick for reassessing narration-based proofs and discovering their impermanence. Today, discussions about reason have become far broader and far more profound than the limited discussions of the past about whether reason was capable of independent judgement on good and bad or not.

At any rate, contemporary Muslims see two lines of thinking in Scripture and Tradition: first, a line of thinking that is compatible with human rights and consists of two types of propositions; i.e. propositions that do not conflict with the notion of human rights and propositions that explicitly affirm that human beings have rights simply by virtue of being human. These kinds of propositions are to be found in the generalities contained in the Mecca Verses and in the Prophet's conduct in Mecca, as well as in the conduct of Imam ʿAli during his time as leader. Secondly, a line of thinking that is incompatible with human rights, including propositions that are explicitly in conflict with human rights, and textual support for distinctions in human beings' rights depending on their religion, gender, whether they are slaves or not, and whether they are *fuqahā'* or not; support for violent and degrading punishment; and the rejection of freedom of religion. These kinds of propositions are to be found in the form of explicit proofs in some of the Medina Verses, parts of the Prophet's conduct in Medina, and some of the Narratives about the Shiʿi Imams.

Faced with these two lines of thinking, traditional Islam has found the evidence for the second stronger, because the proofs for the first are either general, indefinite or brief, whereas the proofs for the second are specific, delineated and detailed. In sum, traditional Islam attaches precedence to proofs that are specific, delineated and detailed. On this basis, all Shariʿa precepts – whether of the first set or the second – are deemed to be unchanging and permanent. This method of adding up the evidence comes into conflict with the notion of human rights in our day. In the solution that we offer, the narration-based proofs of the first set are fortified with reason-based proofs, and reason-based proofs are used as a yardstick for assessing the time frame of the precepts of the second set. Reason discovers that these were bound by interests that no longer apply and have now expired. More precisely, the argument of reason, corroborated by the narration-based proofs of the first set, abrogates the narration-based proofs of the second set, which conflict with human rights, and reports that their terms have expired. With the expiry and abrogation of the conflicting proofs, the conflict itself is fundamentally resolved.

The three preconditions of being rational, just and better than the solutions offered by other religions, did not only pertain in the age of revelation. In any age, the non-worship-related Shariʿa precepts must meet these three preconditions on the basis of the conventions of the wise people of the day. Definite disagreement between a precept and the dictates of reason in our day, a conflict with the norms of justice of our day or the existence of preferable solutions in the modern age reveal that the relevant precept was not permanent and has been abrogated. In other words, these precepts were in keeping with best interests in the age of revelation; they did not rank among the Lawgiver's permanent, unchanging laws. When people start speaking about the implications of time and place, it means that they have accepted the idea that a Shariʿa precept can be temporary. The implications of time and place are not necessarily unchanging; they differ and change. The philosophy behind the presence of these precepts in unchanging Scripture and Tradition was the need to solve the problems of the age of revelation and similar situations. If the Lawgiver had not taken into account the implications of time and place of the Prophet's day and the customs of the time, and had abandoned people to their own devices – at a time when there was great need for such precepts, in view of the limitations of collective rationality in the age of revelation – it would have been out of keeping with God's eloquent wisdom. Despite his perfections, the Prophet would have been unable – without the direct assistance of God – to solve the countless problems related to organising religion and running society. Many was the occasion when he hoped and waited for the blessing of revelation from God. Hence, there was no alternative but to formulate – alongside the unchanging and permanent Shariʿa precepts – temporary precepts that were contingent on the continuation of the underlying best interests, and to include them in Scripture and Tradition. The language of the proof, even if it explicitly conveys everlastingness, does not prevent abrogation if the evidence and proof for one precept is superseded by a subsequent proof. Our distinguished predecessors have unanimously accepted this.

Formulating opinions (*ijtihād*) means distinguishing precepts that were laid down in accordance with the demands of time and place and the conditions of the age of revelation, from the unchanging and permanent precepts of the Shariʿa. Confusing these two types of precepts, and considering all the precepts of Scripture and Tradition to be unchanging and applicable in all times and places, is to fail to understand correctly the meaning of religion, the aim of the Prophetic mission and the objectives of the Shariʿa. People who have elevated secondary precepts and practical forms above the aims and objectives of religion, and who have lent sanctity to the customs of the age of revelation while disregarding the sacred aims of religion and the exalted objectives of the Shariʿa, are at some distance from the correct way of formulating opinions. Constantly rehearsing fatwas that have been issued in the past and glorifying constantly-recurring opinions as the best amounts to nothing more than the imitation of our predecessors in formulating opinions. Shariʿa precepts are accidentally desirable, whereas the exalted aims of religion are essentially so. In other words, Shariʿa precepts are secondary ways or means of attaining religion's main, sacred aims. Any way is only valid as long as it leads us to the destination. The way is not the object, it is the means. If we become certain (not presuming or guessing or assuming) that a precept is no longer the right way and that the best interests on which it was based have expired, it goes without saying that it is no longer valid. If insightful religious authorities (*mujtahids*), informed *fuqahāʾ* and Islamologists who are acquainted with the times fail to rise to this challenge, let them know for certain that serious religious and cultural problems and crises will eclipse religion and the Shariʿa. It goes without saying that deciding which precepts are conditional on mutable best interests, and which are unchanging and permanent, is a specialist task that requires deep knowledge of Scripture and Tradition, on the one hand, and familiarity with the modern achievements of reason (or with the capabilities and limitations of reason in the modern age), on the other. If, per chance, there are people who fear permanent abrogation (despite all the supporting evidence and despite taking every precaution), they can use temporary abrogation, in the sense that they do not rule out that the circumstances may change again and that the abrogated precept may come into force again in a different time and place. The idea of temporary abrogation is not unheard of in Qur'anic studies.

Moreover, the real interests and harms that underpin precepts – which are, on occasion, described as hidden interests and harms and, on other occasions, as intrinsic interests and harms – are completely different from the interests of the state as set out in Ayatollah Khomeini's idea of interest-based *fiqh* or state *fiqh*. In the former case, it is a question of species interests, whereas, in the latter case, it is a question of the interests of a political regime or what the ruler deems to be in the interests of the people. The discernment of species interests is the responsibility of religious experts and conventional wisdom, while the discernment of the state's interests is the responsibility of statesmen and rulers. The former are qualified to formulate Shariʿa precepts, while the latter are in a position to issue state precepts or state decrees.

I hope that readers who have criticisms or suggestions regarding the foregoing material – especially those who are followers of traditional Islam – will be kind enough to inform me of any shortcomings and flaws. The argument will undoubtedly become more cogent in the light of criticism and the clash of ideas.

Peace be upon you.

Translated from the Persian by Nilou Mobasser

Part Two

The Challenge of Equality

5 Classical *fiqh*, contemporary ethics and gender justice

Ziba Mir-Hosseini

In classical Islamic legal texts (*fiqh*), gender inequality is an *a priori* principle that reflects the way in which their authors related to the sacred texts of Islam and the world in which they lived. In this world, inequality between men and women was the natural order of things, the only way to regulate relations between them. Biology was destiny: a woman was created to bear and rear children; this was her primary role and her most important contribution to society. The concepts of equality in law and women's rights – as we mean them today – had no place and little relevance to conceptions of justice in the world of these texts.

By the early twentieth century, with the advent of modernity and the idea that equality is intrinsic to conceptions of justice, and with the emergence of modern Muslim nation-states, the world inhabited by the authors of those classical *fiqh* texts had disappeared. Their intellectual and legal authority waned as secular education expanded and new legal systems were created, inspired by Western models. But the unequal construction of gender rights formulated in those texts lingered on. It was reproduced, though in a modified way, as *fiqh* rulings on family and gender relations were selectively reformed, codified and grafted onto unified legal systems. In the regulation of marriage and gender relations, the statute books took the place of *fiqh* texts, and family law came to be defined by the legislative assembly of a particular nation-state, rather than by private scholars operating within a particular *fiqh* school. As *fiqh* and its practitioners were confined to the ivory tower of seminaries, they lost touch with changing social and political realities and were unable to meet the epistemological challenges of modernity. Thus the *fiqh* tradition lost its dynamism and became a closed book, removed from public debate and critical examination.

In the second part of the twentieth century, with the rise of political Islam and the slogan of "return to Shari'a", the Islamists brought the classical *fiqh* texts out of the closet and – unintentionally – exposed their patriarchal ethos to critical scrutiny and public debate. Some of them defended the *fiqh* rulings as God's will and the authentic "Islamic" way of life, but attempts to translate them into policy provoked many women to increasing criticism and greater activism. Paradoxically, this opened a space, an arena, which has allowed the articulation of an internal critique of patriarchal readings of the Shari'a that is unprecedented in Muslim history. There emerged a new gender discourse that argues for equal rights on all fronts for women within an Islamic framework, various versions of it being labelled "Islamic Feminism".[1] This discourse is nurtured by a feminist scholarship in Islam that is both discovering a hidden history and re-reading the textual sources to unveil an egalitarian interpretation of the Shari'a.

This paper is a contribution to this scholarship, in which I examine, from a critical feminist perspective, the notion of gender rights as constructed in classical *fiqh* texts. I focus on two sets of rulings: those regulating marriage and divorce; and those relating to women's participation in society, or the notion of *ḥijāb* as seclusion. They form two sides of the same patriarchal coin that has legitimated and institutionalised the control and subjugation of women. My objective is twofold: first, to show that these rulings are the products of juristic reasoning and socio-cultural assumptions about the nature of relations between men and women. In other words, they are "man-made" juristic constructs, which were shaped by, and reflected, the social, cultural and political conditions within which Islam's sacred texts were understood and turned into law. My second objective is to show that these rulings are neither defensible on Islamic grounds nor tenable under contemporary conditions.

After a note on my own position and conceptual background, I examine classical *fiqh* rulings on marriage and gender relations, highlighting the theological, philosophical and jurisprudential assumptions that underlie them. I end by considering the challenge that they present to feminist scholars in Islam in their attempts to advance an egalitarian interpretation of the Shari'a.

Approach and conceptual framework

I must stress I am not attempting to emulate Muslim jurists (*fuqahā'*), who extract legal rules from the sacred sources (Qur'an and Sunna) by following juristic methodology (*uṣūl al-fiqh*). Nor is my approach the same as those of the majority of Muslim feminists who go back to the sacred texts in order to "unread patriarchy".[2] I am not concerned – or qualified – to do *ijtihād* or to offer (yet another) new reading of the sacred texts; this is contested terrain, where both those who argue for gender equality and those who reject it can and do provide textual support for their arguments, though commonly taking the texts out of context in both cases. Rather, I seek to engage with juristic constructs and theories and to unveil the theological and rational assumptions and legal theories that underlie them.

I approach classical *fiqh* rulings on gender as a trained legal anthropologist, but also as a believing Muslim woman who needs to make sense of her faith and her religious tradition.[3] I believe in the justice of Islam, and place my analysis within the tradition of Islamic legal thought by invoking two crucial distinctions in that tradition. These distinctions are made by all Muslim jurists and have been upheld in all schools of Islamic law, but have been distorted and obscured in modern times, when modern nation-states have created uniform legal systems and selectively reformed and codified elements of Islamic family law, and when a new political Islam has emerged that uses Shariʿa as an ideology.

The first distinction is between Shariʿa, revealed law, and *fiqh*, the science of Islamic jurisprudence.[4] This distinction underlies the emergence of various schools of Islamic law and within them a multiplicity of positions and opinions. Shariʿa, literally "the way", in Muslim belief is the totality of God's will as revealed to the Prophet Muhammad. *Fiqh*, jurisprudence, literally "understanding", is the process of human endeavour to discern and extract legal rules from the sacred sources of Islam: that is, the Qur'an and the Sunna (the practice of the Prophet, as contained in *ḥadīth*, Traditions). In other words, while the Shariʿa is sacred, eternal and universal, *fiqh* is human and – like any other system of jurisprudence – mundane, temporal and local.

It is essential to stress this distinction and its epistemological and political ramifications. *Fiqh* is often mistakenly equated with Shariʿa, not only in popular Muslim discourses but also by specialists and politicians, who often do so with ideological intent. What Islamists and others commonly assert to be a "Shariʿa mandate" (hence divine and infallible), is in fact the result of *fiqh*, juristic speculation and extrapolation (hence human and fallible). *Fiqh* texts, which are patriarchal in both spirit and form, are frequently invoked as a means to silence and frustrate Muslims' search for this-worldly justice – to which legal justice and equality in law are intrinsic. I contend that patriarchal interpretations of the Shariʿa can and must be challenged at the level of *fiqh*, which is nothing more than the human understanding of the divine will – what we are able to understand of the Shariʿa in this world at the legal level. In short, it is the distinction between Shariʿa and *fiqh* that enables me – as a believing Muslim – to argue for gender justice within the framework of my faith.[5] Throughout this chapter, then, the Shariʿa (as contained in the Qur'an and the Prophetic Traditions) is understood as a transcendental ideal, the path, the way of life, that embodies the justice of Islam and the spirit of the Qur'anic revelations; while *fiqh* includes not only the vast corpus of jurisprudential texts but also the positive laws and rulings that Muslim jurists claim to be rooted in the sacred texts.

The second distinction, which I also take from Islamic legal tradition, is that between the two main categories of legal rulings (*aḥkām*): between *ʿibādāt* (ritual/spiritual acts) and *muʿāmalāt* (social/contractual acts). Rulings in the first category, *ʿibādāt*, regulate relations between God and the believer, where jurists contend there is limited scope for rationalisation, explanation and change, since they pertain to the spiritual realm and divine mysteries. This is not the case with *muʿāmalāt*, which regulate relations among humans and remain open to rational considerations and social forces, and to which most rulings concerning women and gender relations belong. Since human affairs are in constant change and evolution, there is always a need for new rulings, based on new interpretations of the sacred texts, in line with the changing realities of time and place. This is the very rationale for *ijtihād* (literally, "self-exertion", "endeavour"), which is the jurist's method of finding solutions to new issues in the light of the guidance of revelation.[6] Against this background, let me return to classical *fiqh* texts and their rulings on marriage and *ḥijāb*, which in the various *fiqh* schools share the same inner logic and patriarchal conception. If they differ, it is in the manner and extent to which they have translated this conception into legal rules.[7]

Marriage: union or dominion

Classical jurists defined marriage as a contract of exchange whose prime purpose is to render sexual relations between a man and a woman licit. The contract is called *ʿaqd al-nikāḥ* (literally "contract of coitus"). Regardless of how and by whom the marriage proposal is made, the contract itself has three essential elements: the offer (*ījāb*) by the woman or her guardian (*walī*), the acceptance (*qabūl*) by the man, and the payment of dower (*mahr*), a sum of money or any valuable that the husband pays or undertakes to pay to the bride before or after consummation.

In discussing its legal structure and effects, classical jurists often used the analogy of the contract of sale and alluded to parallels between the status of wives and female slaves, to whose sexual services husbands/owners were entitled, and who were deprived of freedom of movement. Al-Ghazali, the great twelfth-century Muslim philosopher, in his monumental work *Revival of Religious Sciences*, devoted a book to marriage, where he echoed the prevalent view of his time:

> It is enough to say that marriage is a kind of slavery, for a wife is a slave to her husband. She owes her husband absolute obedience in whatever he may demand of her, where she herself is concerned, as long as no sin is involved.[8]

Likewise, Muhaqqiq al-Hilli, the renowned thirteenth-century Shi'i jurist, wrote:

> Marriage etymologically is uniting one thing with another thing; it is also said to mean sexual intercourse ... it has been said that it is a contract whose object is that of dominion over the *buzʿ* (vagina), without the right of its possession. It has also been said that it is a verbal contract that first establishes the right to sexual intercourse, that is to say: it is not like buying a female slave when the man acquires the right of intercourse as a consequence of the possession of the slave.[9]

Sidi Khalil, the prominent fourteenth-century Maliki jurist, was equally explicit when it came to dower and its function in marriage:

> When a woman marries, she sells a part of her person. In the market one buys merchandise, in marriage the husband buys the genital *arvum mulieris*.[10] As in any other bargain and sale, only useful and ritually clean objects may be given in dower.[11]

I am not suggesting that classical jurists conceptualised marriage as either a sale or as slavery.[12] Certainly there were significant differences and disagreements about this among the schools, and debates within each, with legal and practical implications.[13] Even statements such as those quoted above distinguish between the right of access to the woman's sexual and reproductive faculties (which her husband acquires) and the right over her person (which he does not). Rather, what I want to communicate is that the notion and legal logic of "ownership" (*tamlīk*) and sale underlie their conception of marriage and define the parameters of laws and practices, where a woman's sexuality, if not her person, becomes a commodity, an object of exchange. It is also this logic, as we shall see, that defines the rights and duties of each spouse in marriage and, in al-Ghazali's words, makes marriage like slavery for women.

Aware of possible misunderstandings, classical jurists were careful to stress that marriage resembles sale only in form, not in spirit, and they drew a clear line between free and slave women in terms of rights and status.[14] The marriage contract is among the few contracts in *fiqh* that crosses the boundary between its two main divisions: *ʿibādāt* and *muʿāmalāt*. The jurists spoke of marriage as a religious duty, lauded its religious merit and enumerated the ethical injunctions that the contract entailed for the spouses. However, these ethical injunctions were eclipsed by those elements in the contract that concerned the exchange and sanctioned men's control over women's sexuality. What jurists defined as the prime "purposes of marriage" separated the legal from the moral in marriage. Their consensus held these purposes to be: the gratification of sexual needs, procreation and the preservation of morality.[15] Whatever served or followed from these purposes became compulsory duties incumbent on each spouse, which the jurists discussed under *aḥkām al-zawāj* (laws of matrimony). The rest, though still morally incumbent, remained legally unenforceable and were left to the conscience of individuals.

For each party, the contract entails a set of defined rights and obligations, some with moral sanction and others with legal force. Those with legal force revolve around the twin themes of sexual access and compensation, embodied in the two concepts *tamkīn* (obedience; also *ṭāʿa*) and *nafaqa* (maintenance). *Tamkīn*, defined in terms of sexual submission, is a man's right and thus a woman's duty; whereas *nafaqa*, defined as shelter, food and clothing, is a woman's right and a man's duty. A woman becomes entitled to *nafaqa* only after consummation of the marriage, and she loses her claim if she is in a state of *nushūz* (disobedience). There is no matrimonial regime: the husband is the sole owner of the matrimonial resources, and the wife remains the possessor of her dower and whatever she brings to or earns during the marriage. She has no legal duty to do housework and is entitled to demand wages if she does. The procreation of children is the only responsibility the spouses share, but even here a wife is not legally required to suckle her child and can demand compensation if she does.

Among the default rights of the husband is his power to control his wife's movements and her "excess piety". She needs his permission to leave the house, to take up employment, or to engage in fasting or forms of worship other than what is obligatory (i.e. the fast of Ramadan). Such acts may infringe on the husband's right of "unhampered sexual access".

A man can enter up to four marriages at a time,[16] and can terminate each contract at will: he needs neither grounds for termination nor the consent or presence of his wife. Legally speaking, *ṭalāq*, repudiation of the wife, is a unilateral act (*īqāʿ*), which acquires legal effect by the declaration of the husband. Likewise, a woman cannot be released without her husband's consent, although she can secure her release through offering him inducements, by means of *khulʿ*, often referred to as "divorce by mutual consent". As defined by classical jurists, *khulʿ* is a separation claimed by the wife as a result of her extreme "reluctance" (*ikrāh*) towards her husband, and the essential element is the payment of compensation (*ʿiwaḍ*) to the husband in return for her release. This can be the return of the dower, or any other form of compensation. Unlike *ṭalāq*, *khulʿ* is not a unilateral but a bilateral act, as it cannot take legal effect without the consent of the husband. If the wife fails to secure his consent, then her only recourse is the intervention of the court and the judge's power either to compel the husband to pronounce *ṭalāq* or to pronounce it on his behalf.

Ḥijāb or seclusion?

Unlike rulings on marriage, classical *fiqh* texts contain little on the dress code for women. The prominence of *ḥijāb* in Islamic discourses is a recent phenomenon, dating to the nineteenth-century Muslim encounter with colonial powers. It was then that there emerged a new genre of literature in which the veil acquires a civilisational dimension and becomes both a marker of Muslim identity and an element of faith.

Classical texts – at least those that set out rulings or what we can call "positive law" – address the issue of dress for both men and women under "covering" (*sitr*), in the Book of Prayer, among the rules for covering the body during prayers, and, in the Book of Marriage, among the rules that govern a man's "gaze" at a woman prior to marriage.[17]

The rules are minimal, but clear-cut: during prayer, both men and women must cover their *ʿawra*, their pudenda; for men, this is the area between knees and navel, but for women it means all the body apart from hands, feet and face. Women's bodies must always be covered in the presence of men who are not *maḥram* (husband or close family members with whom marriage is forbidden); the ban can be relaxed when a man wants to contract a marriage and needs to inspect the woman he is marrying. The rules concerning covering during prayer are discussed under *ʿibādāt* (ritual/worship acts), while rules of "looking/gaze" fall under *muʿāmalāt* (social/contractual acts).

There are also related rules in classical *fiqh* for segregation (banning any kind of interaction between unrelated men and women) and seclusion (restricting women's access to public space). They are based on two juristic constructs: the first is the one that defines all of a woman's body as *ʿawra*, pudenda, a zone of shame, which must be covered both during prayers (before God) and in public (before men); the second defines women's presence in public as a source of *fitna*, chaos, a threat to the social order.[18]

Unveiling the premises

These are, in a nutshell, the classical *fiqh* rulings on marriage and covering, which are claimed to be immutable and divinely ordained. They are claimed to embody the Shari'a notion of gender, and are thereby invoked to legitimate patriarchy on religious grounds. Such a claim needs to be challenged on its own terms; there are two important questions to be asked: How far does this notion of gender reflect the principle of justice that is inherent in the Shari'a? Why and how does classical *fiqh* define marriage and covering so as to deprive women of free will, confine them to the home and make them subject to male authority? These questions become even more crucial if we accept – as I do – the sincerity of the classical jurists' claim that they derive their ideal model of gender relations from the sacred sources of Islam: the Qur'an and the Sunna.

There are two sets of related answers. The first set is ideological and political, and has to do with the strong patriarchal ethos that informed the classical jurists' readings of the sacred texts, eventually leading to women's exclusion from the production of religious knowledge and their inability to have their voices heard and their interests reflected in law. The second set of answers is more epistemological and concerns the ways in which social norms, existing practices and gender ideologies were sanctified, and then turned into fixed entities in *fiqh*. That is, rather than considering practices relating to the "status of women" or "gender" as social issues, the classical jurists treated them as the subject matter of religious rulings (*mawzū' aḥkām*).

The model of gender constructed by classical *fiqh* is grounded in the patriarchal ideology of pre-Islamic Arabia, which continued into the Islamic era, though in a modified form. There is an extensive debate on this in the literature, which I will not enter into here.[19] Suffice it to say that the classical jurists' construction of the marriage contract is based on one type of marriage agreement prevalent in pre-Islamic Arabia. Known as "marriage of dominion", this agreement closely resembled a sale through which a woman became the property of her husband.

Many passages in the Qur'an condemn women's subjugation, affirm the principle of equality and aim to reform existing practices in that direction.[20] But by invoking those few verses that apparently speak of men's authority over women, classical *fiqh* in effect bypassed the spirit of the Qur'anic verses and the direction of reform, and reproduced women's subjugation – though in a mitigated form. Women's financial autonomy and right to control property was recognised, but they were denied the right to control their own bodies or to participate in public life.

What jurists did was to modify the pre-Islamic "marriage of dominion" so as to accommodate the Qur'anic call for reforms to enhance women's rights and protect them in marriage. Women became parties to, not subjects of, the contract, and recipients of the dower or marriage gift. Likewise, by modifying the regulations on polygamy and divorce, the jurists curtailed men's scope of dominion over women in the contract, without altering the essence of the contract or freeing women from the authority of men – whether fathers or husbands. Fathers or guardians retained the right to contract the marriages of their daughters or female wards. While some schools gave a woman the option to annul a contract involving her after she reached puberty, others invested the guardian with the power of compulsion (*jabr*); that is, he could compel his daughter or ward into a marriage without her consent.[21] This went against the very essence of Qur'anic reforms aimed at abolishing the pre-Islamic practice of coercing women into unwanted marriages.

The same can be said of rulings on *ḥijāb*. Compulsory covering and seclusion for women have no basis in the sacred texts that have been invoked to supported them.[22] As recent research has illustrated, these rulings emerged from political and economic developments during the ʿAbbasid period, and were influenced by the presence in public of slave girls and the commoditisation of their beauty and sexuality. It was then that rulings on covering during prayer, which come under *ʿibādāt* (ritual acts), were extended to the realm of *muʿāmalāt* (social acts), but only for free women, to distinguish them from slave women, who were forbidden to cover their hair in public.[23] It was in this context that notions of *ḥijāb* and compulsory covering came about, premised on the imperative of seclusion. The covering or confinement of free women was seen as the best means of protecting them in and from a public space that was deemed contaminated by the presence of slave women and by the commercialisation of their sexuality. Previously, in particular during the era of the Prophet, there was little constraint on women's access to public space or participation in the political and social affairs of the nascent Muslim community. Women took the oath of allegiance to the Prophet as men did, fought in wars and prayed alongside men in mosques.

The further we move from the time of revelation, the more women's voices are marginalised and excluded from political life. By the time the *fiqh* schools emerged, women were already excluded from the production of religious knowledge and their critical faculties were denigrated enough to make their concerns irrelevant to law-making processes.[24] This takes us to the second set of mechanisms by which the egalitarian message of the sacred texts was bypassed: the sanctification of patriarchy through *fiqh* rulings that ensured that women remained subordinate to men. In producing these rulings, classical jurists based their theological arguments on a number of philosophical, metaphysical, social and legal assumptions and theories, which in turn shaped their readings of the sacred texts.[25] Salient philosophical/metaphysical assumptions that underline *fiqh* rulings on gender include: "women are created of and for men", "God made men superior to women", "women are defective in reason and faith". While these assumptions are not substantiated in the Qur'an – as recent scholarship has shown[26] – they became the main implicit theological assumptions determining how jurists discerned legal rules from the sacred texts.

The moral and social rationale for subjugation is found in the theory of difference in male and female sexuality, which goes as follows: God gave women greater sexual desire than men, but this is mitigated by two innate factors, men's *ghayra* (sexual honour and jealousy) and women's *ḥayā'* (modesty, shyness). What jurists concluded from this theory is that women's sexuality, if left uncontrolled by men, runs havoc, and is a real threat to social order. Feminist scholarship on Islam gives vivid accounts of the working of this theory in medieval legal and erotic texts, and its impact on women's lives in contemporary Muslim societies.[27] Women's *ḥayā'* and men's *ghayra*, seen as innate qualities defining femininity and masculinity, in this way became tools for controlling women and the rationale for excluding them from public life and subjugating them in marriage.[28] The sale contract, as already discussed, provided the juristic basis for women's subjugation in marriage, and the legal construction of women's bodies as *'awra* (pudenda) and of their sexuality as a source of *fitna* (chaos) removed them from public space, and thus from political life in Muslim societies.

The new challenge

The genesis of gender inequality in Islamic legal tradition lies in the inner contradictions between the ideals of the Shari'a and the patriarchal structures in which these ideals unfolded and were translated into legal norms. The Shari'a's call for freedom, justice and equality was submerged under the patriarchal norms and practices of seventh-century Arab society and culture and the formative years of Islamic law. In discerning the terms of the Shari'a, and in reading the sacred texts, classical Muslim jurists were guided by their outlook, the social and political realities of their age, and a set of legal, social and gender assumptions and theories that reflected the state of knowledge and the normative values and patriarchal institutions of their time. Their rulings on family and gender relations, which, as we have seen, were all the product of either juristic speculations or social norms and practices, came to be treated by successive generations as though they were immutable, as part of the Shari'a. In this way, what were essentially time-bound phenomena were turned into juridical principles of permanent validity, and consequently "women's status" and gender relations became fixed entities in Islamic legal tradition. This was achieved, first, by assimilating social norms into Shari'a ideals, and second, by classifying rulings pertaining to family and gender relations under the category of *mu'āmalāt* (where the rulings are subject to rationalisation and change) yet treating them as though they belonged to the category of *'ibādāt* (where the rulings are immutable and not open to rational discussion). In short, rather than embodying the principles of justice and equity inherent in Shari'a ideals, *fiqh* rulings on marriage and *ḥijāb* reflect the classical jurists' culture-bound constructions of marriage and gender relations; in their conception of justice, equality, as we understand it, had no place.

Whether these rulings corresponded to actual practices of marriage and gender relations is, of course, another area of inquiry, and that too feminist scholarship in Islam has started to uncover. For example, studies on medieval and Ottoman court archive materials and judgements indicate that the situation on the ground was quite different: women often not only had access to the courts but also could choose between legal schools, and judges generally took a liberal and protective attitude towards women.[29]

How is the new feminist scholarship in Islam to deal with this patriarchal legal heritage? What is one to do with a set of legal rulings and theories whose notions of justice, gender and ethics go against the very grain of the feminist project? Can one argue for gender equality within a legal tradition that is surrounded by an aura of sanctity? How can one bring change and pierce this veil of false sanctity in a legal tradition when one does not have support from the power base of that tradition, i.e. the *ʿulamā'*? Are we to take radical measures, put this heritage aside and replace it by a different code of law, as has been done for instance in Turkey? Or shall we continue the patchwork and piecemeal reforms that started a century ago? Or, as some Muslim feminists have suggested, should we simply acknowledge the fact that *fiqh* marriage laws are so compromised that they are beyond repair – an acknowledgement that can free "progressive Muslims" to "pursue a new marriage law" based on Qur'anic verses that place in the foreground equality between men and women as well as cooperation and harmony between spouses?[30]

For over a century, these questions have been the subject of contentious political debate and argument among the Muslims, and this will undoubtedly continue. There are no easy answers to them, but let me end with two anthropological observations.

First, the very existence of the debate, and the growing literature on "women in Islam" that has emerged since the early years of the twentieth century, are signs of the passing of an era. Available in a variety of languages (and much of it now on the Internet) and ranging from sound scholarship to outright polemics, this literature displays different positions and different gender perspectives, from those who endorse the classical *fiqh* rules, through those who seek their modification with the idea of "complementarity of rights", to those who advocate gender equality on all fronts. Irrespective of their position and gender perspective, all contributors to this literature agree that "Islam honours women's rights" and that justice and fairness are integral to the Shariʿa; they disagree on what these rights are, what constitutes justice for women and how to realise it within an Islamic framework. The intensity of the debate, and the diametrically opposed positions taken by some authors, are indications of a paradigm shift in thinking about gender rights,

Islamic law and politics. Significantly, even those who see classical *fiqh* rulings on marriage and gender roles as immutable, as part of the Shariʿa, are silent on the juristic theories and theological assumptions that underlie them. For instance, they omit the explicit parallels that classical jurists made between the legal structures of sale and the marriage contract, and statements such as those of Ghazali (quoted earlier), which speak of marriage as a type of enslavement for women. Such notions and statements are so repugnant to modern sensibilities and ethics, so alien to the experience of marriage among contemporary Muslims, that no one can afford to acknowledge them. This is clear proof that the *fiqh* definition of marriage has already become irrelevant to the contemporary experiences and ethical values of Muslims, and that the paradigm shift in Islamic law and politics is well underway. We become aware of the old paradigm only when the shift has already taken place, when the old rationale and logic, previously undisputed, lose their power to convince and cannot be defended on ethical grounds. Feminist voices in Islam herald the coming of an egalitarian legal paradigm, a paradigm that is still in the making.

Secondly, legal systems and jurisprudential theories are not unconnected to the cultural, political and social contexts in which they exist and operate. The old *fiqh* paradigm, with its strong patriarchal ethos, as well as the new feminist readings of the Shariʿa, should be understood in this complex double image, as both expressing and moulding social norms and practice. It is important to remember that legal theory or jurisprudence is often reactive, in the sense that it reacts to social practices, to political, economic and ideological forces and to people's experience and expectations. In other words, most often law follows or reflects practice, that is to say, when social reality changes, then social practice will effect a change in the law. Islamic legal theory, or *fiqh*, is no exception – as attested by the way both legal systems and women's lives and social experiences have been transformed in the course of the last century, and by the feminist challenge from within that *fiqh* faces in the new century.

6 Timeless texts and modern morals – Challenges in Islamic sexual ethics

Kecia Ali

This essay takes two propositions as its starting point. First, any discussion of the unchangeable in Islamic contexts must begin – but cannot end – with the Qur'an.[1] Second, sexuality must be integral to the broader reformist quest for gender justice. Mutuality of both desire and satisfaction in intimate relations is intricately intertwined with the aim of recognising women as fully human participants in the family and society. Muslim discourses often highlight the centrality of sexuality to human experience and stress women's sexual rights within marriage as one element of a broader Muslim commitment to women's equality. This treatment of sexuality legitimately draws from elements of both jurisprudence and prophetic Sunna, even as it overlooks certain important tensions within both bodies of literature.[2] Despite the Qur'an-centredness of much feminist and reformist thought, though, Muslim thinkers have paid little attention to the specific content of the Qur'anic discussions of sex, focusing attention instead on other social and familial regulations governing marriage and divorce.

The first section of this essay will discuss reformist and feminist hermeneutic approaches to the Qur'anic text, with special consideration to the double-movement theory of Fazlur Rahman which considers the intention behind specific regulations. The second section will attempt to summarise the content of the Qur'anic discussions of sex. Most of these verses stress maintaining chastity and avoiding indecency, practices which centre on partner choice. Thus, the text is mainly concerned with who one engages with sexually, rather than with the specific acts engaged in or the affective or ethical dimensions of sexual conduct. This is the case in discussions of both male–female and same-sex sexual contact, although this essay is primarily concerned with the former. The third section will consider the limited guidance the Qur'an provides for conduct within the boundaries of approved sexual partnerships. Here, I will highlight both the divine oversight that these verses posit and the androcentric nature of the Qur'anic guidance on sex.

I will argue that the critical principles most often discussed among reformist and feminist interpreters of the Qur'an – mutuality, justice, equality – figure little or not at all in the Qur'anic discussion of sex. This is the case even though these values appear elsewhere in the text: 2:187 posits reciprocity between spouses when it declares "they are a garment for you and you are a garment for them", and 30:21 describes the purpose of marriage as "dwelling" (or finding "tranquillity"), noting that God put "love and mercy" between spouses. Mutuality and love, however, are disconnected from the specific guidelines that the Qur'an establishes for sexual conduct, as is any treatment of consent, which is vital in ethical reflection generally as well as feminist thought specifically. Thus, the strategies of historical contextualisation and principle-extraction that are relevant to discussions of other matters of gender in family and society are not useful in interpreting the Qur'anic regulations on sexual matters.[3] The hermeneutic approach Rahman proposes of looking for "moral injunctions" rather than "legal enactments" does not resolve the difficulty.[4] Interpretations based solely on the Qur'anic discussions of sex – even if one limits oneself to the discussions of virtuous conduct and not the specific regulations regarding punishment for transgressions – cannot comprehend women's desire and active female sexuality in a way congruent with the principles of "protecting chastity" and "avoiding indecency". Androcentric language also constitutes a real barrier to any supposed principle of mutuality.

Rather than seeing the Qur'an's specific guidelines regarding sex as manifestations of overarching principles of equality, mutuality and justice, instead we must confront the absence of those principles from the Qur'anic guidance on sex, which focuses instead on licitness. When the Qur'an discusses sexual conduct apart from its categorisation into chaste and illicit – that is, as it impinges on ritual obligations – it treats men as active and women as passive, rendering claims of mutuality more problematic. I will suggest, though, that the Qur'an does not present objections to locating sex within a broader ethical field – in fact, it alludes to this field without actually describing its nature. It remains for those who view mutuality and consent as vital for morally good sexual relationships to anchor their ethical frameworks outside the Qur'anic discussion of sex.

Reformist methodologies

Before asking how the Qur'an's guidance on matters of sexual morality and conduct is relevant, one must step back to acknowledge that how to treat the Qur'an is a central issue for Muslim thinkers concerned with issues of gender justice and egalitarian family structures. Progressive thinkers, especially feminists, have a tendency to treat the Qur'an in isolation from other authoritative texts. The *ḥadīth* and the works of jurists are recognised to have human, contingent elements, although the extent to which this applies to the Sunna itself (not its recorded form as the *ḥadīth*) is debated.[5] The Qur'an, viewed as a purely divine text, protected and inviolable, is unique in its claim upon Muslim loyalties and it has been the centrepiece of much reformist thought. Scholars have thus faced the question, when confronting once unremarkable and now unacceptable provisions in the Qur'anic text (depending on the interpretive community, these may be slavery, corporal punishments or polygamy): are all of the Qur'an's specific prescriptions unchangeable in their applicability to Muslim life?

Muslim scholars have always recognised that the Qur'an does not explicitly address every possible situation. Implementation of its precepts has been subject to modifications, using Sunna or custom to restrict or expand the application of particular verses to cases not specifically addressed. Likewise, interpreters have disagreed over both the specific meaning of the text and the ways in which it should be applied. How to proceed in such cases gave rise to the genre of theoretical writings on jurisprudential method (*uṣūl al-fiqh*).[6]

In practical terms, too, jurists and judges have been flexible in their implementation of Qur'anic precepts – sometimes to women's advantage, sometimes to women's disadvantage. The codification of "personal status law" in the waning years of colonialism, continuing in today's independent nation states, has had mixed effects for women. Some reforms, such as those increasing women's access to divorce for cause, have improved women's legal standing; other reforms have had the paradoxical effect of restricting women's ability to manoeuvre by reducing judicial flexibility.[7] Among those arguing for further legal reforms to benefit women, it has become commonplace to argue that the scriptural provisions governing female inheritance, divorce and other matters need not always and everywhere be literally implemented, and that fairness may require modifications to the specific guidelines presented in the Qur'anic text. At the same time, advocates for women also confront situations where the text seems to provide a better alternative to repressive social practices. Appeal to the Qur'an (and sometimes *ḥadīth*) as a legitimate authority is often expedient, as for those opposing honour killings. Yet pressing for strict adherence to the text in favour, for instance, of not disinheriting daughters limits one when the time comes to declare that one is in favour of granting equal inheritance rights for children regardless of sex: if one has argued for the timeless supremacy of the text over any specific cultural practices, one cannot argue for moving "beyond" it without being caught in a major contradiction.[8]

Reformists have tried to avoid this trap by arguing for the overriding importance of Qur'anic principles such as justice and equality.[9] These principles, which are themselves assumed to be timeless, take precedence over specific rules, which represent necessary compromises with the conditions of Muhammad's seventh-century Arab environment. At one extreme, this has meant discarding all legislative content and adhering only to theological doctrines. In this view, articulated most daringly by Sudanese scholar Mahmoud Mohamed Taha, some portions of the Qur'an are meant to be timeless (divine Sovereignty, human fallibility, the inexorability of judgement) while others are bounded in time (regulations governing slavery, for instance, or perhaps fighting with unbelievers).[10]

A less drastic approach has sought to treat the Qur'an not merely as a rule book but as a source of guidance for daily life in a much larger sense, by recognising the intent governing its social rules. While it is undoubtedly true that the Qur'anic text contains broad principles, it is also deeply concerned with the specifics of human behaviour. Rather than simply ignore the particular in favour of the general, Pakistani thinker Fazlur Rahman attempted to clarify the relationship between specific provisions and basic aims in his double-movement theory.[11] He advocated analysis of particular regulations to determine their intended purpose during Muhammad's lifetime. Once one had determined their original intent, one would then craft a new regulation to fulfil the same purpose in diverse modern contexts. This approach – which has a parallel in the established jurisprudential technique of analogy (*qiyās*) based on a *ratio legis* (*'illa*) – has been deeply influential in later discussions of matters such as polygamy.[12] However, a reformist approach based on determining and promoting the principles underlying specific Qur'anic provisions on sex is not plausible; the Qur'anic dictates regarding sexual acts are not susceptible to the historical analysis governing Rahman's theory. The Qur'anic approach to sexual contact may be said to be, in a key sense, ahistorical; the rationales behind its specific regulations are not subject to historical shift (except insofar as concubinage with slaves may be relegated to the past, as with slavery more generally). Rather, the Qur'an is concerned with limiting sex to licit partnerships and, to a lesser extent, with keeping it from interfering with matters of purity and ritual.

Chastity and indecency

What are the basic parameters of the Qur'an's approach to sexual intimacy? What principles lie behind its specific rules for sexual relationships? The Qur'an's basic concern regarding sex, as distinct from either the jurisprudential[13] or Sunna[14] approaches, is largely to define the parameters of licit contact – *when* and especially *with whom* – and less with the affective or ethical dimensions of intimate relations. Paradoxically, given that jurisprudence and Sunna are often rejected as patriarchal and thus not useful for a feminist project, in fact they are more concerned with the ethical dimensions of sex than the Qur'anic text. Of course, especially with *fiqh*, these ethical norms are embedded in a larger context that is deeply problematic, as it treats exclusive male dominion of a particular woman's sexual and reproductive capacity as necessary for licit intimacy.[15]

The jurists base their model of lawful and unlawful sex in part on the Qur'anic statements defining good conduct and warning against transgressions. There are two semantic poles here: the virtue of *ḥifẓ al-farj*, chastity, literally "protecting (or guarding) the genitals", stands in opposition to indecency or obscenity (*fāḥisha*), which is broader than lewdness and encompasses non-sexual corruption as well.[16] Sexual morality, then, is embedded in a larger system of righteous and corrupt behaviour.

Protecting chastity is a duty for both men and women (23:5–7, 24:30–1, 33:35, etc.) In 33:35, chastity is a virtue among other virtues; guarding one's genitals, like believing, submitting, having patience, being humble, fasting and remembering God frequently, earns divine recompense. A similar set of virtuous behaviours defines "believers" in 23:1–7. Chastity is connected to other acts of bodily and behavioural modesty: the Qur'an refers to men (24:30) and women (24:31) who cast down their gazes and guard their genitals; in the case of women, the text further stipulates appropriate dress and comportment.[17]

Chaste conduct does not mean complete sexual abstinence, but rather restricting oneself to lawful partners. The Qur'an praises those "who guard their chastity except from their spouses or those whom their right hands own, for they are free from blame. But whoever desires beyond those limits are transgressors" (23:5–7).[18] These verses presuppose two related but distinct types of licit sexual partner (for men). The references to spouses or wives is clear, but "those whom your right hands own" requires further explanation.[19] Although some have argued that the Qur'an uses this term solely for war captives, it came to be understood as encompassing all types of female slaves, including those given as gifts or purchased.[20] The presence of slavery and especially slave concubinage in the Qur'anic text provides a potent case for considering whether all of the Qur'an's provisions are timeless; the existence of these verses is troubling for many today, but relevant to a reformist hermeneutic.[21] Here, I will note only that beyond the basic permission for sexual contact noted above, the Qur'anic text does not state anything specific about sexual contact with unfree women, apart from the injunction not to force slave girls to "whoredom".[22] Notably, related Qur'anic texts permit men to have licit access to more than one woman at a time, but restrict lawful (marital) access to any given woman to one man.[23]

The Qur'anic attention to *fāḥisha* as the opposite of guarding one's chastity lines up with legal prohibitions; what falls outside the lawful – exclusive access to a particular female based on marriage or ownership – is transgression, sometimes with a prescribed punishment. It is also, importantly, sin. The Qur'an treats *fāḥisha* (pl. *fawāḥish*) or *faḥshā'* in a number of verses. These terms refer to indecency but do not always have a sexual connotation, though the former term does in more instances than the latter. In sexual contexts, indecency may refer to either same-sex or, more usually, male–female sexual contact "beyond that" which is permissible.

Just as guarding one's chastity appears in tandem with other virtues on occasion, so indecency may appear with other vices. It is described in conjunction with wronging oneself (3:135), evil (2:169, 12:24), heinous sins (42:37), hatefulness (4:22), dishonour (24:21, 29:45), and dishonour and insolence (16:90). Indecency can be "outward or inward" (6:151, 7:33) and even "flagrant" (4:19, 33:30, 65:1). Most of these characterisations apply to instances of indecency that do not have sexual connotations; the phrase "flagrant indecency", however, seems to be reserved for sexual misconduct. The clearest linkage of "indecency" with the specific sin-crime of *zinā'* (illicit sex) is 17:32: "do not approach *zinā'*; surely it is an indecency."

Approaching indecency is also the subject of three Qur'anic references to the townsfolk of the Prophet Lot, who attempt to commit "indecency" (27:54, 29:28) or transgress God's limits and the design of Creation by approaching "males" (26:165) or "men" (27:55, 29:29) instead of the "women" (27:55) or "mates" (*azwāj*) that "God created for" them (26:166). These verses discussing the appetites of the townspeople surrounding the Prophet Lot specify who may be sexually approached without transgression. They contrast categories of individuals who are not permitted ("males", "men") and those who are ("women", "those [fem. pl.] God created to be your mates"). The Qur'anic discussion of men's approach to other men does not provide any guidelines for conduct, merely a statement of prohibition and a seeming rationale for why that prohibition applies: God created women to be men's mates. Some advocates of accepting same-sex intimate relationships have argued that the Qur'an condemns Lot's visitors' attempted acts not because they involve same-sex contact but because they are non-consensual. In my view, however, this is reading into the text what is not there.[24] The Qur'anic text does not provide any warrant for considering free consent a relevant factor in whether sexual acts constitute chaste or indecent conduct, and this is true not only in these verses but in all cases, whatever the sex of the participants. The Qur'anic text simply does not deal with questions of consent, generosity, affection, or love in its discussion of chastity or licit sex.[25]

The Lot verses, which focus exclusively on the sex of the partners rather than other characteristics, are more general than those commands that delineate which women may be approached without committing transgression: "your women and what your right hands possess". These verses also continue the pattern of addressing commands on sex – who not to approach as well as who may be approached – to men. This pattern continues in those verses that give guidance on sexual conduct beyond the identification of licit partners.

Navigating within the boundaries

The Qur'anic text is clear about boundaries and the consequences of transgressing them but provides little counsel as to how to navigate within the limits prescribed. Two sets of verses, however, do instruct men regarding approaches to their wives. This use of the term "approach", which echoes 17:32 ("do not approach *zinā*") as well as the Lot verses, is important to understanding what the Qur'an has to say about sex beyond its classification into chastity and lewdness: virtuous sexual conduct with spouses. These prescriptions are neither exclusively ethical nor precisely legal, though they fall under the scope of issues regulated by the jurists. Islamic jurisprudence, of course, deals with issues that range beyond law in the sense of enforceable legal codes to both issues of moral behaviour and matters of worship, including ritual purity.[26] Both ethics and worship are linked to sex in the verses under consideration here.

Two discussions of sex (2:187, 2:222–3) specify the time and manner of acceptable sexual approaches by men – who are addressed by the text – to women, presumably wives. Relating sex to the Ramadan fast, 2:187 commands men to approach or remain apart from their wives (literally, "your women", *nisā'ikum*) during certain times, based on the necessity of completing worship.[27] It begins by declaring, "Lawful for you on the nights of the fasts is the approach to your wives. They are garments for you and you are garments for them." It states that men are to "associate with them and seek what God has ordained for you, and eat and drink until the white thread of dawn becomes distinct from the black thread". At this point, contact becomes unlawful and the text issues a positive command – "Then fast until night appears" – followed by a negative command, "and do not touch them while you are in retreat in the mosques".

The other key passage governing men's sexual conduct with wives appears in 2:222–3. In 2:222, the Prophet is given guidance as to how to respond to those who ask about menstruation: "Say: it (i.e. menstruation) is an annoyance, so keep away from menstruants and do not approach them until they are pure. When they have purified themselves, approach them as God has ordered." Following this, the text of 2:223 declares, in part, that "Your wives (again, 'women') are a tilth for you, so come to your tilth as you wish, but do (good) for yourselves (or 'your souls') beforehand, and revere God and know that you will meet Him."

These verses are addressed to men as those with control over the timing and manner of sexual encounters, yet they posit divine assessment of how well men's resulting conduct adheres to divine commands. The first verse refers to God's command ("approach them as God has ordered") and the second refers to men's desire ("come to your tilth as you wish"). Both verses stress God's oversight, emphasising that God will judge men's behaviour ("and know that you will meet Him"). The standards according to which behaviour will be judged, however, are not clearly laid out in the Qur'anic text beyond a concern for purity and the something that men (or perhaps men and women) are to do beforehand for the benefit of themselves or their souls.

In another context, I have suggested a distinction between the androcentrism of certain verses regulating marriage and divorce – which acknowledge patriarchy but seek to promote female autonomy – and those regarding sex which, while likewise androcentric in address and content, do not promote female freedom to act but rather counsel men to behave in particular ways, reaffirming male control over female bodies.[28] Scholars have argued persuasively that the Qur'an addresses certain verses to men, and grants privileges to and imposes responsibilities on them, due to the existence of patriarchy in Arabia of Muhammad's time. Various verses promote female freedom to make certain decisions about remaining married to particular men, or choosing to remarry; the Qur'an thus promotes autonomy for women without challenging the basic patriarchal structure of family or society. But the Qur'anic treatment of women as sexually passive and men as sexual actors, of women's bodies as Other and men's bodies as normative, poses a challenge to understanding the text as purely divine and transcendent.[29]

Sexuality and sexual desire are in part historically produced.[30] It could be argued that female sexual passivity was the norm for seventh-century Arabs, and that therefore the regulations surrounding sex are merely descriptive for the time, and do not reflect normative judgement. Nonetheless, the androcentrism of these passages constitutes one way in which the Qur'anic discourse privileges male experience and highlights male agency. The relationship that Rahman posits between specific provisions and general principles does not explain away the male-centredness of the Qur'anic text, unless one considers androcentrism to constitute a general principle. Rather, this androcentrism stands outside the explanatory power of the double-movement theory, just as the chastity/indecency dichotomy cannot be historically contextualised as a manifestation of principles of justice or equality.

Conclusion

The Qur'an presents two interrelated basic imperatives of "protecting chastity" and "avoiding indecency". For men, this means not approaching partners beyond "wives/spouses" and "what their right hands possess" and not approaching men or males in preference to women. The Qur'an's more specific commands regarding sexual conduct appear within discussions of men's contact with their wives, defining acceptable and unacceptable times for sexual approach: it is unacceptable to approach women during fasting hours, while in retreat in the mosques, or while women are menstruating; presumably, any other time is acceptable. Importantly, the text does not suggest that breaking these commands would constitute indecency. The division of sexual encounters into licit (equivalent to chaste) and illicit (indecent) stands apart from the specific guidance on sex offered in these few verses, which relate to completing ritual obligations or maintaining purity taboos, things that have generally not been considered subject to historical change. These Qur'anic rules regarding times of abstention do not represent the type of broad, transhistorical ethical principles envisioned in Rahman's double-movement theory.

What, though, of the broader categories of chastity and indecency? Are they subject to historical contextualisation? "Protecting chastity" is a virtue, as is "avoiding indecency", but are they critical objectives in themselves, or do they serve other divinely-intended purposes? If one addresses the case of slave concubinage in Rahman's framework, one might argue that the specific permission to have sex with unfree women was part of a broader concern with limiting licit partners as much as possible to contexts where biological paternity could be ascertained and its consequences enforced. Thus, "protecting chastity" in the modern period requires limiting oneself only to spouses. Yet although paternal responsibility and filiation (*nasab*) more generally is acknowledged as an important social objective by Muslim jurists, it seems impoverishing to limit the Qur'anic notion of protecting one's genitals to that concept. In any case, one would have to engage in exegetical gymnastics to link the principle of enforceable paternity to egalitarian visions of gender-justice.

It remains for those who view mutuality and consent as vital for good sex – and here I mean morally good rather than merely pleasurable – to anchor their ethical frameworks outside the Qur'anic discussion of sex. There are a number of possible approaches to this search for an ethical starting point. Of course, on the theory that one first interprets the Qur'an through the Qur'an, one can make a case for relating the discussions of sex to other Qur'anic passages discussing marriage, for instance. This allows one to draw on principles which are clearly present in the text, but it also presents the problem of competing principles. God is said to have placed "love and mercy" between spouses (30:21), and this is certainly a desirable anchor for privileging mutuality in sex. Yet on what basis does one prefer this description of the spousal tie over the *qiwāma* or authority and responsibility mentioned in 4:34 or the "degree" men have over women in 2:228? These questions cannot be resolved by simply privileging principles over specifics, but raise the matter of interpretive choice again, at a slightly different level.

How does one ultimately choose between competing principles? There comes a point at which it becomes necessary to step outside the text. In reality, one always brings elements of one's own formation – social, intellectual, personal – to one's readings. Doing so deliberately, with careful attention to one's conscience, through the lens of other religiously meaningful texts, may prove very important. *Ḥadīth* and jurisprudence are dismissed by some reformers, including some feminists, as corrupted because of human elements in their formulation and transmission – unlike the uncorrupted and pristine Qur'anic text – yet, notwithstanding their patriarchal and even misogynist elements, they may prove important for the working out of ethical approaches to real women's sexuality in real historical situations. Likewise, for many Muslims the texts that have the most meaning may be Sufi writings, poetry, or *qaṣīdas*. There are elements in these works that can provide inspiration and a broader framework for ethical approaches to Muslim life. I have argued elsewhere that reform in sexual ethics must rely on a coherent, consistent, and methodologically rigorous approach to core texts. But situating sexuality within a broader textual base than the Qur'an alone can help relate it to other ethical structures.

In addition to deriving principles from the text, one must also understand that there are limits to what it can provide. If the Qur'an provides only rules about purity and timing and not advice about being a generous lover, committed to caring for one's (licit) partner, that does not mean the latter is not important, only that one must fill in the gaps for oneself in a way that is compatible with, if not explicitly present in, its core guidance.

Those who approach the text as feminists must locate and justify the principles from which they begin. How can one argue persuasively for an egalitarian reading of marriage and gender relationships in the Qur'an without distorting the text? How can one make a strong case for mutuality and partnership as the preferred Qur'anic mode of marriage, and for meaningful consent as a necessary condition for ethical sex? An egalitarian ethics must be grounded in a theological approach to the Qur'anic text, and reformist thought in general must engage more explicitly with theological concerns. Ultimately, it is only at the level of discussions about God and God's relationship to humanity that key questions about basic principles can be addressed. Why does equality matter, besides the fact that some of us have been conditioned by modernity to want it?

I want to conclude by offering one, very preliminary, possibility: an understanding of *tawḥīd* (divine unity) and *islām* (submission), with a lower-case "*i*".

The fundamental individual role of submission to God alone, devotion to the spiritual life, and ordering of one's personal relationships in a way that is pleasing to the divine as well as to one's own sense of spiritual need, can best be accomplished when one has the personal liberty to make particular choices. The radical submission demanded of the individual believer is more meaningful when personal constraints are fewer. The implications of *tawḥīd* for exegesis and ethics remain to be worked out in a comprehensive fashion – and indeed there are other likely points of departure – but in thinking about the union of two selves in physical intimacy, remembering the separateness and Oneness of God to whom all Muslims must ultimately submit as individuals may serve as a place to begin.

The author is grateful for the comments of Ziba Mir-Hosseini, Laury Silvers, Sarah Eltantawi and the organisers and participants of the events in early 2007 where these ideas were discussed: ISAM (Istanbul), Loyola University (Chicago) and the Re-Imagining Muslim Ethics colloquium at Duke University (Durham, NC).

7

Gender equality and Islamic law – The case of Morocco

Aïcha El Hajjami

The principle of equality between men and women as a fundamental value is of recent appearance. The appropriate approach to ensuring enjoyment of this right by women remains a subject of debate and theoretical shifts. The inadequacies of the formal approach initially determine this more suitable approach and have led to the devising of other concepts of material equality with a view to establishing genuine equality between men and women. Presently, this right clashes with social relations between the sexes due to socio-cultural factors.

In Morocco, the right of women to equality as understood in the light of new approaches, especially that of gender, is questioned and contested, placing the issue of women at the centre of the problem of identity, as elsewhere in all Muslim societies. Its articulation with the Islamic frame of reference – in societies where religion is a fundamental component of community identity and a principal source of family laws – arouses much debate and controversy between the advocates of the universality of human rights as enshrined in international treaties and conventions, and the defenders of cultural particularism. Far from engendering objective and rigorous thinking on the issue, these passionate and deeply politicised controversies are exacerbated by the homogenisation of reference models produced by globalisation, and by stereotypes and reductive simplifications combined with conceptual confusions in this area.

Thus, Morocco experienced a virulent clash between the two theses of universalism and particularism during the debate on the reform of the Personal Status Code (the Mudawwana)[1] which dominated the political and social scene in Morocco from the early 1990s until February 2004, when the reform was ratified by the adoption of the new Family Code.

The divergences over the approach to be adopted in the reform of the legal condition of women can be traced to an ambivalence over the frames of reference, a problem experienced by Morocco at every level: institutional, legal and social.[2] It is an ambivalence characterised by the omnipresence of the religious factor in a society that is also strongly influenced by the effects of modernity in all its dimensions.

The condition of women thus bears the mark of the dichotomy within the Moroccan legal system: family space is fully encompassed by Muslim law, whereas public space is dominated by Western-inspired modern law. These two orders draw on two categories of norms that differ in their underlying philosophy, in their source, and in the way they are drawn up: the one considered transcendental and of divine origin, the other wholly dependent on human will for its development.

Taking into account this legal ambivalence that is experienced by practically all Muslim societies – divided between their attachment to the creed of Islam and the community of faith, and the attraction of "modernity" with all its images and notions of liberation – one should explore the scope for developing laws governing the domain of the family in Muslim countries with a view to adapting them to contemporary reality and to the legitimate aspirations of Muslim women to equal citizenship with men. It is likewise legitimate to explore what approaches and tools are conducive to attaining this goal.

How capable is the Islamic frame of reference of taking on board the question of women's rights in relation to the socio-economic and political development of contemporary Muslim societies? What opportunities and potentials does *ijtihād* in fact offer, as a hermeneutics of sacred texts developed by the science of legal foundations (*'ilm uṣūl al-fiqh*), when it comes to the challenge of reconciling two frames of reference that appear completely antinomic and yet deeply rooted in our contemporary Muslim societies?

The problem is all the more thorny since both frames of reference are embedded in the legal system of many Muslim countries. The Moroccan Constitution, for example, refers to Islam as the state religion, and to the King as *Amir Al Mouminine* (Commander of the Faithful), while at the same time affirming Morocco's attachment to "universally recognised human rights". The absence of a hierarchy clearly established by the framer of the Moroccan Constitution between the two frames of reference, makes the problem of harmonising the derived legal orders – especially those relating to women's rights – even more intractable.

Thus, the issue of gender equality calls into question the Islamic frame of reference and places the Muslim world in the dock of nations as a result of non-egalitarian laws governing social relations between the sexes, especially in the private sphere. The upholding of certain discriminatory laws in the legislations of these countries, together with the reservations accompanying their ratification of women's rights conventions, call for discussion of the notion of equality in the sacred texts of Islam, in its relationship with the context of revelation, and the possible prospects for progress offered by the Islamic frame of reference in this area. This would lay the groundwork for narrowing the gap between the principle of gender equality laid down in the international conventions ratified by most Muslim states, and its equivalent in Islam.

The Moroccan example clearly shows the ideological divisions currently fuelled by the issue of women's rights in Muslim societies, just as it epitomises the Islamic frame of reference's potential for innovative thinking on the matter by using the tool of *ijtihād*.

Before tackling the notion of equality in Islam and the approach it has adopted for its construction within a particular social context, we feel it important to elucidate, starting from the Moroccan example,[3] the questions raised and the positions taken on the problem of equal rights for women, and the dangerous tendencies caused by certain conceptual confusions underlying such views.

Equality at the centre of the debate

The polemic surrounding the frame of reference, triggered in Morocco by the demands of women's organisations in March 1992,[4] intensified from March 1999 onwards, when the Prime Minister of the alternating Government[5] announced the draft National Action Plan for the Integration of Women in Development, prepared by the Secretary of State in charge of Social Welfare, the Family and Childhood, in association with representatives from women's associations and human rights and development organisations.

Starting from the principle of equality between the two sexes at all levels of social life, the draft Action Plan, which falls within the scope of the implementation of the recommendations of the Platform for Action of the 1995 Beijing Conference, proposes a number of legal measures consistent with the gender approach.

The legal measures recommended by the draft Action Plan consisted chiefly in reforming the Mudawwana to abolish polygamy, remove the institution of the *walī* (matrimonial guardian), raise the legal age of marriage for girls from 15 to 18 years, establish judicial divorce, and divide property acquired during the marriage between the spouses in the event of divorce.

The Mudawwana as it stood enshrined within its various articles the subordination of woman and her enduring status as an eternal minor. It reflected one of the most retrograde readings of the Islamic frame of reference.

The provisions of the Mudawwana conformed with the legal rules worked out by the jurisconsults of the Maliki school for a bygone time and context, without taking into account the tradition of the founders of that school who advocated recourse to *ijtihād*, and exercised it with a boldness remarkable for their age, in order to adapt Islamic law to the needs of society.[6] Indeed, the Maliki school stands out clearly from other Sunni schools by the adoption of innovative methods of exegesis such as *al-maṣāliḥ al-mursala* (considerations of public interest), or *istiḥsān* (principle of judicial preference), as paradigms of the general concept of *al-maqāṣid al-sharīʿa* (the aims of the Shariʿa). All these concepts allow one to understand the laws concerning Muslim women in the light of the fundamental values of the sacred texts, while taking into account the needs of reality and social changes. Unfortunately, the Mudawwana diverged from this by enshrining in its various provisions a highly unequal relationship between the two sexes within the private sphere. In practice, this contributed to destabilising the family unit and gave rise to situations of institutionalised violence towards women and children.

The propositions of the draft Action Plan aimed to change the provisions of the Mudawwana, drawing inspiration from women's rights as laid down in international conventions, but the reaction from Islamist and traditionalist quarters[7] to the draft was virulent. It was levelled not only against the content of the proposals, which it deemed contrary to the Shariʿa, but also against the procedure for their adoption, which failed to involve the *ʿulamā'* (religious scholars), the only people authorised to reform the Mudawwana. Opposition was similarly focussed on the reference system from which the draft drew its inspiration.

As a result of this opposition, the reform question was reduced to its religious dimension and the modernist movement was obliged to resort to argumentation based on the Islamic frame of reference. The latter was only belatedly and reluctantly used by the great majority of this group, convinced as they were that the religious frame of reference offers no solution to the question of women's rights. Thus, the arguments deployed were limited to simply citing certain verses, *ḥadīth*, or legal rulings underlining the rights of women, in order to legitimate the proposals of the Action Plan against the arguments of the Islamist and traditionalist movements.

The debate was politicised by two broad tendencies that confronted each other over the reform and was often lacking in depth, even though it did have the effect of sensitising different strata of society to the necessity of changing the family laws in a more egalitarian direction.

To get out of this impasse and avoid confrontation,[8] various antagonists, headed by the then Prime Minister, sought the mediation of the King as the "Commander of the Faithful". The King named a consultative commission, tasked with drawing up the draft of the reform, and composed with due consideration to the different tendencies and sensibilities as well as the different areas of expertise of the *'ulamā'*. The nomination of three women to the commission takes on an undeniable symbolic importance. In this way, women were associated with the practice of *ijtihād*, an act hitherto reserved to men. The mission of the commission was to carry out an innovative *ijtihād* while strictly respecting the precepts of Islam, as was underlined in the royal inauguration speech: "I cannot, in my capacity as *Amir Al Mouminine*, allow what God has prohibited, nor forbid what the Highest has allowed." Morocco's commitments to respect universally recognised human rights were likewise referred to.

The draft Family Code drawn up by the commission was announced by the King himself to Parliament in his speech of 10 October 2003, in which every new legal measure in the draft was accompanied by a reference to the religious texts, the Qur'an or the *ḥadīth*. The Code was then debated and unanimously adopted by the vote of the two chambers on 16 January 2004, and gazetted in the *Journal officiel* on 4 February 2004.

This text is egalitarian in inspiration, and is based on a more open reading of the sacred texts, in keeping with the reality of current Moroccan society and its needs, while conforming to the universal values of equality and dignity enshrined in the international conventions signed and ratified by Morocco. Hence, the new Code does away with matrimonial guardianship for adult women, sets the same legal age of marriage for both sexes (18 years), places the family under the joint responsibility of both spouses, imposes strict conditions on polygamy which render its use nearly impossible, grants both spouses equivalent rights as regards the means of dissolving the marriage tie while subjecting it to the control of a judge – the so-called divorce on grounds of discord (*shiqāq*) – and, finally, gives the wife the right to a part of the family's property in case of separation, on certain conditions.

As a result, the new Moroccan Family Code is undeniably a model exercise in innovative *ijtihād* respecting the principles of equality and justice that are extolled by the sacred texts.[9] Nevertheless, despite the consensus reached over the new Family Code, the debate on the issue of the frame of reference is far from closed because, on the one hand, the reform was deemed inadequate by a large part of the modernist movement, and, on the other hand, the issue of the frame of reference transcends the legal frame of the family law reform.

The disagreements surrounding the frame of reference in reality crystallise the ideological clash between two visions of society often perceived and presented by the opponents of each movement as irreconcilably antithetical.[10]

The first vision falls unreservedly within the scope of the so-called universal frame of reference, that of human rights treaties and conventions.[11] Its advocates, drawn from the modernist movement with its roots in women's organisations, human rights organisations and left-wing political parties, are highly sceptical of the ability of the religious frame of reference to keep pace with Moroccan society, as the latter changes and aspires to modernity in all its dimensions, and, primarily, to ensure equality between women and men.

For the radical tendency of this movement, salvation in the sphere of women's rights can only be achieved through modernity, a modernity that breaks with religious thinking by establishing a social conscience freed from the sacred. To do so, it urges ridding family law of religious influence, and abolishing all national rules of law at odds with human rights as laid down in international treaties and conventions, which represent for this movement the reference system *par excellence*.

The second vision, embodied mainly in the Islamist movement and the traditional *'ulamā'*, falls within the Islamic frame of reference and the fundamental values of Islam. Its advocates reject the idea of the universality of human rights as laid down in international treaties and conventions, in the name of cultural authenticity and religious identity. They deem these rights to be incompatible with the fundamental values of Islam and its conception of the universe, be it in terms of its foundations, its methods or its objectives.[12] They say that the genesis and evolution of this so-called universal frame of reference, which is tied to a Western context and to Enlightenment philosophy based on the idea of natural law, conceives of man only as an individual, whereas the Islamic conception of man and society is bound up instead with the notion of community and complementarity.

They clashed all the more vehemently against the recommendations and pressure exerted by international bodies with regard to inter-sex relations that follow from the notion of gender. This approach, which had been incorporated into the draft Action Plan for the Integration of Women in Development, was perceived as a dangerous threat to family structure; its adoption by Morocco would lead to "the sowing of discord among members of the same family and the destruction of the foundations of family life, namely, cordiality, compassion, solidarity and symbiosis".[13]

The attitudes of the two opponents, as expressed during the debate on the draft Action Plan, ultimately reflect the same reductive and narrow perception of Islam. This representation is unfortunately fairly widespread nowadays among a large number of detractors of Islam, as it is among those who, either in good faith or in ignorance, defend in the name of Islam the inequality and exclusion of women. It is fostered and sustained by two dangerous confusions which over the course of history gradually worked their way into Muslim religion as the collective conscience of Muslims.

The first confusion is the widespread one, in the past and present alike, of conflating Shariʿa with *fiqh*, especially in matters concerning the legal and social condition of women. A large number of discriminatory legal rules with regard to women are in reality nothing other than human constructions elevated to the rank of sacred, categorical texts. They are often only a reflection of the hegemony of a patriarchal mentality reluctant to make the changes inaugurated by the Qurʾanic text and the tradition of the Prophet.

The fact that these discriminatory laws and the violent practices resulting from them have become so widespread and commonplace, lies at the heart of another confusion, namely, the equation of social and historical Islam with the Islamic frame of reference, the fundamental values of which unequivocally condemn discrimination based on sex.

The persistence of these two confusions both at the legal level and at the level of mentalities helps not only to perpetuate situations of inequality and violence for Muslim women in the name of a narrow and manipulative reading of the religion, but also to foster a negative view of Islam perceived as the instigator of women's subordination to men.

As a result, it is essential to focus on the distinction between Islam's founding texts, namely the Qur'an and the Sunna which constitute the Shariʿa, and the legal output of Muslim jurisconsults, known as *fiqh*. The *fiqh* represents the full set of legal rules devised long after the revelation of the Qur'an and the Prophet's death by Muslim theologians/jurists (*ʿulamāʾ*), based on their interpretations of the sacred texts and in the light of the social realities and needs of their age.

It is therefore the product of human labour steeped in the circumstances of its creation and the social environment of its authors. Accordingly, it should be open to review, corrected in the light of new social situations and enriched by recent scientific approaches. The confusion between Shariʿa and *fiqh* has gradually led to the latter being regarded as sacred in the conscience of a large swath of Moroccan society, including that of the *fuqahāʾ*,[14] whereas the first founding jurisconsults of the four Sunni schools were modest enough not to claim to hold the truth and often relativised their jurisprudence. Later on, the followers of each school broke with this spirit by elevating the jurisprudence of the founding fathers and the other legal rules of the *fiqh* resulting from it, to a sacred reference neither weakened nor worn over the course of time, in the same way as the Qur'an and the *ḥadīth*.

The *fiqh* in relation to the condition of women has always been the reflection of a prevailing patriarchal mentality, rather than the strict application of the values of equality and justice advocated by the Qur'an and the Sunna.

The approach to equality in Islam

Equality as the foundation

A look at the social context of the revelation of Islam informs us of the revolutionary content of its message with regard to the unequal social relations between men and women in the Arabian peninsula of the seventh century CE. These relations, stemming from the patriarchal mentality and tribal and slave-based organisation of the time, relegated women to an inferior status, with which Islam broke by granting them basic human rights at the same time as it inaugurated a plan to rebuild social relations on the basis of the right to equality.

This right to equality can be seen on two levels:

- On the level of the common origin of all human beings: "Mankind, We have created you from a male and a female, and appointed you races and tribes, that you may know one another. Surely the noblest among you in the sight of God is the most godfearing of you …" (49:13). From this flows a fundamental equality, opposed to every kind of domination or discrimination by sex, race, colour, wealth or rank; each human being is valued solely by merit of piety and good deeds.
- On the level of the equal responsibility of men and women for life on Earth: "The believers, men and women, are protecting friends one of another; they enjoin the right and forbid the wrong …" (9:71).

The tradition of the Prophet, too, bore a vision of profound social transformation. In this sense, the *ḥadīth* says: "women are the uterine sisters of men before the laws". In practice, during the lifetime of the Prophet, Muslim women occupied public spaces such as the mosque, a place of knowledge and state decision-making, and the souks, places of economic exchange where they assumed responsibilities.

For its time, this approach constituted a profound reversal of the socially established division of roles and a rethinking of the separation between the public and the private sphere.

The egalitarian construction of identity in Islam consists in a recognition of sex differences as an unassailable fact, without, however, predetermining any skills or roles whatsoever. Social skills are not regarded as biological attributes and may under no circumstances justify the separation between private space and public space. The same applies to the biological role and function of women and their needs, which are recognised and valued, without, however, using these clear biological differences to erect a hierarchy between the two sexes or to deduce from it any predetermination that would justify discrimination, violence or the exclusion of women.

Hence, the question that arises in the Arab and Muslim world is how to carry on this quest for equality and translate it into legislation concerning family law in general and the inherent rights of women in particular.

Equality as objective

The way Islam took into consideration the socio-cultural context, in order to lay the foundations of profound and progressive social change, must be reflected in *ijtihād* on the sacred texts, with the aim of continuing the advances in the sphere of women's rights that were inaugurated by the Islamic message.

To that end, not only is *ijtihād*, as an effort to clarify and interpret sacred texts with the aim of deducing from them the legal qualifications (*aḥkām*), recommended by the sacred texts, but these possess within themselves the means for ongoing reform in keeping with the development of Muslim societies. This must be achieved in compliance with the aims of the Islamic message, *maqāṣid al-sharīʿa*, which boil down to the fundamental values of equality and justice.

The Qurʾan and the Sunna in fact contain two kinds of teaching: the ahistorical, timeless teachings relate chiefly to creed and ritual practices, *ʿibādāt*, such as prayer, fasting, pilgrimage or compulsory alms-giving (*zakāh*). These are regarded as unchangeable. Conversely, the teachings on social life and the associated human relations, *muʿāmalāt*, must be perceived and understood through the aims of Islam (*maqāṣid al-sharīʿa*) and convey its fundamental values of justice, equality and dignity for all human beings. Without denying these texts their transcendental sacredness, the rules of law resulting from them must give rise, in their elaboration and application alike, to consideration of the social environment of each age.

Family law is not included among the ritual provisions but falls instead within the scope of *muʿāmalāt*, especially since most of its rules were worked out by the *fuqahāʾ* within the framework of *ijtihād*.

It is important to proceed to a profound overhaul of women's legal situation under the current legislation of Muslim countries, with the aim of putting an end to the injustices that tarnish it, and to include in it the right to equality, one of the aims of the Shariʿa.

The concept of *al-maqāṣid* developed by the great jurist-theologians of Islam such as al-Tirmidhi (d. 892), al-Amidi (d. 1232), al-ʿIzz ibn ʿAbd al-Salam (d. 1261), Ibn al-Qayyim (d. 1350), al-Razi (d. 1210), al-Tufi (d. 1316), al-Shatibi (d. 1388) and later Tahir ibn ʿAshur (Tahar Ben Achour, 1879–1973), consists in drawing legal qualifications (*aḥkām*) not from a literal and lexical exegesis of sacred texts, but by seeking in their mediate reasoning (*ʿilla*)[15] the deep and ultimate goal that is *al-ḥikma*, the divine intention. This is and has to be in all cases determined by the one objective which is *jalb al-maṣāliḥ wa darʾ al-mafāsid*, that is, the search for what is useful and good and the rejection of what is harmful. Thus, *maṣlaḥa*, the common good, is the very core of the *maqāṣid*.

Within the sphere of the *maqāṣid*, certain jurist-theologians engaged in bold critical reflection; thus, they managed to push back the barriers of Islamic thought beyond the limits imposed by dogmatic theology. Thus al-Shatibi, one of the precursors of the *maqāṣid al-sharīʿa* approach, developed a method of rational interpretation that was remarkably innovative for his age. The originality of his approach lies in the fact that it falls within a relativism that encompasses both the notion of categorical text (*naṣṣ qaṭʿī*), the authority of the legal qualifications (*aḥkām*) drawn from it, and the exclusive right of the *ʿulamāʾ* to practise *ijtihād*.[16] More recently, Tahir Ibn ʿAshur has commendably broadened the concept of *maqāṣid* to the principles of freedom and equality.

We should, however, note that, generally speaking, these rational and innovative theoretical approaches have not shown through in the *aḥkām* evolved by these eminent jurist-theologians in the sphere of women's rights.

For example, Tahir Ibn ʿAshur, who included in the *maqāṣid* two new principles, freedom and equality, went on to restrict their scope for women. After mentioning the importance of equality as a fundamental principle of the Shariʿa, equally valid for both sexes, he evokes certain exceptional impediments to the application of the principle. Hence, there are certain rights that women cannot seek to exercise, by reason of their innate nature (*jibilliyya*). His examples of rights reserved solely for men are the rights to judicial office, the *khilāfa*, command of the army, and guardianship of children. He gives as another example of an impediment to the application of equality for women:

> the inequality of man and woman whereby the woman is not required to support her husband financially since it has become an established custom that generally it is the man who should maintain the family. This custom is a manifestation of man's inborn disposition enabling him to bear the pain of hard work in earning and accumulating wealth.[17]

It is clear that the reference in this argument is not the scriptural text of the Qur'an nor the tradition of the Prophet, rather, it is nothing other than social custom and tradition elevated to proof: the departure from the principle of equality, hence the superiority of men, draws its legitimacy from the fact that it is the duty and responsibility of men, once again according to custom, to meet the material needs of women.[18]

This clearly shows that even the most innovative theologians of Islam have failed, in their turn, to escape the social construction of sexual relations of their age, according to which the physical and intellectual abilities of women are conclusively determined by their sex.

Among the most limiting restrictions on the practice of *ijtihād* that have severely affected the rights afforded to women by Islam, is the famous rule: *lā ijtihād maʿa wujūd al-naṣṣ* (no *ijtihād* in the presence of a text). This is a rule of the science of legal foundations (*ʿilm uṣūl al-fiqh*), a science that establishes normative methodologies for the deduction of legal qualifications from the sacred texts. It is constantly brandished in order to quell all discussion on the improvement of the condition of women in *fiqh* texts. It has achieved such sacred status among *fuqahā*ʾ that it has succeeded in reducing the hermeneutic operation to a simple literalist reading of the sacred texts, whether it be a categorical (*naṣṣ qaṭʿī*) or conjectural (*ẓannī*) text.

However, this rule should be restricted by specifying the exact meaning of the term *naṣṣ*.[19] A number of conditions must be satisfied for a text to be regarded as categorical and thus immutable. So many apocryphal *ḥadīth* have been raised to the status of sacred texts in order to restrict certain rights afforded to women by Islam, rights from which Muslim women at the time of the Prophet benefited fully!

A further restriction on the scope of *ijtihād* was imposed in the name of *sadd al-dharāʾiʿ* (blocking the means to illicit ends). The concept of *sadd al-dharāʾiʿ* consists of suspending a legal rule in the event that its application might harm someone or cause damage to the community. It was applied felicitously in certain instances to safeguard rights, including those specific to women. Hence under Maliki legal doctrine, a woman repudiated by her dying husband is entitled to inheritance on his death. This is to ensure that a husband at an advanced stage of his disease does not seek to disinherit his wife by repudiating her.

The principle of *sadd al-dharāʾiʿ* was later diverted from its original purpose and became inordinately overused, especially in the area of women's rights, as patriarchal mentality gradually reasserted itself in Muslim societies and strayed from the values of equality and justice advocated by Islam.

This commits Muslim societies to carry out a re-reading of the body of Islamic law in the light of the founding precepts of Islam, so that it can be a vehicle of the universal values of human rights today, as it was at the time of the Revelation.

The Moroccan example of family law reform is undeniably an example of the exercise of an innovative *ijtihād* achieved in compliance with the principles of equality and justice advocated by the sacred texts. This reform is an important step in improving the legal condition of women and in the democratisation process embarked upon by Morocco. Indeed, it is inconceivable for the democratisation of the public sphere to take place independently of that of the private sphere, the place of socialisation and apprenticeship in citizenship *par excellence*. One may thus hope that it will influence social practices and mentalities which are often more restrictive than the rules of law.

An evaluation of the implementation of the new Family Code in Morocco since February 2004 shows that, despite the incontestable amelioration of the legal status of women within the family, there remain a number of obstacles, which are tied to traditions and to economic insecurity, that impede a full application of the new provisions of the Code, especially in the rural environment.

In his legal practice, the judge, whom the legislator has afforded broad powers of discretion in some fields, sometimes has to yield to moral or economic considerations. Permits for polygamy and for the marriage of young female minors, which continue to be very frequently issued in rural areas, are motivated by the wish to protect the first wife or the young girl from the insecurity or degradation they would be exposed to if the permits were refused.

As to the principle of dividing the family property between the spouses, Article 49, aiming to protect the material interest of the spouses when the marriage is dissolved, stipulates that the future spouses may attach to the marriage contract an agreement concerning the management of property acquired by the couple during marital life. However, the weight of tradition means that the future wife and her family do not dare raise the question at the moment the marriage is concluded, for fear of arousing suspicion and mistrust in the future husband. The same article requires the contributions of each spouse to the development of the family property to be taken into account at the moment of separation, on condition that proofs be provided. The requirement of proof renders a just and reasonable measure null and void. The problem of proof arises in the case of a wife who effectively contributes to the maintenance of the home, yet does not keep documentary evidence. It also arises with regard to taking into account the housework of the wife, who in the case of divorce after several years of marriage often finds herself with no resources and unable to work to provide for her needs.[20]

For this reason, alongside legal reform one should work on other factors, such as the resistance of mindsets or the socio-economic situation of the population that the law addresses.

8 Historical and political dynamics of the "women and Islam" issue – The Turkish case

Nazife Şişman

Islam, women and gender equality have been the subject of much discussion in academic circles, especially for the last two decades. However, we can trace this discussion more than a hundred years back in the Turkish modernisation process.

The subject of "women and Islam" can hardly be discussed without referring to the paradigm shift in Islamic thought in general. This is because almost all who wrote or thought about the issue of women inherited a mind-set which was constructed within the context of the modernisation process. In this process, some radical transformations came to the fore in the Muslim world. Religious and traditional structures broke down, roles were turned upside down and statuses became vague. Without taking these vital changes into consideration, the woman question can hardly be placed in an appropriate context.

What is important for the study of "the woman question" in the Middle East is, as Abu-Lughod put it,

> to explore how notions of modernity have been produced and reproduced through being opposed to the non-modern in dichotomies ranging from the modern/primitive of philosophy and anthropology to the modern/

traditional of Western social theory and modernisation theory, not to mention the West/non-West that is implied in most of these dichotomies.[1]

Thus my aim in this paper is to analyse the political and social context of Turkish modernisation in which the "women and Islam" issue became one of the major discussion areas.

In the second half of the nineteenth century, Middle Eastern countries underwent certain radical social transformations. The economic and social parameters of these transformations consisted of the expansion of Western economic powers, the increase in the hegemony of European colonialism in the region, and the rise of modern nation-states. These transformations directly influenced the lives of both men and women.

Women became a theme of nationalist discourse. For the first time in the history of Islam, Islamic practices and Islamic law (e.g. polygamy, divorce, segregation, veiling, etc.) began to be publicly negotiated. The "woman issue" became a major theme in the writings of journalists and politicians in Egypt and in Ottoman society. The discourse on "women and reform" revolved around the argument that European societies had made progress, and that Muslim societies should also seek to achieve that level of progress. This emerging discourse connected the issues of women, nationalism, national progress and cultural change to each other.

Middle Eastern societies gave similar answers to the questions that were raised under the hegemony of the West. They differed over the desired pace of transformation. Whether a country was a colony or not, and its degree of relationship with Europe, also affected the form and pace of the transformation. In other words, different parts of the Muslim world followed different paths to modernisation. However, the dominant element common to all these experiences was the feeling of "backwardness".

The late Ottoman paradigm shift

Ziya Paşa (1825–80), an influential and famous poet in Ottoman times, in a poem of 1870, said, *Diyar-ı küfrü gezdim beldeler, kaşaneler gördüm/Dolaştım mülk-ü İslam 'ı bütün viraneler gördüm* (which may be translated as "I visited lands of unbelief and I saw monumental buildings/When I turned back to the land of Islam I saw ruins"). This intellectual's gaze captured one more difference: the difference between the lives of European women and the lives of Muslim women. When the intellectuals evaluated Western civilisation and progress, the situation and lifestyle of women and the relation between men and women became criteria of comparison between the West and their own society. For as long as human societies and cultures have interacted and compared themselves with each other, the status of women and the rituals of family life have occupied a special place in inter-cultural understanding.

It should be noted that the Muslim intellectuals' comparison of their society with the West came to the fore within a challenging atmosphere. They found themselves in a giving-up process in the name of "progress and civilisation": to what extent they would uphold their own traditions, institutions and lifestyle and to what extent they would give them up, was the main question on their minds. One of the major areas that came up for negotiation was the woman issue. The borders were drawn again and again, and in this process of redrawing borders, the status of women always retained its central role. The question of "to what extent *ala turka* and to what extent *ala franga*"[2] has always been answered through the status of women. This is because "women and their bodies are the symbolic-cultural site upon which human societies inscript their moral order."[3]

What happened in this process was a deep shift in thought and paradigm. The self-perception of Muslims changed radically and dramatically. The West became the context and the frame of reference for the self-evaluation of Ottoman intellectuals and the ruling elite. Şerif Mardin defines the socio-psychological condition in which the Ottoman elite thought and attempted to realise reforms – as in the example of Mustafa Fazıl Paşa (1830–75), who is known as the patron of the founding members of the Young Ottomans[4] – as follows: "the Ottoman elite's internalisation of ideas related to the Ottomans first developed by Westerners." According to Mardin, what defines the condition of our modernisation since the Tanzimat[5] reforms can be expressed as "perceiving ourselves from *their* point of view".[6] In this perception, the social and cultural situation of women in their society seemed backward and barbaric to the reformers. We have to keep in mind the fact that the situation of women, and practices concerning women, were first labelled "barbaric" and "backward" by the Orientalists. Then this became the language of the reformers. The Orientalist narrative concerning the inferiority of Islam was based on the so-called "peculiar practices of Islam with respect to women".[7] Leila Ahmed argues that the thesis of the discourse on Islam "was that Islam was innately and immutably oppressive to women, that the veil and segregation epitomised that oppression, and that these customs were the fundamental reasons for the general and comprehensive backwardness of Islamic societies".[8]

Within this discourse, the veil – the most visible marker of the "difference" and inferiority of Islamic societies – became the symbol of both the oppression of women and the backwardness of Islam. Mohanty[9] and Lazreg[10] have studied how the term "Muslim women" continues to be a synonym for so-called "veiled and oppressed" women in academic writings, and have pointed out the methodological universalism[11] in this approach. The stigmatisation of Muslim women as veiled and oppressed is still the primary operative attitude in cultural relations between the West and the Muslim world.

It was the same cultural basis that shaped the thoughts of nineteenth-century reformist thinkers, no matter whether they had accepted the general evaluation concerning Muslim women, rejected it, or tried to develop responses to it. A prominent writer of the Tanzimat period, namely Ahmed Mithat Efendi (1844–1912), wrote in one of his personal letters as follows: "Ah!!! How I wished to have our women unveiled instead of veiled in the course of such a severe discussion!"[12]

From the beginning of the Tanzimat period almost all thinkers wrote, if not a book, at least a few articles on women and family issues.[13] Their main concern was improving the status of women in society in order to save the family, the society and consequently the nation. The need for a general cultural and social transformation was a central issue in reformists' writings. The arguments regarding women were embedded within the thesis that a general transformation was needed: to change the customs regarding women and their costume, in particular abolishing the veil, was the reformists' key strategy for bringing about the desired general social transformations.

Civilisation and progress, *medeniyet* and *terakki*, were the key terms in their discussions. Civilisations were presented in a hierarchy by both the colonial authorities and the Muslim reformists, and, in this hierarchy, the Muslim civilisation was represented as semi-civilised compared to that of the West. What the Ottoman ruling elite and intellectuals sought was this – to be accepted among the civilised part of the world. Sultan Abdülhamit's strategy in the World Fairs shows this attempt very clearly.[14] In these fairs the "worlding of a world" (Spivak)[15] took place in which the difference was drawn between civilised and primitive or civilised and barbarian.

There is one more feature that characterises the modernisation process in the Muslim world in general, and in Ottoman society in particular. Modernisation movements in the Islamic world were somewhat religious movements, i.e. these movements can be considered as a part of the attempts to reinterpret the religion.[16]

The question, "Is Islam appropriate for civilisation (*medeniyet*)?", was the starting point of the continuing dichotomies: Islam and science, Islam and development, Islam and democracy, Islam and liberalism, and lastly Islam and feminism or Islam and women's rights. These discussions reveal a hegemonic relationship between one side characterised and represented by democracy, science, liberalism, human rights and women's rights, and Islam as the other side. The issue can be formulated as follows: in order for society to reach the ideal side of that dichotomy which the modern Western style represents, the other side, i.e. Islam, must cease to be an obstacle or a handicap. For Islam not to be an obstacle, it must be interpreted in an appropriate way.

Thus for the first time in the history of the Muslim world, Islam was considered as a "problem" that should somehow be solved, and the Qur'an as a burden from which Muslims should be freed. This point in the history of the Muslim world coincides with the colonial era. Throughout Muslim history, however, the Qur'an was on the contrary always considered a blessing and favour (*ni'ma*) and a guide that eased the lives of Muslims. It was not seen as a hindrance nor as something that made life difficult.

Due to these factors, the paradigm changed, and the debate on women's modernisation was centred on the critique of existing practices and on the question of what constitutes "true Islam" in opposition to the centuries of lived, but so-called "wrongly interpreted", Islam. This way of handling history was a strategy to cope with the existing failure that had been recognised not only on the military and political level, but also on the social and cultural level.

The constitutional period

The debate concerning the "woman question" was an arena for political and social criticism in general. Especially during the Second Constitutional Period, from 1908 up to the establishment of the Republic in 1923, the woman question gained great importance, and each school of thought expressed its deliberations on this issue. The existing schools can be classified as Turkish nationalists, Westernisers and Islamists.

To be sure, this classification has some limitations. It does not take into consideration the fact that Ottomans developed these approaches in a struggle for survival in the face of European expansion, and that they accepted these approaches as successive solutions to successive losses. Ottomanism, Islamism and Turkish nationalism follow a chronological line. If we accept these schools of thought as distinct entities, then we will be blind to the historical realities behind this struggle and also to the interpenetration of these approaches with each other in most respects.[17] For instance, Abdullah Cevdet (1869–1932), who was known as a Westerniser, had some thoughts very similar to those of Mehmet Akif (1873–1936), who was known as an Islamist. For example, both of them thought that the argument, "Islam is against progress," was clearly false. For them, the reason for the present failure was despotic rulers and the neglect and mistakes of the *ulema*.[18] However, keeping this limitation in mind and without drawing bold lines between the schools, we may use this classification for the sake of analysis. Concerning the woman question we come across similar views among the nationalists, Islamists and Westernisers, but these three groups also differed to some extent in their approaches.

For Westernisers, civilisation was the European civilisation and it could only be achieved through the emancipation of women. Much like the Egyptian reformist Qasim Amin (1863–1908),[19] Selahattin Asım also saw the reasons for the so-called backwardness of Muslim society in Islamic practices concerning women, such as polygamy, the face veil, unequal share in inheritance, etc. To him, all these religious rules and norms should be rejected for the good of Turkish women and Turkish society.[20]

However, there were others who had internalised Western-inspired politics and at the same time argued for a reform in Islam, rather than for the abolition of Islamic practices. Celal Nuri (1881–1938),[21] Halil Hamit[22] and Ahmed Cevad[23] were among this group who argued that Islam was not against women's rights and pointed to a need for re-interpretation.

The Westernising approach saw women's rights as embedded in Islam. However, their frame of reference was not Muslim, but Western civilisation. What they saw as problematic, such as veiling and polygamy, they held to be particularities of religion, and they tried to solve the problem of such practices by abolishing them.

The nationalists, on the other hand, among whom the writer and sociologist, Ziya Gökalp (1876–1924), was the best known, tried to solve the so-called problematic areas by referring to pre-Islamic Turkish history. Practices such as veiling and segregation, according to him, were not Turkish in origin. Any corruption of the ideal Turkish mores could be attributed to foreign influence, especially Persian and Arabic.

Where the Islamists are concerned, theirs was also a modernist movement, and their understanding of the woman question also had a modernist and apologetic character. Their main cause was to uphold the *din* (religion) and *devlet* (state) and, in their conception, these two terms were necessarily tied to each other. In order to uphold the *din*, it was necessary to uphold the state and because of the experienced military loss and political challenges, their *devlet* was in danger. In such a challenging atmosphere, they started to develop a defence mechanism, basing their arguments on the "right understanding" of Islam. The Islamist intellectuals tended to support the idea that their lived history had been full of superstitions and wrong understandings and practices concerning Islam. Because of the defeat they had experienced, they tried to deny and disown the so-called "history of defeats", and to build a bridge back to a golden age of early Muslim history instead. This was a methodological shift from an organic historical understanding to one that might be called synthetic: they did not ask, "what is our history?" but, rather, "what should our history have been?" It was this understanding which prepared the ground for the discourse of "true Islam".

In their challenging socio-psychological situation, the intellectuals of the time accepted an eclectic and defensive discourse on the woman question. Almost all Islamists argued that Muslim women already had their rights in Islam and that there was no need for a struggle for women's rights. According to them, the only thing that needed to be done was to put an end to the wrong understanding of Islam and give way to "true Islam".

This was a common basis they shared with the nationalists and some of the moderate Westernisers. Although they had a similar view of Islamic history as a history of wrongly interpreted and "wrongly lived Islam", they had different views on practices concerning women, e.g. covering and segregation.

It is not my purpose here to repaint the picture of Ottoman women as passive objects of a transformation regulated by the male intellectuals and propelled by the impetus they had received from Westerners. Of course there was a very active women's movement in Ottoman society, especially during the Second Constitutional Period. Women published newspapers, wrote articles, founded associations and actively took part in this negotiation process. Among others, *Hanımlara Mahsus Gazete* and *Kadınlar Dünyası* were influential and long-lasting magazines and arenas of debate concerning the woman question. So it would be misleading to talk about the way in which Ottoman women, as a single, unified entity, handled the woman question.

For example, Fatma Aliye Hanım (1862–1936), who was known as the first Muslim woman novelist, struggled for women's rights in a conservative way. She tried to find a point of reference from Islamic history and wrote a book on the lives of the most influential women in that history. She tried to put the argument as a struggle not between man and woman, but a struggle between knowledge and ignorance.[24] However, there were others who employed a much more feminist discourse. For example, in the magazine *Kadınlar Dünyası* women voiced their demands based on a shared womanhood.[25]

The characteristic feature of this period was the fact that all of the participants were negotiating in an Islamic atmosphere. Whether you called somebody Westerniser, nationalist or Islamist, they all had to refer to Islam to support their ideas. Women of the time were trying to find a way to practise Islam and be modern at the same time.

The republican period

However, when we come to the Republican Period (from 1923), the debate on the woman question loses its shared Islamic frame of reference. The official discourse on women depended upon the idea that Islam was against women's rights. Kandiyoti argues that the Turkish experience from Ottoman Empire to Turkish Republic can be seen as "a passage from the stance of an enlightened, modernist, Islamist position to a feminism stemming from Turkish nationalism".[26] Islam began to be evaluated as an archaic element that should be kept out of the public sphere. Because of this political preference on the governmental level, an argument such as "Islam acknowledges women's rights" lost its legacy and context.

"Modern women" became the symbol of the level of civilisation, progress and modernity of the new regime. So it became impossible to think of women's rights, women's emancipation and feminism together with the perspectives or understandings of "women and Islam". It was hardly possible to think the rejected past (Islam) and the struggle for an ideal future (i.e. the so-called women's emancipation) together. This negation was a constitutive part of Kemalist woman identity. The new Republican elite stressed the dichotomies of traditional versus modern and progressive versus backward in their definition of the ideal Turkish woman.

In this context, the first female generation of the Republican Period, whom Durakbaşa designates "Kemalist daughters of enlightened fathers",[27] built their image of a new and modern woman identity on the refutation of the Ottoman-Islamic heritage. The new nationalist discourse, while building its national identity and defining the difference between internal and external, between foreign and indigenous, made references to pre-Islamic history and tried to dissociate itself from the Islamic period of Turkish history.

While the Ottoman past was criticised for the backwardness of women and some regulations were made in order to rebuild Turkey as a Western and civilised country, the discourse on women became a central theme. Atatürk's Kastamonu speech (1925) distanced the new Turkish woman from Islamic practices. This approach did not leave any space for a debate that would try to make a correlation between Islam and women's rights or women's emancipation.

> In some places that I visit, I see some women who cover up their faces by a piece of cloth and turn their back when they see a man. O gentlemen! What is the meaning of this behaviour? O gentlemen! Can the mothers and sisters of a nation accept such a barbaric attitude? This is an amusing subject. This situation should be corrected as soon as possible.[28]

Throughout the Republican Period, the debate on women depended on the dichotomy of traditional versus modern women. The still ongoing headscarf issue both reveals this dichotomy and gives clues concerning how the notions of modernity have been produced. Since Turkey's experience of modernity was an experience of Westernisation, the headscarf is always held up as a symbolic reminder that Turkish society has failed to adopt the Western style of life. Because of this, the modernising elite always considered the headscarf guilty of keeping society "backward" and as the symbol of the old regime – the Ottoman State – that the new regime disowned.

Hence in the rhetoric of modernisation, emerging concepts such as emancipation of women, "new women" and "modern women" were conceptualised in opposition to the traditional women who were covered. So throughout Turkey's modernisation period, the head cover has been perceived as a low-status symbol.

It has always symbolised either backwardness or *irtica*, i.e. going back to the old days, to the Ottoman-Islamic days.

Another point that should be stressed is the fact that in the Turkish experience, the public sphere is not seen as a common domain that should be discussed and defined. Rather, it is seen as a domain in which modernity reveals itself, as "a sacred temple of modernity".[29] Because of the symbolic meaning attributed to "modern" women, throughout the Republican period the headscarf has been defined as an element that should not enter into the public sphere, since the public sphere has a hierarchical structure and its definition is based on banning and filtering out things that are seen as non-modern. Because of this hierarchy and filter, women with head covers who try to enter into the public sphere are perceived as a challenge to the foundations of the Republican regime.

In such a line of thinking, of course there was no way to talk about Islam and women with a positive attitude. Another factor that has made it difficult to correlate these two is the stress of the Republican regime on secularism. Even keeping in mind that the relationship between feminism and Kemalism in Turkish history is a controversial issue, it can safely be said that for the Kemalist regime, secularism has always had a higher priority than feminism and women's rights. So in this context, it became irrelevant to discuss women's issues in relation to Islam.

The period of "women and Islam" books

After the 1960s, the "women and Islam" issue regained its unique position on the agenda of the Islamists due to changes in the social and political atmosphere. In this period, many books were written under titles like "Women and Islam".[30] A considerable part of these books were of Pakistani and Egyptian origin. Including the ones written by Turkish authors, they all stressed the woman's role as mother and tried to build a comparison and contrast with the European/Western women. On the one hand, Western women were drawn as victims of consumerism and capitalism, of which Muslim women were considered to be free. On the other hand, feminism was seen as a necessary solution only for Western women, because of their cultural and historical baggage of misogyny, of which, again, Muslim women were considered to be free. One of the motives behind this line of thinking was Muslim unease with the developments in Europe, especially after 1968, in terms of sexual freedom and anti-family propaganda.

However, we do not find a conceptual framework and a theoretical analysis in these evaluations. Without having a sophisticated philosophy behind it, some of them rewrote the old *fiqh* books, others criticised so-called "corrupted Western women" and yet others gave apologetic answers to the centuries-old discourse of "oppressed Muslim women".

The debate in this period, if it is appropriate to call it a debate, was held only in closed religious circles. It was not carried to the larger society as a public debate, since the mainstream official attitudes were the same as in the first years of the Republic.

The male as the "Other" for Muslim women

In the late 1980s, a paradigm shift took place in the "women and Islam" issue. A series of articles that were published in a religious newspaper in 1987 was the starting point of this paradigm shift.[31] The writers of these articles did not see feminism as necessary only for European women, in contrast to their predecessors in the 1970s. On the contrary, they internalised feminist arguments as useful instruments for all women who are confronted with inequality and injustice in modern social life.

A male Islamist writer and sociologist, Ali Bulaç (b. 1952), wrote an article in which he argued that feminism was a type of modernism and a danger for Muslim women, because feminist demands led to a struggle between men and women that was going to disturb the harmony within the family and would lead in the end to a homosexual society. He was proposing a contradiction between the covered Muslim women and feminist women.[32] However, a series of articles written by several "Islamist" women as an answer to this article made it apparent that these women accepted a line of thinking similar to feminism, especially in their analysis of patriarchy and in basing their analysis on a shared position of womanhood.[33]

Theirs was a parallel discourse to the new women's movement in Turkey that took inspiration from the second wave of the feminist movement worldwide. In the authoritarian atmosphere of the 1980s after the military coup, the women's movement had a unique status as the only political movement not being hindered by the semi-military government.[34] Islam continued to have a negative connotation within this movement's thoughts and actions. The employment of "women and Islam" in the same phrase, as if hinting at a negative relationship between the two, did have its political usefulness. The ones who claimed to be the heirs of the Republican regime and the guardians of laicism used this negative connotation when they tried to find justification for their bans on religious acts and symbols in the public sphere.

Within this rising trend of women's rights discourse, the so-called Islamist women who were not allowed to enter into universities because of the headscarf ban became a part of the women's agenda, either as victims of the headscarf ban or as a "different group" in its pejorative sense. Academicians "discovered" a new area of research, and studied it in cooperation with the media. For example, while

Nilüfer Göle was doing her research for her book *Forbidden Modern*,[35] she did not neglect to collaborate with an influential magazine of the day. *Nokta* was a weekly news magazine, which was known for its leftist or social democratic tendency, and it covered the "women and Islam" issue in a popular and sometimes pejorative way. One of its cover titles was "feminists with turbans".[36]

From then on, the "women and Islam" issue began to be discussed frequently in the mainstream media. In this process, women with headscarves have continued to suffer being the objects of representation and discussion up till the present. The issue was discussed only on a cultural level, since discussing Islamic law on the legal level was and still is irrelevant to the present Turkey. This is because the secular civil code and the existing practices make it pointless to discuss the long-standing "women and Islam" issues such as polygamy, inheritance, divorce, etc. In this situation, the headscarf retained its exclusive status as the unique field of discussion as far as Islamic practices were concerned.

With the 1990s, a considerable shift was experienced in handling the woman issue among the Islamists. What was novel for the religious community was the fact that they entered into the public sphere as men and women. The rhetoric of solidarity yielded to a discourse of competition. The brothers and sisters of the former community life became rivals as men and women in the public arena.

The long-lasting ban on the headscarf had led to a displacement psychology among the covered women. Women felt anger at the state for banning headscarves, but redirected their anger at Islamist men, since the men were not directly experiencing the same discrimination. Though men were not innocent of the charge of discriminating against Islamist women, there was a discrepancy in the attitudes of covered women. It was apparent that not only women suffered: a considerable number of men in the military were dismissed because of their religious tendencies, and mostly because women in their family were wearing the headscarf, typically their wives. A considerable number of men failed to get promotion in universities or in governmental offices for the same reasons, but although both men and women suffered for their so-called Islamist tendencies, especially after the 1997 "post-modern coup", when the Army forced the resignation of an Islamist government led by the Refah Party, the limitations were felt especially sharply by women. A new discourse emerged: not only the authorities, but also the Islamist men were discriminating against Islamist women, since they did not face a ban similar to theirs. This discourse first found expression in some secularist writings[37] and then became the language of some women wearing the headscarf. This was an important point of separation in the experiences and positions of men and women among the religious/Islamist community.

During the struggle against the headscarf ban, some new strategies were employed. The ban on the headscarf began to be criticised as a form of discrimination against women. Non-governmental organisations struggling against the ban tried to cooperate with other women's organisations on the basis of a shared womanhood. What was interesting in this process was the fact that not the relationship of the headscarf with religiousness, but rather the relationship of the headscarf with womanhood was stressed. Thus the conceptual framework of feminism concerning a common ground of womanhood was used, even if not consciously.

However, the ban on the headscarf was not the only factor differentiating the experiences of men and women among Islamists. From the 1990s on, Islamist women started to take part in public life. In 1994 an Islamist Party, Refah, won the municipality elections in big cities. Although female party members had undeniably played a considerable role in the election victory, they were not allowed their share of the administrative posts. Taking part in politics without gaining equal positions on the administrative level led most of the female members of the party to question both the party's policy, and women's issues in general, in terms of gender discrimination.

With the accelerating impact of capitalist market conditions, especially after the 1990s, the number of working Islamist women – or to put it differently, head-covered women – increased. The language of solidarity yielded to a language of competition. In this atmosphere, a new wave of literature emerged among the Islamist women that accepted the historiography of feminism. This group of women writers started to employ terms such as patriarchy, historically universal misogyny and the misinterpretation of religion by the male elite, etc.[38] This was a development parallel to the globalisation of feminism and its claim to be the only way to the well-being of women, or its claim to be "the end of history" for women. Among Islamists there emerged a group that gave up the arguments that "Islam approves women's rights", that feminism is "the struggle of Western women" and that feminism is unacceptable because it contradicts the idea of complementary gender roles and does not value the importance of male and female principles in Islamic intellectual tradition. Of course, it was a little early for the argument that "Islam has been interpreted within a patriarchal conception throughout history". However, the "other" of the religious Islamist woman was no longer the "modern and secular woman"; instead, it was the Islamist man.

Conclusion

We are at a new stage of modernisation, and at this stage, the challenge for the Muslims is much more complex. In the first decades of the twentieth century, while Islamists were arguing that Islam recognised women's rights, they took an apologetic attitude vis-à-vis Western civilisation. The formulation they found in the end was taking the technology of the West and preserving their own indigenous culture. Just like the nationalists, they tried to preserve their culture through women, but their frame of reference was "true Islam".

For the Islamists, from the nineteenth century onwards, the "other" in the context of "women and Islam" gained different connotations. Sometimes Western women, sometimes so-called traditional Muslims who were ignorant of "true Islam" and sometimes extremely modernised women were positioned as the "other" in relation to Muslim women.

Recently a new dichotomy has been added to the list: man and woman. Defining the male as the "other" is a new stage, or a new paradigm, in the history of modern Islamic thought. It is this paradigm shift that has led a group of women to advocate genealogically Western notions of "gender" and "patriarchy" without much revision and criticism.

The experience of Islamist men with Islamist women in Turkey's public sphere is a recent development. This has led to a political and social stress that has caused polarisation between men and women. At the same time, it has aroused a need for redefinition of statuses and gender roles. Probably, this is a general scene in almost all Islamic countries. However, there is something that makes the Turkish experience unique: Islamist women in Turkey live with the difficulties of secularism, not the difficulties of so-called "Islamic law". Since Turkey has a secular civil law, Islamist women have not carried the burden of the wrongly practised so-called "Islamic law of Islamists". Their burden was to be blamed by the secularists for backwardness and to suffer bans in the public sphere. This factor may lead the discussion of "Islam and women" towards a moderate position. This unique situation will help Turkish Islamist women both criticise the Western notions of gender politics and negotiate the changeable and unchangeable in Islamic thought and practice at the same time.

Part Three
Authority and Islamic Normativity

9 Islamic authority

Khaled Abou El Fadl

In formulating Islamic law, it has become common in the modern age to use the authority of the Author (God) to justify the despotism of the reader. In effect, by claiming that the only relevant consideration is the Will of the Author, the reader is able to displace the Author and set himself as the sole voice of authority: the reader becomes God, as it were. The replacement of God's authority with that of the reader is an act of despotism and a corruption of the logic of Islamic law.

Islamic law is founded on the logic of a Principal who guides through the instructions set out in texts. Those instructions are issued to the agents who have inherited the earth and who are bound to the Principal by a covenant. The point of the covenant is not to live according to the instructions, but to *attempt* to do so. Searching the instructions is a core value in itself – regardless of the results, searching the instructions is a moral virtue. This is not because the instructions are pointless, but because the instructions must remain vibrant, dynamic, open and relevant. It is impossible for a human being to represent God's Truth – a human being can only represent his or her efforts in search of this truth. The ultimate and unwavering value in the relationship between human beings and God is summarised in the Islamic statement, "And, God knows best".

Deferring to God and honouring the text requires a human being to exercise self-restraint in speaking for God and the text. But discharging the obligations of human agency mandates that the reader (agent) take his or her role very seriously by aggressively and vigorously investigating both God and God's instructions. "God knows best" is not an invitation to intellectual complacency and smugness, but, as the Qur'an states, to realise that "over every knowledgeable person is One more knowledgeable" (12:76). Submission to God is at the core of the Islamic creed, but it does not mean blind submission to those who claim to represent God's law, and it does not mean submitting to the contentment and comfort of arrogant self-reference. Submission to God means the will and act of engaging the intellect and body in the pursuit of God, but also the humility of knowing that no intellect or body can ever fully represent God. The Qur'an sums up this point by reminding the Prophet that even he has not been sent to control or dominate people, but to admonish and teach (88:21–2).

This reminder is particularly pertinent to those who place themselves in the position of the devoted sages of the Divine instructions. As special agents, they accept the responsibility of doing what is not feasible for everyone to do: they devote a lifetime to the study of the instructions. As the Qur'an states, the task of these special agents is to study the instructions and to share the results of their search with the common agents who ultimately bear the responsibility of acting according to the dictates of their conscience (9:122). The authority of these special agents is not inherent or institutional – it is persuasive. The common agents will and should defer to the determinations of these special agents, but only to the extent that the special agents are honestly and diligently representing what the special agents believe to be the Will of the instructions.

There are implied conditions that define the authoritativeness of the special agents. These serve as the basis for the deferential relationship between the special agents and common agents. They are: honesty, diligence, self-restraint, comprehensiveness and reasonableness. Violating these contingencies is a breach of responsibility and a betrayal of the trust that the common agents have placed in the special agents. These conditions act as constraints on the special agents, and as controls against possible abuses of authority and, ultimately, despotism. A violation of one of the enumerated conditions is an abuse that threatens to become a usurpation of the Principal's authority. Authoritarianism of the special agent takes place when such an agent speaks for God without being authorised by the instructions to do so. This is well-represented by the Qur'anic concept of *idhn*, according to which it is a grave violation to speak for God's law without proper authorisation (10:59, 42:21). At least when it comes to law, the primary form of authorisation is the instructions contained in texts. This necessarily means that the five conditions do not only apply to determining the meaning of the text, but also to verifying that the text has legal competency, which means verifying that the text is qualified to act as part of God's instructions.

Special agents, like all readers, work within the context of interpretive communities. Interpretive communities develop habits, and these habits could be a line of precedents that are considered dispositive of an issue, or factual beliefs about social practices or propensities, or the method by which an interpretive community analyses an issue. The existence of assumptions within an interpretive community, in itself, is not authoritarian. However, these assumptions could lead to a breach of the conditions of authority pursuant to which the common agent defers to the determination of the special agent. If the special agent dogmatically treats these assumptions as part of the Principal's instructions, or considers such assumptions to be indisputable or immutable, this is likely to lead to the corruption of the process and to authoritarianism. This is especially the case when the special agent refuses to acknowledge that assumptions are merely enabling or efficient tools and treats them as sacrosanct, or when the special agent fails to disclose the existence and the nature of these assumptions to the common agents.

Faith-based assumptions are always the most challenging and the most dangerous. By nature they are not accessible or sufficiently accountable to others. Faith-based assumptions are like saying, "I love God", "God is most merciful", or "God loves all people". Such statements must be believed and felt to mean anything. They could be engaged and debated, and one can attempt to refute them, but fundamentally, they rely on what I call a collateral relationship with God. If, for example, I believe that God cannot and will not command anything that is immoral and ugly, there is no doubt that this will affect all my interpretive activities and legal determinations. I am not arguing that it is inappropriate or futile to argue about faith-based matters – far from it. Faith-based assumptions are influenced by a variety of human experiences including textual evidence, sociological experience, human temper and individual dialectics, but they are not determined by any of them. As such, faith-based assumptions do run the very high risk of becoming authoritarian. We witness this particularly in sectarian debates. Historically, Sunni scholars have rejected the determinations of Shiʿi narrators of *ḥadīth* and vice versa. In addition, the scholars known as *ahl al-ḥadīth* dismissed the transmissions of the Muʿtazila, Khawarij and Shiʿa as palpably false. Yet, faith-based assumptions are a matter of conscience and conviction, and so they cannot be dismissed as irrelevant.

The question becomes: what does a special agent do with faith-based assumptions? At a minimum, they must be honestly disclosed so that common agents may decide whether they share these assumptions or not. Moreover, it is important to remember that faith-based assumptions have a rather limited scope. If something is established in an interpretive community through rational analysis, factual determination or methodological choices, in most circumstances it is impeachable on the same grounds. Since faith-based assumptions are always at risk of being whimsical, they should be utilised sparingly. The reliance on whimsical beliefs or determinations is treated in the Qur'an as an abomination and a sin. Therefore, a cautious and wise agent will not hastily claim a faith-based determination, but will first pause and then honestly, diligently, comprehensively, reasonably and humbly scrutinise the evidence before deciding to reach an opinion. If the evidence reasonably supports his or her claim, then there is no issue, but if it does not, the agent may be forced to revise his or her beliefs or decide to become a conscientious objector. This becomes the case especially when deciding the competence of instructions that warrant a conscientious pause.

A person develops a relationship with God perhaps through prayer and supplication, by reflecting upon creation, or by reflecting upon history. These various avenues to the knowledge of God exist apart from the indicators of the text, but they work in conjunction with the text to formulate a conviction about the nature and normativities of the Divine. Although the text plays a role in forming these convictions, one cannot exclude the possibility that the conviction which has been formulated might come into friction with certain determinations of the text. A person can read a text that seems to go against everything that he or she believes about God and will feel a sense of incredulous disbelief, and might even exclaim, "This cannot be from God, the God that I know!"

What does one do in such a case? The appropriate response is to exercise what I call a conscientious pause. Having experienced this fundamental conflict between a conscientious conviction and a textual determination, a responsible and reflective person ought to pause. The point of the pause is not to simply dismiss the text or the determination, but to reflect and investigate further. It is akin to flagging an issue for further study and suspending judgement until such study is complete. After due reflection, a person might conclude that the conflict is more apparent than real, or that this determination does not do justice to the text, or might conclude that in good conscience, he or she ought to yield and defer to the textual determination. All of these and other ways of resolving the conflict are possible. But it is also possible that an adequate resolution would not be found, and that the individual conscience and the textual determination continue to be pitted in an irresolvable conflict. I argue that as long as a person has exhausted all the possible avenues towards resolving the conflict, in the final analysis, Islamic theology requires that a person abide by the dictates of his or her conscience. A faith-based objection to the determination might be necessary. Faith-based objections are founded on one's sense of *īmān* (conviction and belief in and about God), and it seems to me that after all is said and done, it is this sense that ought to be given deference.[1] But a faith-based objection that is not preceded by a diligent and exhaustive investigation runs the serious risk of being a simple exercise of capricious whimsy.

Determinations and traditions demeaning to women

I fear that Islamic jurisprudence, as an epistemology and as a methodology of inquiry, has become dominated by authoritarian discourses. If Islamic jurisprudence basically consists of rules (*aḥkām*), then one must conclude that Islamic law is thriving in the modern age. I do not believe there is a shortage of individuals, organisations, or countries willing to enter into a mass production of *aḥkām*, and even live by them. However, if Islamic jurisprudence is about a methodology for a reflective life that searches for the Divine, and about a process of weighing and balancing the core values of Shariʿa in pursuit of a moral life, then I think one would have to concede that it has disintegrated and disappeared in the last three centuries, but particularly in the second half of the twentieth century. I think that the results can be clearly observed when one considers the impact of contemporary Islamic rules on women.

I will take as examples certain traditions (*ḥadīth*) cited by the Permanent Council for Scientific Research and Legal Opinions (hereafter: CRLO), the official institution in Saudi Arabia entrusted with issuing Islamic legal opinions. This is not because I wish to discredit the CRLO or its long list of affiliated jurists, but because it is my belief that the methodology utilised by the CRLO has become very widespread in the Muslim world today. Their *responsa* on women both have wide impact in Muslim societies and provide powerful demonstrative case studies in the construction of authoritarian discourses.

As a means of being conscientious about our reliance and presentation of the instructions of the Principal, I argue for a relationship of proportionality between our assessment of the instructions (mostly Sunna and *ḥadīth*) and their theological, legal and sociological impact. The greater the anticipated impact of a tradition, the more assured and confident should we be of its competence.

Pleasing husbands and entering heaven

One set of traditions cited by the CRLO makes a wife's religious salvation explicitly contingent on her husband's pleasure. For example, a tradition narrated by Abu Dawud, al-Tirmidhi, Ibn Maja, Ibn Hibban and al-Hakim claims that Umm Salama, the Prophet's wife, reported that the Prophet said, "Any woman who dies while her husband is pleased with her enters Heaven."[2] Even if we say, like some commentators, that the tradition only applies to pious women, it is still problematic because God's pleasure is still contingent on the husband's pleasure, regardless of how impious the husband might be. This is a revolutionary concept with profound theological and social implications. Before it can be recognised as setting a theological foundational principle, it must be of the highest degree of authenticity, which it is not.

Other traditions relied upon for the same obedience determination include one that claims that the Prophet stated, "A woman's prayers or good deeds will not be accepted (by God) as long as her husband is upset with her."[3] Another tradition reportedly transmitted by ʿAbd Allah b. ʿUmar claims that the Prophet proclaimed, "God will not look at a woman who is not grateful to her husband despite her reliance on him."[4] Yet another report claims that the Prophet said, "If a woman upsets her husband, his angelic wife in Heaven (*ḥūr al-ʿayn*) will say, 'May God confound you! Do not upset him [the husband]! He is but a visitor with you who is about to leave you and join us.'"[5]

These traditions should invoke a conscientious pause – they trouble the conscience, contradict other portrayals of the Prophet's character and conflict with the Qur'anic spirit. With a minimal amount of reflection, one can see a conflict between the fundamental principles set by the Qur'an and the traditions of subservience and obedience. The Qur'an talks of love, compassion, friendship and virtuous women who are obedient to God – not to husbands (33:35, 4:34). In my view, the Qur'anic conception of marriage is not based on servitude, but on compassion and cooperation; and the Qur'anic conception of virtue is not conditioned on the pleasure of another human being, but on piety and obedience to God.

Classical and modern jurists argue that if there is a conflict between the sources, one must reconcile them – not use one source to trump the other. This is a well-established principle in Islamic jurisprudence, so consequently the obedience traditions would serve to specify or particularise the broader discourses in the Qur'an and Sunna about friendship and companionship. This is the logic that the CRLO uses. According to this reasoning, Islam requires the establishment of friendship and companionship, but through obedience. However, one should ask the following methodological question: Should traditions of divergent versions, of singular (*āḥādī*) transmissions, which do not reach the highest level of authenticity and which have suspect theological logic and profound social implications, be allowed to conflict with the Qur'an in the first place? In fact, and more importantly, should such traditions be recognised as establishing laws, let alone foundational principles, for something as essential as marriage? I propose that a rationale of proportionality must be adopted, which would necessarily require only those traditions of the highest degree of authenticity to be recognised as foundational in matters of crucial religious or social implications.

The CRLO, and those who follow their school of thought, agree with the group of scholars known as *ahl al-ḥadīth* in allowing *āḥādī* traditions to be dispositive in all fields of law as well as in matters of faith and conviction. To a large extent, this position justifies the majority of their determinations, especially on issues related to women. Furthermore, this position seems to have gained widespread currency. However, it is important to note that, other than *ahl al-ḥadīth*, the vast majority of classical Muslim jurists wanted to limit the scope of *āḥādī* traditions. Since *āḥādī* traditions cannot lead to certain knowledge of the Prophet's utterances, they cannot be relied upon to the same extent as *mutawātir* traditions (*ḥadīth* reported by a large number of people and considered of certain attribution). *Āḥādī* traditions, the majority argued, could be used to establish branches (*furūʿ*) of the religion, but not the fundamentals (*uṣūl*). Although the majority of jurists struggled with the distinction between fundamentals and branches, the fact remains that they did not consider *āḥādī* traditions of sufficient probative value to establish matters that are essential to religion. Therefore, it makes perfect sense to argue for a proportional relationship between the authenticity of traditions and their effective scope. I cannot claim that the logic of proportionality is explicitly endorsed by the discourses of the classical jurists, but I believe that proportionality is the clear import of their debates on *āḥādī* traditions. However, to limit the logic of proportionality to the dichotomy between *uṣūl* and *furūʿ* is not plausible. The distinction between *uṣūl* and *furūʿ* is itself problematic. More importantly, the issue is not whether a problem could be technically classified as part of *uṣūl* or *furūʿ*. Rather, the issue is the existence of proportionality between our knowledge of the source of a text, and the impact of the text. The greater the potential impact of a textual source, the more one should insist on its authenticity.

By the same token, the analysis should not simply be limited to whether a tradition is *mutawātir* or *āḥādī*. Especially in cases of the conscientious pause, whether a tradition is *mutawātir* or *āḥādī* is only the beginning of the inquiry. The point in question is not only how many people from the first generation of Muslims transmitted a particular tradition. Rather, when a tradition has serious social, theological or political implications, the inquiry should be whether the totality of the evidence could provide us with a clear sense of the role of the Prophet in what is attributed to him. The totality of the evidence would include the authenticity and trustworthiness of the transmitters, the number of transmitters from the early generations, the number of versions of the traditions, the factual contradictions between the different versions, the substance of the tradition, the relation between the tradition and more authentic or less authentic reports from the Sunna, the Qur'anic evidence (in terms of contradictions or consistencies), the historical context of the tradition, and the practices of the Prophet and Companions in related contexts. By their very nature, *mutawātir* traditions will be able to withstand greater scrutiny than their *āḥādī* counterparts. Ultimately, however, even after evaluating the totality of the evidence, one might have to take a faith-based stand in rejecting a particular position. Importantly, if this stand is taken by a special agent who has fulfilled the five contingencies, including disclosing his or her conscientious objection, one cannot describe the special agent's behaviour as authoritarian. After all, the special agent has shown humility, self-restraint and diligence in exploring all the possibilities, and, after disclosure, the common agents are free to affirm or withdraw their trust and deference.

The fitna traditions

The issue at the core of most juristic determinations mandating the exclusion of women from public places is the issue of *fitna* (seduction or seductive acts). The problem of *fitna* overlaps in important respects with the issue of the veil (*al-ḥijāb*), but conceptually it remains a separate field of inquiry. *Fitna* connotes the notion that certain things or acts produce the type of sexual arousal that is conducive to the commission of sin. Certain acts, such as *khalwa* (privacy and seclusion between a foreign man and woman) are presumed to be inherently dangerous because they produce the type of *fitna* that is conducive to the commission of unlawful sexual acts.

The most pronounced feature of the legal determinations that exclude women from public life is their obsessive reliance on the idea of *fitna*. In these determinations, women are persistently seen as a walking, breathing bundle of *fitna*. One can hardly find a *responsum* that deals with women without the insertion of some language about the seductions of womanhood. So, for instance, according to the CRLO, women may attend mosques only if it does not lead to *fitna*; women may listen to a man reciting the Qur'an or give a lecture, only if it does not lead to *fitna*; women may go to the marketplace only if it does not lead to *fitna*; women may not visit graveyards because of the fear of *fitna*; women may not do *tasbīḥ* or say amen aloud in prayer because of the fear of *fitna*; a woman praying by herself may not raise her voice in prayer if it leads to *fitna*; a woman may not even greet a man if it leads to *fitna*; and every item and colour of clothing is analysed under the doctrine of *fitna*.[6] It does not seem to occur to the jurists who make these determinations that this presumed *fitna* that accompanies women in whatever they do or wherever they go is not an inherent quality of womanhood, but is a projection of male promiscuities. By artificially constructing womanhood into the embodiment of seductions, these jurists do not promote a norm of modesty, but, in reality, promote a norm of immodesty. Instead of turning the gaze away from the physical attributes of women, they obsessively turn the gaze of attention to women as a mere physicality. In essence, these jurists objectify women into items for male consumption, and in that is the height of immodesty.

The challenge, however, is that the jurists who make these determinations find support in a range of traditions that position women as an inexhaustible source of seduction and temptation for men. The CRLO jurists unfailingly cite these traditions in arguing for the seclusion of women and in prohibiting the mixing of the sexes in public forums (*ikhtilāṭ*). There is a plethora of traditions that convey the same basic message: women are an unadulterated *fitna*. In some of the most common versions of this genre of traditions, we encounter the following: Abu Saʿid al-Khudri reports that the Prophet said,

> This earth is lush and pretty, and God has entrusted you (in this earth) to see what you will do. When it comes to (the temptations of) this world be cautious, and as to women be cautious (as well) for the first *fitna* that befell the Israelites was (the *fitna* of) women.[7]

In another oft-quoted version, the Prophet reportedly said, "I have not left in my people a *fitna* more harmful to men than women".[8] In a report from a related genre of traditions, the Prophet reportedly said, "Women are the snares of the devil."[9] In a tradition that draws a connection between *ʿawra* (private parts that must be covered) and *fitna*, it is transmitted that ʿAbd Allah b. ʿUmar narrated that the Prophet said: "[The whole of] a woman is a *ʿawra* and so if she goes out, the devil makes her the source of seduction."[10] A particular genre of reports takes the message of these traditions to its logical extreme. This genre effectively declares that women ought to be either married or dead. In a version transmitted through Ibn al-Abbas, the Prophet reportedly said, "A woman has ten *ʿawras*; when she marries, her husband covers one of her *ʿawras*, and when she dies, the grave covers the rest."[11]

Not surprisingly, these traditions lay the foundations for most of the determinations regulating a woman's appearance and conduct, regardless of whether a particular woman has covered her private parts. Therefore, even if a woman has covered her private parts, she may still not mix with men in all public forums and some private forums. Importantly, these traditions become the vehicle for symbolisms placing women in the role of the distrusted or treacherous, and for associating them with the construct of a menace that must be restrained. Consequently, in classical commentaries on these traditions, it is not unusual to find the following language:

> Since God has made men desire women, and desire looking at them, and enjoying them, women are like the devil in that they seduce men towards the commission of evil, while making evil look attractive (to men). We deduce from this that women should not go out in the midst of men except for a necessity, and that men should not look at their cloth and should stay away from women altogether.[12]

One serious conceptual and moral difficulty with the idea of *fitna* concerns the principle that no one can be called to answer for the sins of another, which is a core Shariʿa value. In Qurʾanic discourses, one person or set of people cannot be made to suffer because of the indiscretions, sins, or faults of others – each individual is responsible and accountable only for his or her own behaviour.[13] In fact, when addressing issues of modesty, the Qur'an is quite careful to place the blame on those it labels the hypocrites, who harass or molest the innocent (33:58–60).[14] The jurisprudence of *fitna*, however, runs the risk of violating this principle. For example, assume that the reason we are confronted with a *fitna* situation is because of men with an overactive libido, or who are impious or ill-mannered. Demanding that women should suffer exclusion or limitations would violate the principle that the innocent should not pay for the indiscretions of the culpable, yet most *fitna* determinations rely on the dubious logic that women should pay the price for the impious failures of men. Furthermore, in these determinations, as far as women are concerned, *fitna* emerges as the core value of Islam. Therefore, women's education, mobility, safety and even religious liberty should be restricted in order to avoid *fitna*. Hence, we observe that women can be banned from driving, working, serving in the military, or appearing in public life on the pretext of averting *fitna*.

The first point of inquiry is to ask, do the *fitna* traditions make an empirical claim or a normative claim? Are these traditions saying that as an empirical matter women will always have this effect on men? If the answer is yes, then the question is, what if the empirical reality contradicts the claim of the tradition? In the science of *ḥadīth*, any tradition that contravenes human experience cannot be accepted as valid. So, for instance, if a tradition says that the people of Yemen walk on three legs, since the tradition is empirically incorrect it cannot be relied upon in legal determinations. Therefore, if human experience reveals that men are the sources of as much evil as women, how do we then deal with these traditions? Arguably, the *fitna* traditions are not describing an empirical state of affairs, but are setting a normative principle. The normative principle is that women are dangerous – whether you can empirically verify this or not, you must accept it, believe it and act on it. This, of course, takes us full circle through the construction of reality – by prophesying that women are dangerous and treating them as dangerous, we are never able to realise any reality other than that women are dangerous.

As argued earlier, however, traditions of singular transmissions should not support determinations of faith. Because of this, it is important to ask – if these traditions cannot establish points of conviction or faith, then what claims do remain? Once we disqualify these traditions from establishing points of faith (*'aqīda*), what remains of the tradition? What remains is the empirical claim – what remains is sociology. Since under a proportionality analysis, these traditions only qualify to make empirical claims, they become empirically verifiable. Human experience can either confirm or completely refute their credibility. If the tradition is empirically unbelievable, then it cannot be relied on and cannot be enforced either. But even assuming that we are able to empirically verify that women are the source of *fitna*, that is not the only consideration. The ending of seduction must be weighed against the principles of Islamic justice. Consequently, if the core of the problem is the promiscuities of men, then women should not be made to suffer for the faults of men. Furthermore, in all cases higher values, such as education or health, cannot be sacrificed in order to guard against dangers of *fitna*.

The *ḥadīth* literature should properly be seen as the product of an authorial enterprise. It is an authorial enterprise because of the widespread participation of so many individuals from a variety of socio-historical contexts, with their own sense of values, levels of consciousness, and memories, who engage in the process of selecting, remembering and transmitting the memory of the Prophet and the Companions.

We should assess the issue of the authorial enterprise as it relates to the *fitna* traditions. I start the analysis with the following speculation: Is it possible that the Prophet in one or more contexts warned against sexual promiscuities and immodesty, and that this warning was remembered and reconstructed into a warning against women? This speculation is warranted because it is entirely possible that the Prophet would counsel modesty and virtue, and it is also plausible that the patriarchal society receiving the Prophet's counsel redirected this counsel into a statement against women.

One of the most problematic aspects of the *fitna* traditions and their determinations is that they make a good part of the Islamic historical experience in Medina appear a corruption. It is difficult to reconcile the traditions of *fitna* and exclusion with the numerous reports about the active participation of women in public life during the life of the Prophet and after his death as well. In fact, the reports that document incidents of seclusion of women are few in comparison with the reports documenting the opposite. The reports of public participation are too numerous to report here.[15] In none of these reports about the historical practice is there a hint of obsession about *fitna*. Conversely, the overwhelming majority of the traditions of the *fitna* genre do not purport to describe a historical practice. Rather, they present declarations, aspirations, claims, or normative prescriptions. If these traditions are to be believed, then there was an enormous disparity between the normative declarations of the Prophet and the actual historical practice in Medina. Seen differently, either the reports that describe the historical practice are exaggerated or the traditions of *fitna* are exaggerated. It is implausible that the Companions and the Prophet, himself, consistently chose to ignore the Prophet's normative injunctions about *fitna* in actual practice.

The typical CRLO response to this type of argument is to claim that all such incidents took place before the imposition of the *ḥijāb*. Once the *ḥijāb* was imposed, all such incidents became irrelevant. However, considering that the *ḥijāb* was introduced in the very last years before the death of the Prophet, we end up with the peculiar result that most of the Islamic historical experience, as far as gender relations are concerned, becomes an utter nullity. In addition, most Qur'anic commentaries explicitly state that the *ḥijāb* was imposed only on the Prophet's wives. In fact, the verse explicitly addresses itself to the wives of the Prophet and comments that the wives of the Prophet are unlike other women in the Muslim community (33:32, 33:53).[16] Furthermore, many of the reports about the historical practice describe numerous incidents of public participation by women in the last years of the Prophet's life and after his death.

Moreover, even assuming that the law of *ʿawra* was revealed in the last year or two of the Prophet's life, the issue of *ʿawra* is separate from the issue of *fitna*. Although the issue of *ʿawra* needs a separate treatment, it is significant that according to the authorial enterprise that conveyed the laws of *ʿawra*, the *ʿawra* of female slaves are different from the *ʿawra* of free women. A female slave does not require the covering of the hair, the arms, or part of the legs. If the discourse of *ʿawra* was related to the discourse of the *fitna*, there would be no grounds for distinguishing the two. In my view, the mere fact that the authorial enterprise distinguished between the *ʿawra* of free and non-free women is sufficient in itself to warrant a complete re-examination of the *ʿawra* laws.

There are six main elements that, I believe, warrant careful examination in trying to analyse the laws of *ʿawra*, and that invite us to re-examine the relationship between *ʿawra* and *fitna*. First, early jurists disagreed on the meaning of *zīna* (adornments) that women are commanded to cover. Secondly, the jurists frequently repeated that the veiling verse was revealed in response to a very specific situation. Corrupt young men would harass and, at times, assault women at night as these women headed to the wild to relieve themselves. Apparently, when confronted, these men would claim that they did not realise that these women were Muslim but thought them non-Muslim slave girls, and, therefore, not under the protection of the Muslim community. Thirdly, as noted above, Muslims jurists consistently argued that the laws mandating the covering of the full body did not apply to slave girls. Fourthly, the jurists often argued that what could be lawfully exposed in a woman's body was what would ordinarily appear according to custom (*ʿāda*), nature (*jibilla*), and necessity (*ḍarūra*). Relying on this, they argued that slave girls do not have to cover their hair, face, or arms because they live an active economic life that requires mobility, and because by nature and custom slave girls do not ordinarily cover these parts of their bodies. Arguably, women in the modern age too live an economically active life that requires mobility and, arguably, custom varies with time and place. Fifthly, several early authorities state that the Qur'anic verse primarily sought to have women cover their chests up to the beginning of the cleavage area. Sixthly, there is a sharp disjunction between the veiling verses and the notion of seduction. A man could be seduced by a slave girl, and a woman could be seduced by a good-looking man, yet neither slave girls nor men are required to cover their hair or faces.[17]

In order to evaluate the authorial enterprise behind the *fitna* traditions, we need to examine the totality of the evidence including the rhetorical dynamics of these traditions along with their functions and potentialities. For instance, in one of the traditions that the CRLO jurists frequently cite in support of their argument for the exclusion of women, Ibn ʿUmar narrates that the Prophet said: "Do not forbid your women from going to the mosque, but praying at home is better for them." A version of this report purportedly transmitted from the Prophet by ʿAbd Allah b. ʿUmar, becomes more extreme. It states: "The prayer of a woman in her room is better than her prayer house and her prayer in a dark closet is better than her prayer in her room."[18] These reports coexist with other traditions that assert that the mosque of the Prophet was full of rows of women lining up for prayers. At times, men arriving late for prayer would pray behind women and their prayers were considered valid.[19] Furthermore, there are reports that some women would stay for long periods and even sleep in the mosque.[20] Of course, reports of widespread attendance of prayers by women in mosques create a rather untenable situation. One would have to conclude that all these women ignored the Prophet's advice to pray in dark closets. In response to this tension, we find reports that try to rehabilitate the situation, somewhat. For instance, a report attributed to ʿA'isha asserts that ʿA'isha said, "If the Prophet had seen what women are doing in mosques today, he would have prohibited them [from attending the mosque] as the women of Israel were prohibited [presumably, by Jewish law]." The importance of this tradition is the fact that it is attributed to ʿA'isha, who led an active political life and continued to pray and teach in the mosque in Medina after the Prophet's death.

Such various traditions allow us to observe a vibrant historical dynamic in which a social issue is being negotiated through the subtleties of language. Observing this social dynamic allows us to assess the authorial enterprise behind the *fitna* traditions in a more reasonable, comprehensive, diligent and honest assessment.

Part of the historical negotiation process was the co-option and redirecting of reports that described a historical practice into reports of normative warnings against the *fitna* of women. In several traditions, ʿA'isha reports that women of the time of the Prophet would attend morning prayers wearing their cloaks. The women would attend and leave without being recognised because of the darkness. ʿA'isha reportedly says this in the context of arguing that morning congregational prayers should be performed early, at dawn, when it is still dark. Her point is technical and related to the proper timing of prayer.[21] Remarkably, however, this tradition becomes co-opted by some early and modern authorities into a statement against *fitna*. According to these sources, and according to the CRLO, the lesson of these traditions is that women should not be seen going to and coming from the mosque, or that if they go to the mosque, they should thoroughly wrap themselves in clothing so that no one will recognise them.

The issue is not simply who said what, or who said what about whom, the relevant issue is to investigate thoroughly, comprehensively and diligently the totality of contextual evidence that might enlighten us about the motives, dynamics, values, memory and the construction of reality. For example, noticing that many of the reports that demean, and sometimes honour, women are consistently attributed to Abu Hurayra, ʿAbd Allah b. ʿUmar, and Abu Saʿid al-Khudri, a diligent agent must ask, why? Is it possible that these traditions were the legal opinions of these Companions, and that these individual legal opinions were misremembered by later generations, and attributed to the Prophet? Is it possible that people tended to attribute opinions that expressed a conservative view about women to these particular Companions who were collectively remembered as conservative men? Someone like Abu Saʿid al-Khudri was an honoured and revered Companion of the Prophet, and we find that 1,170 traditions were attributed to him. Out of these, al-Bukhari accepted only sixteen traditions as authentic, and Muslim accepted fifty-two.[22] For someone to come in the contemporary age and argue that perhaps al-Bukhari and Muslim could have included some or excluded others of the traditions attributed to al-Khudri, is not heresy – it is simply a diligent discharging of the burdens of special agency.

In my view, these traditions are not only demeaning to women, but are also demeaning to men. The often graphic and repulsive nature of these reports is evidence of the fact that they were produced in the context of highly contentious social dynamics. Their wording and style seem intended to shock, challenge and frustrate a particular social strata or set of interests. Quite aside from the issue of the technical, chain-of-transmission-focused authenticity of these traditions, they are indicative of a dynamic and highly negotiative historical process. If one adopts the faith-based conviction that the Prophet was not sent by God to affirm and legitimate conservative and oppressive power structures, traditions that affirm the hegemony of patriarchy would have to pass the strictest level of scrutiny. However, applying this level of scrutiny to these traditions would reveal that there were too many patriarchal vested interests circulating, advocating and embellishing these types of reports. Consequently, one would have to conclude that the voice of the Prophet in the authorial enterprise behind these traditions has been hopelessly drowned out.

Serving justice

What is problematic about such determinations as the *responsa* of the CRLO on women is not only that they are often blatantly result-oriented, nor that they are remarkably careless and uncritical in handling the evidence, nor that they are not clear or forthright about their sociological and factual assumptions, but also, and even more importantly, that they fail to integrate or give due weight to moral assessments. I realise that in the contemporary age it is not fashionable to speak about morality when discussing Islamic law, except to adopt a vulgar form of legal positivism which declares that whatever the rule of law, therein lies the moral imperative. It is also not fashionable to speak of intuitive morality or the application of reason to God's law. Very few contemporary Muslim authors attempt to rekindle and develop the classical discourses on the role of *ʿaql* (intellect), *fiṭra* (intuition), or *ḥusn* and *qubḥ* (the moral and the immoral) in the process of developing God's law.[23] Even rudimentary notions of moral awareness, such as being aware of the value of fairness, dignity, and truthfulness, are hardly given any weight by bodies such as the CRLO, especially in determinations that deal with women. Since no legal system functions in a moral vacuum, serious thought needs to be given to the visions of morality that might guide Islamic law in the contemporary age.

I am painfully aware that the reactions of some fellow Muslims to these ideas are going to be somewhat unpleasant. However, I feel that Muslims in the present age are going through their intellectual dark ages, and this creates an added burden on Muslim intellectuals. In the same way that Muslims of previous generations reached the awareness that slavery is immoral and unlawful, as a matter of conscience, I confess that I find the virtual slavery imposed on women by the CRLO and like-minded special agents to be painfully offensive and unworthy of Shariʿa. To claim that a woman visiting her husband's grave, a woman raising her voice in prayer, a woman driving a car, or a woman travelling unaccompanied by a male is bound to create intolerable *fitna*, strikes me as morally problematic. If men are so morally weak, why should women suffer? Besides, doesn't this assumed moral weakness run contrary to the assumption that men should be the heads of the family and the leaders of society because they are of a stronger and more enduring constitution? Doesn't this also contradict the assumption that men are more rational and less emotional than women? Furthermore, arguing that women should pray in the most inaccessible area in a home, or should walk next to a wall to the point of rubbing against it, or should physically submit whenever it fits the husband's whimsy, or that women's salvation is contingent on the pleasure of their husbands, or that women will form most of hell's population, or that a woman is a walking, talking bundle of seduction, again, strikes me as morally offensive.

Because of the drastic normative consequences of traditions such as this, they require a conscientious pause. If by the standards of age and place, or the standards of human moral development, traditions lead to *wakhdh al-ḍamīr* (the unsettling or disturbing of the conscience), the least a Muslim can do is to pause to reflect about the place and implications of these traditions. If a Muslim's conscience is disturbed, the least that would be theologically expected from thinking beings who carry the burden of free will, accountability and God's trust, is to take a reflective pause, and ask: To what extent did the Prophet really play a role in the authorial enterprise that produced this tradition? Can I, consistently with my faith and understanding of God and God's message, believe that God's Prophet is primarily responsible for this tradition?

If my analysis is correct, the evidence, itself, does not warrant these misogynistic determinations. The question remains: what solicits or generates these types of determinations? If one apologetically says that culture is the culprit – that these determinations have nothing to do with the religion, but are the product of highly patriarchal cultural settings – I would politely have to say, I agree. However, I agree in a different way, and with a different claim. It would be dishonest to claim that these determinations find no support in Islamic sources, for they clearly find support in a variety of traditions and precedents. However, one can justifiably argue that these determinations are inconsistent with Qur'anic morality, and that other Islamic sources challenge these determinations, at least as much as they lend them support.

In my view, herein is the true Divine test and challenge. One of the most fascinating, and understudied, aspects of the Qur'anic text is its discourse on the idea of justice.[24] The Qur'an connects the idea of bearing witness upon humanity with the idea of balance. For instance, the Qur'an states in part: "Thus, We have made you Muslims a nation that must be justly balanced, so that you may bear witness over humanity" (2:143; cf. 22:78). Elsewhere, the Qur'an interchanges the obligations towards justice with the obligations towards God. For instance, it states, "O you who believe, *stand firmly for God as witnesses for justice*, and let not the hatred of others to you make you swerve to wrong and depart from justice" (5:8), and then, "O you who believe, *stand firmly for justice as witnesses for God*, even as against yourselves, or your parents, or your kin, and whether it be against rich or poor" (4:135).[25] It seems to me that standing firmly for God or standing firmly for justice are one and the same, or, at least, coexist in the same moral plane. Furthermore, without being themselves morally balanced, Muslims cannot discharge their obligation to bear witness upon humanity, let alone to bear witness upon themselves. It strikes me as unjust to bear witness upon others according to a balance that is neither accessible, nor understandable, nor accountable to those others. If Islam is a universal message, its language of morality and justice ought to make sense beyond the limited confines of a particular juristic culture in a particular cultural setting. I am not advocating a universal law, and I am not advocating the abolition of all cultural participation, but, at a minimum, it seems that serving God means serving justice, and serving justice necessarily means engaging in the search for the just, moral and humane. The test and the challenge to our sense of balance and equanimity is, regardless of the socio-historical circumstances, or textual and doctrinal indicators, to try always to pose the questions: Is it fair? Is it just? – and, at the end of every conscientious and diligent process, to close with, "And, God knows best".

10 A theory of Islam, state and society

Abdullahi A. An-Naʿim

The main objective of the argument I will make here is to promote the view that the future of Shariʿa, the normative system of Islam, lies among believers and their communities, and not in the enforcement of its principles by the coercive powers of the state.[1] By its nature and purpose, Shariʿa can only be freely observed by believers, and its principles lose their religious authority and value when enforced by the state. The institutional separation of Islam and the state is necessary for Shariʿa to have its proper positive and enlightening role in the lives of Muslims and Islamic societies. This view can also be called "the religious neutrality of the state", whereby state institutions neither favour nor disfavour any religious doctrine or principle. The object of this neutrality, however, is precisely the freedom of Muslims in their communities to live by their own belief in Islam, while other citizens live by their own beliefs. The proposed neutrality of the state does not mean that Islam and politics should be separated, because that is neither possible nor desirable. The separation of Islam and the state, combined with the regulation of the connection between Islam and politics, would make it possible to implement Islamic principles in official policy and legislation through general political deliberation, but not as imperative religious doctrine.

The religious neutrality of the state

A point of terminology that should be briefly clarified concerns the relationship between the propositions I am trying to advance and the notion of "secularism". The separation of Islam and the state, which constitutes the first part of my main proposition, sounds like secularism as that notion is commonly understood and rejected by many Muslims. The connection between Islam and politics, which is emphasised in the second part of the proposition, is an attempt to address the concerns of Muslims about secularism. The common negative perception of secularism in much of the Muslim world does not distinguish between the separation of Islam and the state, on the one hand, and Islam's connectedness to politics, on the other. Failure to appreciate this distinction leads to the assumption that the separation of Islam and the state can only mean the total relegation of Islam to the purely private domain and its exclusion from public policy. Since this is not what I am proposing, it might be wise to use the term pluralism instead. This usage would be appropriate because secularism is in fact necessary for the practical and sustainable realisation of pluralism as the unqualified and institutionalised acceptance of religious, cultural and other forms of diversity as positive social and political values. Indeed, both secularism and pluralism require the religious neutrality of the state. However, I will use the term secularism as defined here, in order to rehabilitate the concept and keep possibilities of comparative reflection among various parts of the world.

The proposed relationship between Islam, state and politics is premised on a combination of theoretical clarifications and practical safeguards for the actual practice of mediation and negotiation amongst them over time. It is not possible to cover all relevant concepts and arguments here, but some basic terms and themes can be briefly explained. In particular, it may be helpful to clarify the basic paradox that Islam and the state can be separated, even though Islam and politics are connected and even though the nature of the state is political. That is, how can we secure the religious neutrality of the state against those who seek to use the political process to enforce their view of Islam? This is the basic question I will be addressing in various ways in this chapter, in an effort to mediate a paradox.

The state is a complex web of organs, institutions and processes that are supposed to implement the policies that are adopted through the political process of a society. In this sense, the state should be the more settled and deliberate operational side of self-governance, while politics is the dynamic process by which society makes choices among competing policy options. The state is reflected in the continuity of institutions like the judiciary, civil and foreign or diplomatic services, while politics are reflected in the government of the day. To fulfil its own functions, the state must have what is known as a monopoly on the legitimate use of force, the ability to impose its will on the population at large without the risk of counter-force being used by those subject to its jurisdiction. This coercive power of the state, which is now more extensive and effective than ever before in human history, will be counterproductive when exercised in an arbitrary manner or for corrupt or illegitimate ends. That is why it is critically important to keep the state as neutral as humanly possible, which requires constant vigilance by the generality of citizens acting through a wide variety strategies and mechanisms, political, legal, educational, etc. If the government of the day, however popular it may be, is allowed to take over the institutions of the state, it will manipulate them to advance the political and economic interests of the ruling elite.

The distinction between the state and politics therefore assumes constant interaction among the organs and institutions of the state, on the one hand, and organised political and social actors and their competing visions of the public good, on the other. This distinction is also premised on an acute awareness of the risks of abuse or corruption of the necessary coercive powers of the state. It is necessary to ensure that the state is not simply a complete reflection of daily politics because it must be able to mediate and adjudicate among the competing visions and policy proposals, which requires it to remain relatively independent from the different political forces in society. Since complete independence is not possible either, it is sometimes important to recall the political nature of the state, because it cannot be totally autonomous from those political actors who control the apparatus of the state. Paradoxically, this reality of connectedness makes it necessary to strive for separating the state from politics, so that those excluded by the political processes of the day can still resort to state organs and institutions for protection against excesses and abuses by state officials.

Failure to observe the distinction between the state and politics tends severely to undermine the peace, stability and healthy development of the whole society. This is because those who are denied the services and protection of the state as well as effective participation in politics will either withdraw their cooperation or resort to violent resistance in the absence of less drastic remedies. The question should therefore be how to sustain the distinction between state and politics, instead of ignoring the tension between them in the hope that it will somehow resolve itself. This necessary, though difficult, distinction can be upheld through principles and mechanisms to safeguard and promote constitutionalism and the protection of the equal human rights of all citizens, but these principles and institutions cannot succeed without the active and determined participation of all citizens, which is unlikely if people believe them to be inconsistent with the religious beliefs and cultural norms that influence their political behaviour. The principles of popular sovereignty and democratic governance presuppose that citizens are sufficiently motivated and determined to participate in all aspects of self-governance, including taking organised political action to hold their government accountable and responsive to their wishes.

A major conceptual contradiction in the dangerous illusion of an Islamic state is the notion that Shariʿa principles can be enforced through the coercive power of the state. This belief is contrary to the nature of Shariʿa itself as well as the nature of the state. To begin with, the wide diversity of opinion about every aspect of public policy or legislation among Muslim scholars and schools of thought (*madhāhib*) means that whatever action is undertaken through state institutions would have to select among competing views that are equally legitimate from one Islamic view or another. Moreover, there are simply no generally agreed-upon standards or mechanisms for adjudicating between the views of various schools of thought, let alone between those of different sects, such as Sunnis or Shiʿa. Secondly, whatever standards or mechanisms are imposed by the organs of the state to determine official policy and formal legislation will necessarily be based on the human judgement of those who control those institutions.

If this is true, why did the early Muslim jurists insist on the need for a ruler to be responsible for the enforcement the Shariʿa? Several factors should be noted in response to this question. First, early Muslims jurists never conceived of the centralised enforcement of Shariʿa by the state as such. Instead, they called for an effective ruler who would enforce Shariʿa as determined by the scholars (*ʿulamāʾ*), and not as legislated by the state. It should be recalled here that the first codification of Shariʿa principles was done by the Ottoman Sultan in the mid-nineteenth century, and was limited to some aspects of the Hanafi school of thought. The idea of enactment of Shariʿa for centralised enforcement was simply incomprehensible to Muslim jurists and scholars. Moreover, the early jurists called on the ruler to enforce Shariʿa but had no institutional means of compelling him to do so short of calling for rebellion, but that was not peculiar to Islamic jurisprudence at the time, as institutional limitations on the powers of the ruler were unknown anywhere in the world for the next thousand years. Whatever may have been the situation in the pre-modern era, it has been drastically transformed by the unprecedented power of the modern state. Any alleged enforcement of Shariʿa by the modern state can only be selective and partial, reflecting the political will of the ruling elite, and not the integrity and coherence of Shariʿa as a comprehensive normative system.

Consequently, whatever the state enforces in the name of Shariʿa will necessarily be secular, the product of coercive political power and not superior Islamic authority, even if it is possible to ascertain what that means among Muslims at large. To enable Muslims and other citizens to live in accordance with their religious and other beliefs, we must categorically repudiate the dangerous illusion that an Islamic state can coercively enforce Shariʿa principles. In fact, the notion of an Islamic state is a post-colonial idea that is premised on a European model of the state and a totalitarian view of law and public policy as the instruments of social engineering by ruling elites. The proponents of a so-called Islamic state seek to use the powers and institutions of the state, as constituted by European colonialism and continued after independence, to regulate individual behaviour and social relations coercively in the specific ways selected by ruling elites. It is particularly dangerous to attempt such totalitarian initiatives in the name of Islam, because it is far more difficult to resist than when used by a state that openly identifies itself as secular without claiming religious legitimacy for its totalitarianism. At the same time, it is clear that the institutional separation of any religion and the state is not easy, because the state will necessarily have to regulate the role of religion in order to maintain its own religious neutrality.

The religious neutrality of the state is necessary for it to play its role as mediator and adjudicator among competing social and political forces in the daily implementation of policies and administration of justice. This role includes regulating and organising religious activities, such as whether to grant tax exemption for religious educational institutions. But there is also the broader question of how to regulate political parties which have a strong religious dimension, to prevent them from imposing their religious agenda in the name of democratic governance. In other words, the state is responsible for sustaining and safeguarding the requirement of public reason to ensure that public policy and legislation are adopted for broad civic justifications and not for narrow religious demands. At the same time, there is always the risk of religious groups taking over the state precisely in order to pre-empt or manipulate this regulatory role of the state.

Moreover, the religious neutrality of the state is a necessary condition for compliance with Islamic precepts and their implementation as religious obligations for individual Muslims. Such compliance must be completely voluntary because it requires pious intention (*niyya*), which is negated by the coercive enforcement by the state. Moreover, when Muslims wish to propose policy or legislation out of their religious or other beliefs, as all citizens have the right to do, they should support such proposals with what I call "public reason". The word "public" here implies that reasons of policy and legislation should be publicly declared, as well as that the process of reasoning on the matter should be open and accessible to all citizens. The rationale and purpose of the public policy or legislation must be based on the sort of reasoning that the generality of citizens can accept or reject, and about which they can make counter-proposals through public debate, without exposing themselves to charges of disbelief, apostasy or blasphemy. Public reason and reasoning, not personal beliefs and motivation, are necessary because even if Muslims are the predominant majority, they would not agree on what policy and legislation would necessarily follow from their Islamic beliefs.

It is not possible here to attempt to explain, or engage in, the intense debate among Western political philosophers about the notion of "public reason", except to note its main meaning and how it is similar to, or different from, what I mean.

According to John Rawls, the leading scholar in this field, public reason is the reason of free and equal citizens, its subject is the public good concerning questions of fundamental political justice, and its contents are expressed in public reasoning by a family of reasonable conceptions of political justice reasonably thought to satisfy the criterion of reciprocity.[2] The proper domain of public reason according to Rawls is the "public political forum", which provides for three different discourses to take place:

> the discourse of judges in their decisions, and especially of the judges of a supreme court; the discourse of government officials, especially chief executives and legislators; and finally, the discourse of candidates for public office and their campaign managers especially in their public oratory, party platforms, and political statements.[3]

Habermas has criticised some aspects of Rawls' arguments, such as his distinction between comprehensive doctrines and political values.[4]

Rawls and Habermas would probably support my main proposition about the role of public reason, namely, the requirement that the rationale and purpose of public policy or legislation must be based on the sort of reasoning that the generality of citizens can accept or reject, and use to make counter-proposals through public debate, without being open to charges of disbelief, apostasy or blasphemy. Their views and debates, however, seem to assume a developed and stable constitutional order and stable society which are wealthy enough to support debate around public policy and public reason, which is hardly the case anywhere in the Muslim world. I would therefore prefer to draw on the work of Western political philosophers like Rawls and Habermas in general, without closely identifying with any of them or joining the debate among their Western audiences.

While the requirement of public reason in public policy may sound reasonable, it is unrealistic and unwise to expect people to comply fully with this requirement in the choices they make within the realm of inner motivation and intentions. It is difficult to tell why people vote in a particular way or justify their political agenda to themselves or to their close associates. Still the objective should be to promote and encourage public reason, while diminishing the exclusive influence of personal religious beliefs. The requirement of public reason does not assume that people who control the state can be neutral. On the contrary, the operation of the state must be held to this requirement precisely because people are likely to continue to act on personal beliefs or justifications. The requirement of public reason will, over time, encourage and foster a broader consensus among the population at large, beyond the narrow religious or other beliefs of various individuals and groups. The ability to present public reasons and debate them publicly is already present in most societies; what I am calling for is further development of this ability, consciously and incrementally, over time, rather than suggesting that it is totally absent now, or expecting it to be fully realised immediately.

Islam, Shari'a and the state

The premise of Islam is that each and every Muslim is personally responsible for knowing and complying with what is required of him or her as a matter of religious obligation. The fundamental principle of individual and personal responsibility that can never be abdicated or delegated is one of the recurring themes of the Qur'an, as in 5:105, 41:46, 4:79–80, and 53:36–42. Yet, when Muslims do seek to know what Shari'a requires of them in any specific situation, they are more likely to ask an Islamic scholar (*'ālim*, plural *'ulamā'*) or Sufi leader they trust, rather than to refer directly to the Qur'an and Sunna themselves. Whether personally or through an intermediary, Muslims necessarily make reference to the Qur'an and Sunna through the structure and methodology they have been raised to accept. This would normally happen within the framework of a particular school (*madhhab*) and its established doctrine and methodology, but never in a totally fresh and original manner, without preconceived notions of how to identify and interpret relevant texts of the Qur'an and Sunna.

In other words, whenever Muslims consider these primary sources, they cannot avoid the filters not only of layers of experience and interpretation by preceding generations, but also of an elaborate methodology that determines which texts are deemed to be relevant to any subject, and how they should be understood. Human agency is therefore integral to any approach to the Qur'an and Sunna at multiple levels, ranging from centuries of accumulated experience and interpretation to the current context in which an Islamic frame of reference is invoked. The next question to clarify briefly is how an Islamic frame of reference can be invoked from an institutional perspective of state policy and legislation.

As a political institution, the state is not an entity that can feel, believe or act. It is always human beings who act in the name of the state, exercise its powers or operate through its organs. Thus, whenever a human being makes a decision about a policy matter, or proposes or drafts legislation that is supposed to embody Islamic principles, this will necessarily reflect his or her personal perspective on the subject, and never that of the state as an autonomous entity. Moreover, when such policy or legislative proposals are made in the name of a political party or organisation, such positions are also taken by the human leaders speaking or acting for that entity. It is true that specific positions on matters of policy and legislation can be negotiated among critical actors, but the outcome is still necessarily the product of individual human judgement and the choice to accept and act upon a view that is agreed upon among those actors.

For instance, a decision to punish the consumption of alcoholic drinks as a *ḥadd* crime as defined by Shariʿa is necessarily the view of individual political actors taken after weighing all sorts of practical considerations, and the language used in drafting the legislation and the measures taken in implementing it are similarly the product of human judgement and choice. For our purposes, the point here is that the whole process of formulating and implementing public policy and legislation is constantly subject to human fallibility, which means that it can always be challenged or questioned without violating the direct and immediate divine will of God. This is part of the reason why matters of public policy and legislation must be supported by public reason, even among Muslims, who can and do disagree in all such matters without violating their religious obligations. Debates among believers about the doctrine of their religion will of course continue, and a secular state as defined here will facilitate such internal debates. My concern here is about public policy and legislation, which I believe should be supported by public reason, as explained above. The fact that believers may have their own religious reasons for supporting a policy or legislation is in fact welcome, provided that other citizens accept such proposals without having to rely on the religious convictions of some believers.

I should emphasise here that it is of course possible to develop institutional influence and constraint on the subjective judgement of human agents acting in the name of the state. Neither am I claiming that the risks of bias or oppression of dissent do not apply to supposedly democratic and public reason-based legislation as well as so-called Islamic legislation. Such issues of political philosophy and constitutional and political practice will remain relevant to the struggle of all societies for justice, stability and development. It is just that the Islamic dimension of these fundamental issues is my subject here, and I do believe that religion adds a more complex dimension that is harder to deal with than matters of purely political or economic power relations. It may therefore be helpful to see why so-called Islamic legislative or policy propositions should not be permitted to transcend or avoid the safeguards I am proposing.

The structure and methodology known as *uṣūl al-fiqh*, through which Muslims can comprehend and implement Islamic precepts as conveyed in the Qurʾan and Sunna, was developed by early Muslim scholars. In its original formulations, this field of human knowledge sought to regulate the interpretation of these foundational sources in light of the historical experience of the first generations of Muslims. It also defines and regulates the operation of such juridical techniques as *ijmāʿ* (consensus), *qiyās* (reasoning by analogy) and *ijtihād* (juridical reasoning).[5] These techniques are commonly taken to be methods for specifying Shariʿa principles, rather than substantive sources as such. However, *ijmāʿ* and *ijtihād* had a more foundational role beyond that limited technical meaning. It is that broader sense that can form the basis of a more dynamic and creative development of Shari'a now and in the future.

The consensus (*ijmā'*) of generations of Muslims from the beginning of Islam that the text of the Qur'an is in fact accurately contained in the written text known as *al-Muṣḥaf* is the underlying reason why that text is accepted by Muslims at any time and place. The same is true of what the generality of Muslims accept as authentic reports of what the Prophet said and did (the Sunna), though that took longer to establish and is still controversial among many Muslims. In other words, our knowledge of the Qur'an and Sunna is the result of inter-generational consensus since the seventh century. This is not to say or imply that Muslims manufactured these sources through consensus, but simply to note that we know and accept these texts as valid because generation after generation of Muslims have believed that. Moreover, consensus is the basis of the authority and continuity of *uṣūl al-fiqh* and all its principles and techniques, because this interpretative structure is always dependent on its acceptance as such among the generality of Muslims from one generation to the next. In this sense, *ijmā'* is the basis of the acceptance of the Qur'an and Sunna themselves, as well as the totality and detail of the methodology of their interpretation.

For Muslims, the significant difference distinguishing the Qur'an and Sunna from the techniques of *uṣūl al-fiqh* is that there is no possibility of new or additional texts, because the Prophet Muhammad is the final prophet and the Qur'an is the conclusive divine revelation. In contrast, there is nothing to prevent or invalidate the formation of a new consensus around techniques of interpretation or innovative interpretations of the Qur'an and Sunna which would thereby become part of Shari'a, in the same way that existing techniques or principles came to be part of it in the first place. It may be argued here that what I am proposing goes against the fairly entrenched view among traditional Muslim scholars that certain interpretations of the Qur'an and Sunna are not open to debate because previous generations reached a sure consensus on them.

To be clear on this point, I am saying that that view is wrong and, in fact, inconsistent with the rationale of consensus itself. Consensus, as a wide-ranging or even universal agreement among Muslims, can only be binding subject to the individual responsibility of each and every Muslim to accept and act on what is proposed. Since all Muslims are personally accountable for what they do or fail to do, regardless of the unanimous agreement of all other Muslims, the consensus of previous generations cannot be binding unless it is accepted as such by every generation for itself, with all due critical reflection and debate. The safeguards of separating Islam from the state and regulating the political role of Islam through constitutionalism and protection of human rights are necessary for ensuring freedom and security for Muslims to participate in proposing and debating fresh interpretations of these foundational sources.

Any understanding of Shari'a is always the product of *ijtihād* in the general sense, that reasoning and reflection by human beings, as ways of understanding the meaning of the Qur'an and Sunna of the Prophet, are forms of *ijtihād*. Whether or not any text of the Qur'an or Sunna applies to an issue, whether or not it is categorical (*qaṭ'ī*), who can exercise *ijtihād* and how: these are all matters that can only be decided by human reasoning and judgement. Therefore, imposing prior censorship on such efforts violates the premise for deriving Shari'a principles from the Qur'an and Sunna. It is illogical to say that *ijtihād* cannot be exercised regarding any issue or question, because that determination itself is the product of human reasoning and reflection. It is also dangerous to limit the ability to exercise *ijtihād* to a restricted group of Muslims who are supposed to have specific qualities, because that will depend in practice on those human beings who will set and apply the criteria of selecting who is a qualified *mujtahid*. To grant this authority to any institution or organ, whether official or private, is dangerous because that power will certainly be manipulated for political or other reasons. Since knowing and upholding the Shari'a is the permanent and inescapable responsibility of every Muslim, no human being or institution should control this process for Muslims. In other words, it is inconsistent with the Shari'a itself to restrict free debate by entrusting human beings or institutions with the authority to decide which religious views are to be allowed or suppressed. It is clear that there is an urgent need to continue the processes of Islamic reform to reconcile the religious commitment of Muslims with the practical requirements of their societies today. The main premise of a viable reform process, in my view, can be stated as follows. While the Qur'an and Sunna are the divine sources of Islam according to Muslim belief, the meaning and implementation of these sources in everyday life is always the product of human interpretation and action in a specific historical context. It is simply impossible to know and apply Shari'a in this life except through human agency. Any view of Shari'a known to Muslims today, even if unanimously agreed upon, necessarily emerged out of the opinions of human beings about the meaning of the Qur'an and Sunna, as accepted by many generations of Muslims and the practice of their communities. In other words, opinions of Muslim scholars became part of Shari'a through the consensus of believers over many centuries, and not by the spontaneous decree of a ruler or the will of a single group of scholars.

The future of Shari'a in a secular state

Various understandings of Shari'a will remain, of course, in the realm of individual and collective practice as a matter of freedom of religion and belief, but will also be subject to established constitutional safeguards. What is problematic is for Shari'a principles to be enforced as state law or policy on a religious basis, because once a principle or norm is officially identified as "decreed by God", it will be extremely difficult to resist or change its application in practice. At the same time, the integrity of Islam as a religion will decline in the eyes of believers and non-believers alike when state officials and institutions fail to deliver on the promise of individual freedom and social justice. Since Islamic ethical principles and social values are indeed necessary for the proper functioning of Islamic societies in general, the implementation of such principles and values would be consistent with, indeed required by, the right of Muslims to self-determination. This right, however, can only be realised within the framework of constitutional and democratic governance at home and international law abroad, because these are the legal and political bases of this right in the first place. The right to self-determination presupposes a constitutional basis that is derived from the collective will of the totality of the population, and can be asserted against other countries because it is accepted as a fundamental principle of international law.

The paradox that Islam and the state must be separate (that the state must be religiously neutral), yet are unavoidably connected through politics, can only be mediated through practice over time, rather than resolved once and for all by theoretical analysis or stipulation. The question is therefore how to create the most conducive conditions for this mediation to continue in a constructive fashion. First, the modern territorial state should neither seek to enforce Shari'a as positive law and public policy, nor claim to interpret its doctrine and general principles for Muslim citizens. Second, Shari'a principles can and should be a source of public policy and legislation, subject to the fundamental constitutional and human rights of all citizens, men and women, Muslims and non-Muslims equally and without discrimination. This will require reform of certain aspects of Shari'a, as explained later, but even reformed principles of Shari'a should not be enforced by the state. In other words, Shari'a principles are neither privileged or enforced as such nor necessarily rejected as a source of state law and policy. The belief of Muslims that these principles are binding as a matter of religious obligation should remain the basis of individual and collective observance among believers, but is not accepted as sufficient reason for their enforcement by the state as such.

Since effective governance requires the adoption of specific policies and the enactment of precise laws, the administrative and legislative organs of the state must select among competing views within the massive and complex corpus of Shari'a principles, as noted earlier. That selection will necessarily be made by the ruling elite. For example, there is a well-established principle of Shari'a, known as *khul'*, whereby a wife can pay her husband an agreed amount (or forfeit her financial entitlement) to induce him to accept the termination of their marriage. Yet, this choice was not available in Egypt until the government decided to enact this Shari'a principle into law in 2000. The fact that this principle was part of Shari'a did not make it applicable in Egypt until the state decided to enforce it.[6] Moreover, this legislation certainly gave Egyptian women a way out of a bad marriage, but the condition that this was possible only at a significant financial cost for the wife could not be contested, because the legislation was made in terms of "enacting" Shariʿa, rather than simply as a matter of good social policy. Since the legislation was framed in terms of binding Islamic principles, the possibility and requirements of the legal termination of marriage remain limited to general principles of Shariʿa as formulated by Islamic scholars a thousand years ago. The broader point for my purposes here is that the inherent subjectivity and diversity of Shariʿa principles mean that whatever is enacted and enforced by the state is the political will of the ruling elite, not the normative system of Islam as such. Yet, such policies and legislation are difficult for the general population to resist or even debate when they are presented as the will of God.

To avoid such difficulties, I am proposing that the rationale of all public policy and legislation should always be based on what might be called "public reason", as explained earlier. Muslims and other believers should be able to propose policy and legislative initiatives emanating from their religious beliefs, *provided* they can support them in public, free and open debate by reasons that are accessible and convincing to the generality of citizens, regardless of their religion or other beliefs. But since such decisions will in practice be made by majority vote in accordance with democratic principles, all state action must also conform to basic constitutional and human rights safeguards to protect against the tyranny of the majority. Thus, for example, the majority would not be able to implement any policy or legislation that violates the fundamental requirements of equality and non-discrimination. These propositions are already supposed to be the basis of legitimate government in the vast majority of present Islamic societies. Yet they are unlikely to be taken seriously by most Muslims unless they are perceived to be consistent with their understanding of Islam. This reality is the underlying reason for insisting on presenting my theory from an Islamic perspective, including calling for the reform of certain traditional interpretations of Shariʿa.

Moreover, secularism as simply the separation of religion and the state is not sufficient for addressing any objections or reservations believers may have about specific constitutional norms and human rights standards. For example, since discrimination against women is often justified on religious grounds in Islamic societies, this source of systematic and gross violation of human rights cannot be eliminated without addressing the commonly perceived religious rationale. This must also be done without violating freedom of religion or belief for Muslims, which is also a fundamental human right. While a secular discourse in terms of separation alone can be respectful of religion in general, as can be seen in West European and North American societies today in contrast to the present practice of Islamic societies, it is unlikely to succeed in rebutting religious justifications of discrimination without invoking a counter-religious argument. The principle of secularism, as I am defining it here, includes a public role for religion, and it encourages and facilitates internal debate and dissent within religious traditions to enable believers to overcome religiously-based objections. When a society ensures that the state is neutral in regard to religion, the coercive power of the state cannot be used to suppress debate and dissent. However, that safe space still needs to be actively used by citizens to promote religious views that support equality for women and other fundamental human rights. In fact, such views are needed for promoting the religious legitimacy of the doctrine of separation of religion and the state itself, as well as other general principles of constitutionalism and human rights.

Allowing Shariʿa principles to play a positive role in public life, without permitting them to be implemented as such through law and policy, is a delicate balance that each society must strive to maintain for itself over time. For example, such matters as dress style and religious education will normally remain in the realm of free choice, but can also be the subject of public debate, even constitutional litigation, to balance competing claims. This can happen, for instance, regarding dress requirements for safety in the work place or the need for comparative and critical religious education in state schools to enhance religious tolerance and free debate. I am not suggesting that the context and conditions of free choice of dress or religious education will not be controversial. In fact, such matters are likely to be very complex at a personal and societal level. Rather, my concern is with ensuring, as far as humanly possible, fair, open and inclusive social, political and legal conditions for the negotiation of public policy in such matters. Those conditions include, for instance, the entrenchment of such fundamental rights of the persons and communities as the right to education and freedom of religion and expression, on the one hand, and due consideration for legitimate public interests or concerns, on the other. There is no simple or categorical formula to be prescribed for automatic application in every case, though general principles and broader frameworks for the mediation of such issues will emerge and continue to evolve within each society.

Need for Islamic reform

My call for recognising and regulating the political role of Islam is untenable without significant Islamic reform. I believe that it is critically important for Islamic societies today to invest in the rule of law and the protection of human rights in their domestic politics and international relations. This is unlikely to happen if traditional interpretations of Shariʿa that support principles like male guardianship of women (*qiwāma*), sovereignty of Muslims over non-Muslims (*dhimma*), and violently aggressive *jihād*, are maintained. Significant reform of such views is necessary because of their powerful influence on social relations and the political behaviour of Muslims, even when Shariʿa principles are not directly enforced by the state. One premise of my whole approach is that Muslims are unlikely to support actively the principles of human rights and to engage effectively in the process of constitutional democratic governance, if they continue to maintain such views as part of their understanding of Shariʿa. The Islamic reform methodology I find most appropriate and effective in achieving the desired objectives is the one developed by *Ustādh* Mahmoud Mohamed Taha.[7] Other approaches can be applied, provided they can also achieve the desired objectives.

Whatever possibilities of change or development are proposed must begin with the reality that European colonialism and its aftermath have drastically transformed the basis and nature of political and social organisation within and among territorial states where all Muslims live today. This transformation is so profound and deeply entrenched that a return to pre-colonial ideas and systems is simply not an option. Any change and adaptation of the present system can only be sought or realised through the concepts and institutions of this local and global post-colonial reality. Yet many Muslims, probably the majority in many countries, have not accepted some aspects of this transformation and its consequences. This discrepancy seems to underlie the apparent acceptance by many Muslims of the possibility of an Islamic state that can enforce Shariʿa principles as positive law, and the widespread ambivalence about politically motivated violence in the name of *jihād*. Significant Islamic reform is necessary to reformulate such problematic aspects of Shariʿa, but that should not mean the wholesale and uncritical adoption of dominant Western theory and practice in these fields. To illustrate the sort of internal Islamic transformation I am proposing, I will briefly review here how the traditional Shariʿa notions of *dhimma* should evolve into a coherent and humane principle of citizenship. Such evolution should take into account the following considerations.

First, human beings tend to seek and experience multiple and overlapping types and forms of membership in different groups on such grounds as ethnic, religious or cultural identity, political, social or professional affiliation, economic interests and so forth. Second, the meaning and implications of each type or form of membership should be determined by the rationale or purpose of belonging to the group in question, without precluding or undermining other forms of membership. That is, multiple and overlapping memberships should not be mutually exclusive, as they tend to serve different purposes for different persons and communities. Third, the term "citizenship" is used here to refer to a particular form of membership in the political community of a territorial state in its global context; "citizenship" should therefore be related to the specific rationale or purpose of such membership, without precluding other possibilities of membership in other communities for different purposes. Proposing this threefold premise is not to suggest that people are always consciously aware of the reality of their multiple memberships, or appreciate that they are mutually inclusive, with each being appropriate or necessary for its different purpose or rationale. On the contrary, it seems that there is a tendency to collapse different forms of membership, as when ethnic or religious identity is equated with political or social affiliation. This is true about the coincidence of nationality and citizenship in Western political theory that was transmitted to Muslims through European colonialism and its aftermath.

Thus, official or ideological discourse regarding the basis of citizenship as membership in the political community of a territorial state did not necessarily coincide with a subjective feeling of belonging or an independent assessment of actual conditions on the ground. Such tensions existed in all major civilisations in the past and continue to be experienced in various ways by different societies today, as illustrated by struggles over national unity and minority rights. To determine citizenship by a contrived and often coercive membership in a "nation" on the basis of shared ethnic and religious identity and political allegiance would be oppressive on those who do not belong to that dominant ethnic or religious group. In other words, the coincidence of citizenship and nationality was not only the product of a peculiarly European and relatively recent process, but was often exaggerated in Europe at the expense of other forms of membership, especially of ethnic or religious minorities. I prefer to use the term *territorial* state to identify citizenship with territory, as the term nation-state can be misleading, if not oppressive toward minorities.

The term citizenship is also used here to indicate an affirmative and proactive sense of belonging to an inclusive pluralistic political community that affirms and regulates possibilities of various forms of "difference" among persons and communities to ensure equal rights for all, without distinction on such grounds as religion, sex, ethnicity or political opinion. By an "affirmative and proactive" sense of belonging I mean the personal confidence and legal safeguards that enable each citizen to seek out possibilities of democratic participation and civic engagement in the daily affairs of the community. This requires citizenship to be premised on a shared cultural understanding of equal human dignity and effective political participation for all. In other words, citizenship is defined here in terms of the principle of the universality of human rights as "a common standard of achievement for all people and all nations", according to the Preamble of the 1948 United Nations Universal Declaration of Human Rights.

The desirability of this understanding of citizenship is supported by the Islamic principle of reciprocity (*muʿāwaḍa*), also known as the Golden Rule, and emphasised by the legal and political realities of self-determination. Persons and communities everywhere have to affirm this conception of citizenship in order to be able to claim it for themselves under international law as well as domestic constitutional law and politics. That is, acceptance of this understanding of citizenship is the prerequisite moral and political basis of its enjoyment. Muslims should strive toward this pragmatic ideal from an Islamic point of view, regardless of what other peoples do, or fail to do, in this regard.

Moreover, there is a dialectical relationship between domestic and international conceptions of citizenship, whereby citizens at the country level exercise their rights at that level and thereby contribute to the determination and practice of the international standards that define citizenship at that local level. In other words, any limitation or restrictions on the rights of citizens at the local level can be corrected through the participation of the same people in setting the international human rights standards that will address their concerns. The same human rights principles underlie the proposed definition of citizenship in domestic politics as well as international relations, whether expressed in terms of fundamental constitutional rights or universal human rights. Citizens acting politically at home participate in determining and implementing universal human rights which, in turn, contribute to defining and protecting the rights of citizens at the domestic level. Citizenship and human rights are therefore inherently related and mutually supportive.

These reflections clearly emphasise the importance of creative Islamic reform that balances the competing demands of religious legitimacy and principled political and social practice. These demands are simply inconsistent with the notion of an Islamic state. But this notion is so appealing to Muslims in the present domestic and global context that other possible justifications for an Islamic state must also be confronted. For example, it may be suggested that it is better to allow the idea of an Islamic state to stand as an ideal while seeking to control or manage its practice. This view is dangerous because as long as this notion stands as an ideal, some Muslims will attempt to implement it according to their own understanding of what it means, with disastrous consequences for their own societies and even beyond. It is impossible to control or manage the practice of this ideal without challenging its core claims that human views of Islam enjoy religious sanctity. Once the possibility of an Islamic state is conceded, it becomes extremely difficult to resist the next logical step of seeking to implement it in practice, because that would be regarded as a heretical or "un-Islamic" position.

Maintaining this ideal of an "Islamic state" is also counterproductive, because it will preclude debate about more viable and appropriate political theories, legal systems and development policies. Even if one overcomes the psychological difficulty of arguing against what is presented as the divine will of God, charges of heresy can result in severe social stigma, if not prosecution by the state or direct violence by extremist groups. As long as the idea of an Islamic state is allowed to stand, societies will remain locked in stale debates about such issues as whether constitutionalism or democracy are "Islamic", and whether interest banking is to be allowed or not. Such fruitless debates have kept the vast majority of present Islamic societies locked in a constant state of political instability and economic and social underdevelopment since independence, instead of getting on with securing constitutional democratic governance and pursuing economic development. The real issues facing Islamic societies today cannot be resolved by futile debates about an incoherent and counterproductive notion of an Islamic state which enforces Shariʿa as the automatic basis of public policy and law.

11 A call for a moratorium on corporal punishment – The debate in review

Tariq Ramadan

On 30 March 2005, I launched an international call for a moratorium on corporal punishment, stoning and the death penalty in the Islamic world (hereafter referred to as "the Call"). The Call did not come out of a vacuum. I had been discussing such a proposal with Muslim scholars (*'ulamā'*) around the world for the previous seven years. Privately, many agreed with me or at least found the subject well worth discussing. In public, however, the voice of Muslim scholars and community leaders remained silent and apologetic about the matter. But I think that it is impossible for us as Muslims to remain silent as irreversible injustice is done to the poorest and weakest members of society in the name of our religion.

I will not repeat here the full text of the Call, which can be found on the Internet[1] along with many of the discussions I refer to. I will only briefly summarise the key points, before moving on to address the responses from the Muslim leaders and scholars.

The Call for an immediate moratorium

The Call addresses the *ḥudūd* or "limits", which in the specialised language of the Muslim jurists (*fuqahā'*) refer to the Islamic penal code. The classical *ḥudūd* include the punishments of flogging for fornication, false accusation of illicit sex and consumption of alcohol, stoning to death for adultery and amputation of the hand for theft. The call also addresses other corporal punishments and the death penalty which are, in one way or in another, related to the Islamic penal code.

All the *'ulamā'* recognise the existence of scriptural sources that refer to such punishments. They diverge over their interpretation, the conditions of the application of the derived Islamic penal code, and its degree of relevance to the contemporary era. The majority of the *'ulamā'* hold that these penalties are on the whole Islamic, but that the conditions under which they should be implemented are nearly impossible to re-establish – they are "almost never applicable".

Yet behind this "almost never", the sombre reality is that women and men are punished, beaten, stoned and executed in the name of *ḥudūd*.[2] Worse, these penalties are applied almost exclusively to women and the poor, not to the wealthy and powerful. More unjust still, the accused often have no access to defence counsel or other fundamental legal safeguards.

The international community's denunciations of these penalties have been selective and calculated for the protection of geostrategic and economic interests. A poor African or Asian country trying to apply the *ḥudūd* will face the mobilisation of international campaigns, while their ongoing and well-known application in oil-rich monarchies and allies of the West is condemned only reluctantly, if at all.

As for Muslim conscience, it appears untouched by these facts, betraying the message of the justice of Islam. Everywhere, there is increasing devotion to Islam and its teachings, but this devotion is not always followed by a real understanding of the texts and of the scholarly discussion of their contexts and conditions. There is sometimes popular support for the literal and immediate application of *ḥudūd*, because it is seen to guarantee the "Islamic" character of society. This is, first, because the punishment provides a visible reference to Islam that, by its harshness, would indicate fidelity to the Qur'anic injunctions. Second, the literal application of *ḥudūd* is taken to be authentically Islamic for the simplistic reason that it is denounced by the West. Popular passion responds to frustration and humiliation by asserting an Islamic (anti-Western) identity. This formalistic and binary reasoning is dangerous, because it grants an Islamic quality to laws and governments not for what they promote, but for what they are antithetic to. It is not based on a comprehension of the objectives (*maqāṣid*) of Islamic teachings or the interpretations and conditions relating to *ḥudūd*.

The *'ulamā'* should stand against formalism and binary reasoning because they should be the guardians of fidelity to the objectives of justice and equality and proponents of a deep reading of the texts and of the analysis of conditions and social contexts. But unfortunately, the majority of the *'ulamā'* are afraid to confront these popular and passionate demands for fear of losing their status and credibility with the masses. Moreover, we observe a crisis of religious authority accompanied by an absence of internal debate among the *'ulamā'*, leading to a chaos of disparate and contradictory Islamic legal opinions. Lacking proper guidance, the Muslim public satisfies itself with measures that can give an appearance of fidelity. In fact, there is a multi-faceted crisis: of closed and repressive political systems, religious authorities upholding contradictory juristic positions, and populations swept up in religious fervour but lacking the knowledge to be truly faithful to the teachings of Islam.

Under these conditions, it becomes the responsibility of each *'ālim* (scholar) to speak up. In fact, it becomes the responsibility of every woman and man with a conscience, wherever they are, to realise that Islam is being used to degrade and subjugate women and men in certain Muslim-majority countries, and to act accordingly. Therefore, the Call was launched toward the conscience of each individual, to mobilise ordinary Muslims to call on their governments to place an immediate moratorium on the application of these punishments, and to call on Muslim scholars for the opening of a vast intra-community debate on the matter.

Underlying this Call were two central considerations. First, the opinions of scholars regarding the understanding of the texts and the application of *ḥudūd* are often not explicit, and these opinions are neither unanimous nor held by even a clear majority. Second, the political systems and the state of the Muslim-majority societies do not guarantee a just and equal treatment of individuals before the law.

The Call therefore posed a series of questions to the Islamic religious authorities of the world. First, what are the texts that make reference to these punishments? How authentic are they recognised to be, what is the margin of interpretation and on what points is there clear divergence (*ikhtilāf*), historically and in the contemporary era? Second, what are the conditions (*shurūṭ*) stipulated for each of these penalties by the sources and the scholars? Where do these stipulations diverge and what extenuating circumstances have been elaborated? Third, in what socio-political context (*wāqi'*) is it possible to apply the *ḥudūd* today? What would be required of political systems and legislation, regarding freedom of expression, equality before the law, public education and eradication of poverty and social exclusion – and again, where do the *'ulamā'* diverge?

The purpose of these questions was to start a reflection from within the community on the texts and their context. This undertaking will require rigour, time and spaces for dialogue and debate, nationally and internationally, between the *'ulamā'*, Muslim intellectuals, and Muslim communities. In the meantime, before this debate has clarified what is, and what is no longer, applicable under contemporary conditions, there can be no justification for applying these penalties.

As the Call made clear, imposing a moratorium and debating these questions is not to disrespect the scriptural sources of Islam. On the contrary, the legal texts must be read in light of the objectives (*maqāṣid*) that justify them, first and foremost the protection of the integrity of the person (*nafs*) and the promotion of justice (*ʿadl*). A literal and non-contextualised application of *ḥudūd* without regard for the strictly stipulated conditions is a betrayal of the teachings of Islam, because it produces injustice. The Call noted that the second caliph, ʿUmar ibn al-Khattab, recognised this when he suspended the punishment for thieves during a famine, when social conditions meant applying the punishment would have been unjust, even though it was clearly stated in the sources.

Reactions to the Call

Within a month, the Call had elicited reactions from some leading Islamic scholars and bodies around the Muslim world, while others have remained silent. Many of these reactions to date have been negative, though they have also established important points of agreement. Quite a few have misunderstood the content of the Call, attributed to me meanings I never expressed and intentions I never held, conflated this initiative with unrelated ones, denied the importance or priority of the matter, and generally evaded the actual issues raised in the Call. This kind of reaction was expected, though it is disappointing that some scholars and leaders seem to have reacted only to a media distortion of the Call. A few have been thoughtful and serious.

Many of the reactions appeared on the *Islam Online* website. On 19 April, it reported the comments of Dr Ahmad al-Rawi, chairman of the Federation of Islamic Organisations in Europe.[3] I was surprised to read that he rejected my justification of the Call as a means of combating the vilification of Islam in the West, since I have never justified the Call in those terms, whether in private or in public. I also found unfair and unacceptable his remarks associating the Call with recent unrelated controversies concerning women and prayer in the United States and Holland. I had to ask him whether he considered this Call a *bidʿa* (illicit innovation in religion), and how he could justify such a claim. According to Dr al-Rawi, further, one should have "consulted specialised scholars and jurists" before launching a call through the media, and should refer such questions to bodies like the European Council for Fatwa and Research (ECFR). Leaving aside the question of my scholarly qualifications, and the fact that the ECFR does not consider *ḥudūd* to be its concern, since Muslim minorities do not have to apply them, this misses the essential point that the Call does address *ʿulamāʾ* and requests that they engage profoundly in a debate on all levels. Most disappointingly, Dr al-Rawi was reported as asking, "Where on earth are such *ḥudūd* applicable?" and adding, "They are not implemented in all Muslim countries and there are some reservations on the application of these *ḥudūd* in Saudi Arabia." To minimise the facts about the daily practice of corporal punishments and the death penalty – whether directly or indirectly justified by Islam – in such a way is not intellectually acceptable.

If I was disappointed by Dr al-Rawi, I was shocked to see the respected Dr Taha Jabir al-ʿAlwani, president of the Graduate School of Islamic and Social Sciences, headline his comment "Unacceptable Allegation" and start it by stating "Fabricating lies against the Muslim nation is unacceptable ..."[4] I do not know where in the Call he found these lies or allegations, since he cited no example. Nor do I know where he found any "plot to efface our identity, culture and tradition" through a claim that "we Muslims are no longer [in] need of the Shariʿah." To the contrary, the Call argues that it is urgent to reconcile ourselves with the true meaning of the Shariʿa by reforming our practices. Dr al-ʿAlwani asserts that we live in the world where Shariʿa "is almost not applied". However, in this world, we have a few known, and many less known, cases of stoning; we have the corporal punishments inflicted on poor Pakistani and Filipino workers in the petro-monarchies; and we have unjust executions, whether applied in the name of Islam or indirectly sanctioned by it. Dr al-ʿAlwani's further statement that some people due to ignorance understand Shariʿa as penal law was wide of the mark, as he would have realised from a careful reading of the Call, which clearly frames the punishments as only a part of the Shariʿa. His reference to the controversy over women's *imāma* (leadership in prayer) was likewise not pertinent to the Call. Like Dr al-Rawi, he questioned my credentials and said I should have directed my questions to the *ʿulamāʾ*. I explained that this was what I had been doing for years and what I was continuing to do through the Call; again, I repeated the three questions posed by the Call.

Dr Muzzamil Siddiqi, the president of the Fiqh Council of North America, gave a more careful reply.[5] He noted that corporal punishments are only one aspect of the Shariʿa, the purpose of which includes the protection of religion, life, mind, honour and property. He agreed with the Call that in many places the *ḥudūd* are applied unjustly and that most of the time the weak and poor are punished, while the rich and powerful remain free to break the laws. Indeed, as Dr Siddiqi put it, very often governments apply the *ḥudūd* before taking care of the *ḥuqūq* (rights) of the people. However, he felt that a public call for a moratorium might encourage others to disrespect the laws of Allah. I responded to Dr Siddiqi, among other points, that the call for a moratorium has the virtues of stopping immediately the unjust acts perpetrated in the name of Islam and of opening an in-depth debate that is not just a reaction to individual events.

On 28 April 2005, the al-Azhar University's Legal Research Commission (Lajna al-Buhuth al-Fiqhiyya) published an official statement opposing the Call.[6] The Commission primarily advanced three arguments. First, "whoever denies the *ḥudūd* … or demands that they be cancelled or suspended, despite final and indisputable evidence, is to be regarded as somebody who has forsaken a recognised element which forms the basis of the religion." Second, I was demanding that the *ḥudūd* be stopped "because this is hurting the message of Islam", which the Commission considered a "refuted matter". Third, as to the specific example of ʿUmar ibn al-Khattab, the Commission argues that he suspended the punishment in a time of war, and that we are not today in a situation of war that would allow us to suspend the punishments.

In response, I again pointed out that the Call never denied the texts exist, are authentic and form an essential part of the religion. Nor did the Call ever state as the reason for suspending the *ḥudūd* that they are hurting Islam; rather, it stated that it is a betrayal of Islam to apply them in current social and political contexts, where the conditions for their application are not met. Finally, scholars diverge over the exact justifying cause (*ʿilla*) for ʿUmar's moratorium on the *ḥadd* for theft: whether it was the war, or the famine, or, as I humbly submit, because the required conditions for its application were impossible to meet. I concluded by once again reiterating the questions posed by the Call to the *ʿulamāʾ* and urging the Commission to respond.

After this, I was relieved and grateful to welcome the meticulous, insightful and closely argued response of Shaykh Dr ʿAli Jumʿa, Mufti of Egypt.[7] The Shaykh, for whom I have the highest respect, was once my teacher in a private intensive course of study in Islamic law and jurisprudence. His comments raised fundamental points as to the understanding of the Shariʿa, the conditions under which it is applied, the times we live in, and the universal spirit of the message of Islam.

Dr Jumʿa defined the Shariʿa in broad terms, restoring to its proper place the debate on the criminal code, which he further noted is intended as a deterrent against crimes, and is not "inherently unjust nor violent in and of itself". Noting that the Islamic legal system has provided conditions for the application of *ḥudūd*, he forcefully concluded: "When these conditions are not fulfilled, when these situations or states cannot be established, the application of *ḥudūd*, in the absence of these elements, is considered a transgression of the Shariʿa." This is precisely what the Call draws attention to: for Muslims, there exist a Revelation and texts whose authenticity is beyond dispute, but there also exist conditions and requirements whose existence cannot be denied except at risk of transgressing the message of Islam itself.

Dr Jumʿa went on to note that necessity (*ḍarūra*), doubt (*shubha*), public interest (*maṣlaḥa*) and the absence of the required conditions (*shurūṭ*) have always been invoked to suspend practices or establish exemptions from a literal application of Islamic regulations. Unlike some scholars who have referred to this as "rational abrogation", Dr Jumʿa preferred the more appropriate expression, "the consequence of the absence of conditions in [the application] of judgement". It is impossible for reason to abolish established and definite rules, but it is possible for human rationality to refrain from applying a law or a rule if the conditions for its application are absent. This is precisely the position defended in the Call.

Through several examples from the time of the Prophet and the Companions, Dr Jumʿa demonstrated that "the Islamic legal system is more interested in forgiveness, clemency, and the overlooking of faults than in the applications of penalties and punishments." This fundamental teaching of goodness, readiness to pardon and respect for privacy requires painstaking examination of the forces that shape Islamic societies. Again, this directly reflects the meaning of the considerations and proposals in the Call.

Giving a precise inventory of the Muslim-majority countries where the *ḥudūd* in the strict sense are applied, Dr Jumʿa concluded that this concerns only a minority of Muslim countries. With respect to one of these countries, Saudi Arabia, he further wrote that there exist "no demands nor influential trends calling for the [annulment], cessation or suspension of such application", except perhaps among elements of the political opposition. He concluded that the matter of the *ḥudūd* is not an urgent one or a priority, and that raising it at the present time "would do more harm than good".

As I will further discuss below, I am not convinced by this quantitative argument: the conscience of Muslims must reject and condemn any betrayal, large or small, of Islam's message of justice. The application of a penalty in the absence of the necessary conditions must be considered as a "transgression of the Shariʿa" whether or not such penalties are instituted in the name of Islam, and for that matter, whether or not the country in question is predominantly Muslim.[8] As to the lack of opposition to such penalties in Saudi Arabia, we know that, for political, economic, or financial reasons, criticism by Muslims as well as by the West is timid or altogether absent. Yet we are well aware how unpleasant it is to be a Pakistani or Filipino guest worker in certain petro-monarchies. Such criticism cannot be left to the political opposition alone; Muslims who live in countries where the freedom of expression is protected have a greater responsibility to deplore the betrayal perpetrated in the name of Islam in the heartland of the Muslim world.

As to the urgency and priority of the issue and the propriety of raising it at the present time, in my reply to Dr Jumʿa I asked: What is the proper moment to take up such matters? The Muslim world is in such a state, and there are so many new problems in the news each day, that we might well conclude there never is a proper moment.

Space does not permit discussing in detail every response from the Muslim scholars and leaders to the Call, but the above may serve as a representative sample. Beside these responses, there have also been many reactions from the public, from ordinary Muslim men and women, as well as non-Muslims. Some have agreed with and endorsed the Call, declared their personal support, and expressed their satisfaction that this issue is finally being raised and moving forward. Others have responded with shock or puzzlement, wondering what I am trying to do, or have attacked the Call with second-hand arguments from scholars who themselves do not seem to have read it carefully.[9]

Many Islamic organisations decided not to invite me any more because of my stand on "*ḥudūd*": I have been facing a clear boycott from some organisations which used to invite me to speak before I launched the Call. According to them, I was acting against the "Shariʿa" and this was not acceptable! When I have been invited to speak and explain my position, it has been clear that my arguments are heard and understood by the public and ordinary Muslims. More than two million have visited my website where the Call is posted: the comments are diverse, but the debate is open and, as we knew, changes will take time.

Over the past three years, I have had many personal meetings with Muslim scholars (among whom is Shaykh Yusuf al-Qaradawi[10]) and have attended many councils or meetings with *ʿulamāʾ* (in Morocco, Jordan, Qatar, Pakistan, Canada and Europe). We have been discussing this issue further. When the meaning of the Call was explained in private session, with all the arguments, the great majority of the scholars understood it better and accepted its Islamic rationale. Many scholars said the way it was presented misled them, while others confided to me that they were not going to champion the Call in public (for many reasons ranging from "it is not our priority" to "it is going to be misunderstood").

What the Call reveals

I have spoken several times of how the Call acts to reveal the nature of a common intellectual attitude among contemporary Muslims: it is an evasive, reactive and uncreative mentality. Except for a few rare voices, the *ʿulamāʾ* have not offered a serious public response to the questions raised in the Call. Various types of opposition to the Call have appeared. Some have dismissed it by misinterpreting its meaning, some have responded by avoiding the subject altogether and others have simply made broad and emotional statements. Recurrent elements of the negative reactions include the following five points.

First, there is the insistence on understanding the Call for a moratorium as a call to set aside the texts or to set aside the Shariʿa, though nowhere does the Call make such proposals. I have said very clearly that the texts concerning these punishments exist, that some of them are definitive as to their authenticity and their meaning (*qaṭʿiyya al-thubūt wa al-dalāla*), and that they are determined to be an essential part of the religion (*maʿlūm min al-dīn bi-darūra*). The Shariʿa is "the path to faithfulness" for Muslims, which cannot be reduced to the *ḥudūd* and the "penal code". The Call is clearly not for setting aside the Shariʿa, but for understanding the conditions without which its literal application in the social and political contexts we live in becomes a betrayal of Islam's message of justice.

Second, those prepared to grant the first point then put forward the argument of a slippery slope. If we suspend the *ḥudūd* today, they say, tomorrow there will be a call for suspending Islamic family law, or business law, and so on. One *ʿālim* was reported as saying: "If we call today for an international moratorium on corporal punishment, stoning and the death penalty, then tomorrow I am so worried that they may ask Muslims to suspend their Friday prayer."[11] We should avoid this kind of exaggeration. It is understandable, however, that Muslims worry where "innovations" and ideas of a "progressive Islam" could lead. Therefore, we have to be explicit about our faithfulness to the fundamentals of Islam and the classical tradition. We have to be clear that the fundamentals are fundamentals, and we have to say "no" to any attempt to destroy Islam from within. That is exactly why we cannot accept that our message be betrayed, just because we are afraid of exaggerations and a slippery slope. Suspending the application of the *ḥudūd*, the farthest "limits" of Islamic law, and the harshest – to stop irreversible injustices – is not to do away with the Shariʿa, nor even to say we should not think of an adapted penal code in the meantime.

By an accident of timing, the Call was made shortly after the controversial public event in the US when Dr Amina Wadud led a congregation of men and women in Friday prayer. To support their argument, many scholars have associated the Call for a moratorium with the case of Dr Wadud calling for women's *imāma*. I have stated, regarding Dr Wadud's views on the *imāma*, that I think she is wrong according to the teachings of Islam about the field of *ʿibādāt* (and more importantly, she was not targeting the right issues as to women and religious authority in Islam).[12] In any case, the Call has nothing to do with that debate, and the comparison has no merit.

Third, the Call is dismissed as coming from the West, being influenced by the West, or designed to please the West or to protect Islam from the attacks of Westerners. We are so afraid to be influenced by the Western culture and lifestyle that we only care that whatever action we promote should not appear to be "Westernised". This binary reasoning and antithetical understanding is dangerous. Both Muslims and non-Muslims, both in the West and in the Muslim-majority countries, have a responsibility, and we should listen to each other. The responsibility of Muslims in the West is all the greater because they have the political freedom to act and to criticise. But in any case, there is nothing Westernised in this Call: it is wholly a reflection from within the Islamic tradition. If I had wanted to please those who attack Islam, I would have called for rejecting the texts, and for condemning and abolishing the *ḥudūd*, rather than for suspending them out of respect for the texts.

Fourth, it is argued that these punishments are not an urgent matter or a priority. To support this argument, the extent to which corporal punishments and the death penalty are applied in Muslim countries is minimised. In response, it must first be said that the problem is greater than the critics allow: corporal punishment is practised in numerous Muslim countries and the death penalty is applied in the majority of these countries. There are hundreds of such cases every year, as well as a smaller number of stonings and other strict applications of *ḥudūd*. Even those punishments that are not applied as *ḥudūd* are perceived, by analogy or extension, as accepted Islamic prescriptions, due to the fact that Islamic texts speak of corporal punishments, and due to the silence or lack of clarity of the opinions of the *ʿulamāʾ* on their application in the contemporary period. This opens the door to the violation of the physical integrity of individuals by national or local authorities under judicial systems with little or no respect for the rights of the accused, whether the accused are criminals or political opponents. Moreover, such a purely quantitative argument is not morally satisfactory, even if it were true. Even if with such a moratorium we could save but a single life, protect one woman or man from unjust punishment or death, it might be enough to please Allah and be accepted in His mercy when, on the Day of Judgement, we are asked about our poor brothers and sisters who were punished and killed in the name of Islam. As to questions of priority and urgency: almost every day we witness acts undertaken in the name of Islam that betray its true message of mercy and justice. Is this not a priority? By introducing a moratorium, lives can be saved. Is this not urgent?

Fifth, many have argued that this Call should not have been launched through the media. They say the question should have been posed, quietly, to authoritative and reliable *ʿulamāʾ* and to bodies such as the al-Azhar Shariʿa Council, the Saudi Legal Councils, the ECFR, the Fiqh Council of North America, and others. Before launching this Call, I had been raising these questions and discussing a moratorium around the world for seven years. Whether in Indonesia, Pakistan, Morocco, Jordan or in Europe and in North America, I met many *ʿulamāʾ* who understood and agreed with the approach and the proposal. However, as the Call notes, many are afraid to speak and remain silent on a very sensitive topic. Today, the *ʿulamāʾ* usually do not react except under the pressure of the media or under the pressure of the community, which itself does not react except under the pressure of the media. It was with these realities in mind that the Call was launched, to attract worldwide media coverage as a first step to make the Muslim communities aware of the problem, so that as a second step, ordinary Muslims might be mobilised to ask the *ʿulamāʾ* to tackle the issue. To keep silent while injustices continue is not the way our Prophet acted.

Some of these arguments countering the Call evade the issues altogether; some are critical of the approach and the tactics adopted. They do not go to the heart of the substance of the Call. The more thoughtful critics, however, express themselves in terms commensurate with the meaning of the Call on several points.

First, we agree that the *ḥudūd* and the "penal code" are but one aspect or part of the Shariʿa, the path to faithfulness. The Shariʿa includes both ritual, ethical and legal rules. It must be understood in the light of its global objectives (*maqāṣid*), which traditionally include the protection of the religion (*dīn*), the person's integrity (*nafs*), the intellect (*ʿaql*), family ties (*nasl*), property (*amwāl*), and the person's dignity and honour (*ʿirḍ*).[13]

Second, we agree that the Shariʿa stipulates not only the *ḥudūd,* but also the conditions for their application, and that the punishments should not be literally applied in the absence of these conditions. There are many examples from Islamic history of how these punishments have been suspended in practice, because of the element of doubt (*shubha*), necessity (*darūra*), the public interest (*maṣlaḥa*), or because the conditions (*shurūṭ*) could not be met. The tradition has not been about literally applying these punishments under any and all circumstances, but about readiness to pardon and reluctance to condemn, respect for privacy and respect for a deep reading of the texts in their context.

Third, many of us agree that the present social and political context in Muslim-majority countries is not conducive to a just application of the *ḥudūd*. We agree that corporal punishments, stoning and the death penalty are in fact being unjustly applied to the weakest and poorest segments of society, to guest workers, women, and even minors, in the absence of proper defence counsel and other basic legal safeguards. The punishments are being applied by governments that have not taken the necessary steps to ensure justice through education, social and economic development, or promotion of the moral climate that would ensure justice. Indeed, as one critic put it, governments are applying *ḥudūd* before taking care of people's *ḥuqūq* (rights). The necessary conditions for a just application of these punishments simply do not exist in Muslim-majority countries today.

Concluding remarks

I am grateful to the scholars and the *ʿulamāʾ* who have taken the time to read and to comment on the Call. From the bottom of my heart, I value these comments, and I respect their criticisms, which I had expected. My intention was and remains to initiate a debate. Only a very few scholars have given a deep and serious response. The challenge still stands to the rest of the *ʿulamāʾ* to stand up, to speak up and to commit seriously to engaging in a critical and honest debate.

Several important scholars have publicly disagreed with the conclusions of the Call, while showing themselves to be in substantial agreement with its description of the problem and with its understanding of Islam's message of justice, of Shari'a and the texts. This is encouraging and is a foundation that we can build on. The differences come down to choices – the choices of priority, timing, approach and strategies. Instead of calling for change through the media, the critics say, one should refer the question to scholars, and meanwhile work for a more just implementation of these punishments, criticising their faulty aspects, but not suspending them across the board.

Should we be satisfied with the frequent pronouncement that the implementation should be fairer? Is it not time to propose a reform project for Muslim-majority societies that is more coherent and consonant with our dignified Islamic message? The great majority of the *'ulamā'* with whom I spoke privately for seven years before I made the Call in March 2005, as well as after, agreed that our message is being betrayed and that things needed to change – but when there is no "media noise", everyone keeps silent, and the injustices continue. This question remains: Can we as Muslims, whether scholars or ordinary people, continue to hide behind general statements that the *ḥudūd* are almost never applied, or that the applications we see are not the "true implementation" of the Shari'a, while poor innocent people continue to be unjustly punished and killed? If this is wrong, let us say that it is wrong: let us stop it now.

12 Negotiating gender rights under religious law in Malaysia

Zainah Anwar

The Islamic resurgence that has engulfed most Muslim countries today has led to tension and an ideological contest over what Islam – and whose Islam – is the right Islam. The status and rights of women have become the first casualty on this battleground.

The struggle for equality and justice for Muslim women must therefore be placed within the context of an Islam that is increasingly shaping and redefining the lives of women living in Muslim societies. Since the early 1970s, Muslim societies in all parts of the world have been caught up in the throes of a resurgent Islam. All too often, in the turn to Islam as a way of life and the source of solutions to the ills and injustices that beset our societies, it seems that the subordination of women has become the first (and easiest) measure of a group's or society's commitment to the faith. It is as if those who have turned to Islam cannot cope with the monumental challenges posed by the outside world that is galloping ahead and changing in ways and directions that are beyond their control. Instead, they target the disempowered and the weakest in society to prove their power and ability to dominate and bring about change, allegedly in the name of Islam.

It is therefore not surprising that in these countries, from Egypt to Iran, Pakistan, Indonesia and Malaysia, women's groups are at the forefront in challenging traditional authorities and political Islamist groups and their use of religion to justify women's subordination and inferior status, and, most perniciously, to use religion to silence any dissent and to defame or incite hatred against those who offer alternative views or protect and promote the rights of women.

For most Muslim women, rejecting religion is not an option. We are believers: as believers we want to find liberation, truth and justice within our own faith. We strongly feel we have a right to reclaim our religion, to redefine it, to participate in it and to contribute to an understanding of what Islam is and how it is codified and implemented – in ways that take into consideration the realities and experience of women's lives today.

For too long, men have defined for us what it is to be a woman and how to be one. Men have used religion to confine us to these socially constructed limitations that reduce us to being the inferior half of the human race. Today, however, we live in an era where women are educated, travel the world and hold positions of power and responsibility in increasing numbers. Today's Muslim women in countries like Malaysia and Indonesia – countries that are rapidly modernising and industrialising – will no longer accept their inferior status, not even when it is justified in the name of religion. Women will not accept that Islam actually promotes injustice and ill-treatment of half the human race. Today's women are challenging the values of patriarchal society where power and authority reside exclusively with the husband, father and brother, to whom the wife, daughter and sister owe obedience.

In Malaysia today, women form the majority of students in the public universities and an even higher percentage of the graduating class, as the drop-out rate among boys is higher. In 2004 the female labour force participation stood at 47 per cent and was rising. It can only be expected that women, with increasing knowledge and education, with economic independence, will gain more confidence and courage to speak out in the face of injustice. If the injustice is committed in the name of religion, then today's women will go back to the original source of the religion to find out for themselves whether such a great religion could indeed be so unjust to half of its believers.

Of course, there are many other Muslim women activists who have decided it is futile to work within the religious framework because they believe that all religions, including Islam, are inherently patriarchal and unjust: that to work within religion would only serve the interest of the male oppressors who use religion to control women and maintain their subjugation. To those activists, the choice to work within the religious framework, which groups like Sisters in Islam – an NGO in Malaysia – have made, is a losing battle. For every alternative interpretation that women can offer to justify equality and justice in Islam, they say, the *'ulamā'* will offer a hundred others to challenge that interpretation. They have therefore chosen to struggle for women's rights within the framework of universal values and principles.

However, in the past 10–15 years, progressive scholars have challenged the Islamic agenda of the traditionalist as well as the fundamentalist *ʿulamāʾ* and activists and their intolerance and outright oppression of women. These scholars recognise equality between men and women in Islam, argue for the imperative of *ijtihād* (juristic effort to deduce law from its sources), address the dynamics between what is universal for all times and what is particular to seventh-century Arabia, look at the socio-historical context of revelation and articulate the need to differentiate between what is revelation and what is a human understanding of the word of God.[1] Research, methodology and conceptual frameworks developed to deal with the challenge to Islam of modernity have enabled more and more Muslim women activists all over the world to realise the validity and possibility of working within the Islamic framework – that they can indeed find liberation from within Islam. Besides beginning to read the works of these new scholars, they have also unearthed classical texts and arguments of scholars of the early centuries of Islam that were marginalised and silenced for their progressive views on women, rights and freedom. Women have begun to study the Qur'an and the traditions of the Prophet for themselves, to better understand Islam. With this knowledge and new-found conviction, they have begun to stand up to fight for women's rights to equality, freedom and justice within the religious framework.

Our strength comes not just from the realities of our lives today, but also from our conviction and faith in an Islam that is just, liberating and empowering to us as women. Through groups like Sisters in Islam, we are reclaiming for ourselves the Islam that liberated women and uplifted our status by giving us rights considered revolutionary 1,400 years ago.

It is this ethical vision of the Qurʾan that insistently enjoins equality and justice – it is this liberating and revolutionary spirit of Islam that today guides our quest to be treated as fellow human beings of equal worth.

The challenges

As a feminist and an activist, I am concerned with the practice of Islam in Malaysia because of the injustice women suffer in the name of Islam. In the public sphere, Muslim women are striding forth into the world in the name of development and modernisation, but, in the private sphere, in dealings with the religious authorities and under personal status laws, women are often discriminated against in the name of Islam.

Where is the justice of Islam when women have to suffer in silence because Islam supposedly demands that they be obedient to their husbands, or because Islam grants men the right to beat their wives or to take second wives? Muslim women are told again and again that in Islam men are superior to women, that men have authority over women, that the testimony of two women equals that of one man, that a wife has no right to say 'No' to sex with her husband, that hell is full of women because they leave their heads uncovered and are disobedient to their husbands ...

Civil law in Malaysia is slowly being amended to recognise equality between men and women, reflecting the realities of women's lives and gender relationships today, but Muslim women are excluded from these changes. Islamic law, as interpreted and codified by men, has sanctified a patriarchal ideology. In fact, in the 1990s and 2000s, the government of Malaysia introduced new Muslim laws or amendments to existing ones that were more punitive and discriminatory against Muslim women in particular, and against Muslims in general.[2]

The Islamic Family Law, one of the most enlightened personal status laws in the Muslim world when it was enacted in 1984, was amended in the 1990s to make divorce and polygamy easier for men and to reduce men's financial responsibilities towards women. Further discriminatory amendments were made in 2005, which led to loud public protests.[3] New Shariʿa criminal laws[4] were passed to ensure that the lifestyle of Muslims would not transgress Islamic teachings. New offences were created that criminalise indecent behaviour, eating in public during the month of Ramadan, missing Friday prayers, etc. Surveillance and enforcement of morality were expanded, and Muslims were made liable to more severe punishment.

The Administration of Islamic Law Act was amended in the 1990s to automatically give the force of law to a fatwa[5] issued by the state Mufti once it is gazetted, without going through the legislative process. Only the Mufti has the power to revoke or amend a fatwa. This was accompanied by new amendments to the Syariah [Shariʿa] Criminal Offences Act, which provided that any violation of a fatwa, as well as any effort to dispute or to give an opinion contrary to a fatwa, constitutes a criminal offence. To even possess books on Islam that are contrary to a fatwa that is currently in force is also an offence.[6]

In the states of Kelantan (1993) and Terengganu (2002), laws codifying traditional *ḥudūd* punishments were passed by the state governments under PAS (Parti Islam SeMalaysia) control. These laws contain contentious classical provisions for *ḥudūd* punishments such as flogging, amputation of limbs, stoning to death and crucifixion, and they discriminate against Muslim women and non-Muslims.[7]

In the context of Malaysia, it is a "holier than thou" contest between the dominant ruling party in the coalition government, UMNO (United Malays National Organisation) and the Islamist party PAS, that has led to this escalation of discriminatory amendments against Muslim women, moral policing and harsh punishments, all in the name of being "authentically" Islamic. This race to measure one's piety and Islamic credentials by the control of women and by the severity of the punishment imposed on supposed transgressors of the teachings of the religion, demonstrates what happens in many Muslim societies when religion is transformed into an ideology for political struggle and a source of legitimacy.

As Muslim countries increasingly turn to Islam as a source of law and public policy, women's groups and human rights groups are becoming very concerned about the impact of these laws on women's rights and human rights in general, as well as the impact on the law-making process and the implications for democratic governance. This impact should not be underestimated.

The misogynistic bent

The amendments to the Islamic Family Law since the early 1990s are a major instance of discrimination against Muslim women. For instance, the amendments allow a polygamous marriage contracted without the permission of the court to be registered, upon payment of a fine or jail sentence; delete the condition that a proposed polygamous marriage should not directly or indirectly lower the standard of living enjoyed by the existing wife and dependents; and allow the registration of divorces pronounced outside court.

Further amendments passed by Parliament in 2005 discriminated against women, ironically, through the use of gender-neutral language. Rights traditionally given to women, for example the right to *fasakh* divorce (divorce for cause) were extended to men, within a legal framework that already grants men the unilateral right to divorce their wives at any time, without cause.[8] The only conceivable reason for extending such grounds for divorce to men is to enable them to escape paying compensation if the divorce is caused by the wife's fault. While a woman was given the right to claim her share of the matrimonial assets should her husband take a second wife, the use of gender-neutral language also enables the husband to claim his share of the matrimonial assets upon taking another wife. These amendments provoked a public outcry that led to the unprecedented move by the government to review the discriminatory amendments in full consultation with women's groups.

Such discriminatory amendments to the Islamic Family Law were made at the same time as the government – in response to long-standing demands from women's groups – was taking steps to amend laws that discriminated against women in the civil sphere. In the name of Islam, Muslim women were denied the enjoyment of the legal rights and protection granted to women of other faiths.

For example, in early 1999, the Guardianship of Infants Act, a civil law, was amended to give non-Muslim mothers equal rights with fathers to guardianship of their children, but no similar amendment was made to the Islamic Family Law to accord the same right to Muslim mothers. The argument used was that guardianship in Muslim families is under the Islamic Family Law jurisdiction, while the Guardianship Act can only apply to non-Muslims. Because this was deemed to be a "sensitive issue", no attempt was made to negotiate with the religious authorities to effect the same amendments to the guardianship provisions under Islamic Family Law. This reflects the propensity among many in government to declare any matter which touches on religion as sensitive and therefore untouchable, even when other Muslim jurisdictions have progressive alternative interpretations and legal provisions which recognise equality and non-discrimination.

One wonders, what are Muslim women expected to do while their non-Muslim sisters are increasingly accorded greater rights to be treated as equal to men? Sisters in Islam protested and successfully lobbied the Federal Government to ensure that Muslim mothers can benefit from the effect of the civil law reform until the Islamic Family Law is amended. The Cabinet issued a policy directive that all official documents to manage the affairs of children which require the consent of the guardian (under the Islamic Family Law, this means the father) will now read "father/mother/guardian". This policy decision now enables Muslim mothers to make decisions on their children's applications for passports, school registration and transfer, and permission for surgery, which in the past could only be done by the father.

The negotiations for a Domestic Violence Act in the early 1990s also saw attempts to exclude Muslims from the jurisdiction of the Act because of the widespread belief that Muslim men have a right to beat their wives. Again, the women's groups had to lobby the government for several years to make domestic violence a crime whether it is committed by a Malay, a Chinese, or an Indian man.[9] Even after the law was passed by Parliament in 1994, we had to go through two more years of pressure and lobbying to get it implemented. This time, those opposed to the application of the law to Muslims shifted their argument to asserting that domestic violence was a family matter that should come under the Shariʿa jurisdiction of the states, rather than a criminal matter under federal jurisdiction.

The *ḥudūd* laws of Kelantan and Terengganu grossly discriminate against women by disqualifying women (and all non-Muslims – which in sum means three quarters of Malaysia's population) as eyewitnesses in *ḥudūd* crimes. These laws assume that an unmarried woman who is pregnant or has delivered a baby has committed *zinā*ʾ (adultery/illicit sex). If she claims she has been raped, the burden of proof lies on her.

The original draft of the Terengganu law provided that a woman who reports rape would be charged with *qazaf* (Arabic *qadhf*, slanderous accusation) and flogged 80 lashes if she was unable to prove the rape (through four Muslim male eyewitnesses). It caused such an outrage that the PAS government was forced to amend the law to allow for circumstantial evidence. Even so, the burden of proof remains on the woman.

All these new laws and amendments to existing laws reflect the misogynistic bent of those in religious authority, whether in government or in opposition. At a time when the Malaysian government, at least at the leadership level, recognises equality between men and women in the country and is slowly responding to calls by women's groups to amend all laws that discriminate against women, other parts of that very same government do not share this egalitarian vision.

The 2002 amendment to Article 8 of the Federal Constitution to prohibit discrimination on the basis of gender poses a special challenge to the Islamic religious authorities and the Syariah Court in Malaysia that steps be taken to end all forms of discrimination against Muslim women in law and in practice, that are committed in the name of Islam.

Groups like Sisters in Islam do not believe that there is a conflict between the constitutional guarantees of equality and non-discrimination and the teachings of Islam. However, many obstacles lie in the way of those working for the principles of equality and justice to guide the policy and law-making process in the name of Islam.

A shroud of silence

Until recently, what has been remarkable about the making of Islamic laws in Malaysia is the silence that surrounds the whole process, both at the drafting and legislative levels.

First, there is a lack of consultation and public debate in the law-making process, even though such personal status laws have widespread impact on the private and public lives of some 60 per cent of the Malaysian population who are Muslims. This means that very often laws are made without any public knowledge that they even exist or that such a process was taking place – until there is a public outcry when they are passed by Parliament or when they are enforced by the religious authorities.

For example, most Malaysians did not know that the Administration of Islamic Law Act provides, that upon publication in the Government Gazette, a fatwa is binding on all Muslims as a dictate of their religion. Most Malaysians were also not aware that the Syariah Criminal Offences Law was amended to provide that it is an offence to violate or dispute a fatwa and to dress indecently – until this law was enforced in 1997, when three Muslim girls were arrested and charged for taking part in a beauty contest and for indecent dress. Given the complexities of law reform and the lack of media coverage, it is quite common to meet political leaders in government or in opposition and even legislators who are not aware that these grossly discriminatory provisions exist.

Second, there is a lack of substantive debate in the legislatures when Islamic laws are tabled. Most elected representatives are too fearful to speak out and to question or to debate – let alone criticise – Islamic bills, be it on constitutional, theological or Islamic jurisprudential grounds. Non-Muslim opposition MPs are cautious about commenting on any matters relating to Islam. – When they do speak out, they are often silenced by their fellow Muslim MPs, because the latter do not recognise the right of non-Muslims to speak on Islam, which they regard as the exclusive preserve of the Muslims.

However, this has begun to change since 2004, under the leadership of the new Prime Minister, Datuk Seri Abdullah Ahmad Badawi. There is now more vigorous debate in Parliament and this new openness has enabled more effective lobbying by women's groups. A cross-party Parliamentary Gender Caucus has also been formed and MPs have taken the initiative to speak out on gender-discriminatory laws and policies. MPs are more open to input from women's groups. The fears of rising conservatism and extremism have also pushed non-Muslim MPs to carve out a space to speak on Islamic laws from justice and constitutional perspectives.

The authority to speak on Islam

Who has a right to speak on Islam is a major contentious issue in Malaysia and other Muslim countries today. Traditionally, most Muslims have believed that only the *'ulamā'* (religious scholars) have the right to speak on Islam, and that those not traditionally educated in religion do not have the right to engage publicly in the debate about religion. Therefore, very few Muslims have the courage to question, challenge or even discuss matters of religion, even when they are concerned about unjust teachings and practices. They have been socialised to accept that those in religious authority know best what is Islamic and what is not.

A major reason for the silence that surrounds law-making in the name of Islam, then, is fear and ignorance. The bifurcation of the modern education system means that those trained in secular schools have little knowledge of religion and those trained in religion have little understanding of the world outside. As Islam increasingly shapes and redefines our lives today, many Muslims who are concerned about the intolerant and extremist trends are too fearful to speak out about their concerns because they feel they do not know enough about Islam. Their tentative attempts to raise questions and express concern are often silenced by the pronouncement that they should desist, lest their faith be undermined.

Even those who are knowledgeable about Islam are often reluctant to speak out, especially if their views do not coincide with the mainstream orthodox view. They fear that they will be embroiled in a controversy or that they will be labelled as anti-Islam and accused by the extremists of questioning the word of God. It is not that they do not have the knowledge to defend themselves, but that they would rather hide in the safety of their ivory tower than be embroiled in any kind of controversy, especially when they live in a working and social environment dominated by orthodoxy.

Thus, when women's groups or lay intellectuals speak about Islam, their credentials, their right and their authority to speak publicly are questioned. Thus, for instance, in early 2002 the Ulama Association of Malaysia attempted to charge six writers, including myself, with insulting Islam. To me, this is nothing more than an attempt to monopolise the public discourse, meaning and content of Islam to serve a political agenda.

In actual practice, however, it is not because of one's education or competence that one is accorded the right to speak on Islam, but because of one's position on various issues in Islam. If one supports the death penalty for apostasy, the *ḥudūd* law and the Islamic state, then one will be given the freedom and space to speak on Islam, even if one is only a third-class engineering graduate from a third-rate university.

Sisters in Islam takes the position that when Islam is used as a source of law and public policy, with widespread impact on the lives of the citizens of a democratic country, then any attempt to limit writing, talking and debate about Islam to only the *ʿulamāʾ* or those with supposedly "in-depth knowledge" of Islam is really tantamount to the rule of a theocratic dictatorship. Why is it that all citizens have the right to speak on political, economic and social issues that impinge on our well-being and rights, but, when it comes to matters of religion, we must be silent and defer to the *ʿulamāʾ*? In a democracy, public law must be opened to public debate, even if that law is made in the name of Islam.

The conservatives like to argue that religion is like medicine: it takes an expert to dispense opinion. This is a misguided analogy for many reasons, but most importantly because, if the client does not like the opinion and treatment of one doctor, he is free to go to another. He will not be declared an apostate or accused of insulting the profession and the expertise of the doctor; he will not be incarcerated at best, or sentenced to death at worst. To earn the respect and continued patronage of their patients, top doctors keep abreast with the latest developments in their specialisation, but the same cannot be said of many of those who monopolise the decision-making process in religion.

A "Holier-Than-Thou" competition

Whether in the area of fundamental liberties or women's rights, the tendency displayed by the religious authorities is often to codify the most conservative opinion into law. For example, traditionally there are three juristic positions on apostasy. The first position is that all unrepentant apostates deserve the death penalty (the Shafi'i school prevalent in Malaysia makes no distinction as to gender). The second view prescribes the death penalty only if apostasy is accompanied by rebellion against the community and its legitimate leadership. The third view holds that even though apostasy is a great sin, it is not a capital offence in Islam. Therefore, a personal change of faith merits no punishment.[10] The Qur'an is explicit in its recognition of freedom of religion, and there exists within the Islamic juristic heritage a position that supports freedom of religion. This position is further strengthened by the official al-Azhar position under the current Shaykh, Dr Muhammad Sayyid Tantawi.[11]

However, PAS in its vision of Islam has chosen the most extremist juristic opinion to codify into law: death for apostasy, while the government's religious authorities have supported a compromise position: one-year compulsory rehabilitation instead of death. This outcome stems from the political power-struggle over religious legitimacy.

When Islam is used as a political ideology in the contest for power, rival parties descend into a holier-than-thou battle for the hearts and minds of the Muslim voters. In Malaysia, the PAS and UMNO parties are engaged in a one-upmanship game to dispute each other's religious credentials. This is dangerous to democratic governance. In giving in to the demands of the religious ideologues, the government continually legitimises them and becomes hostage to the PAS agenda.

In Malay villages, the PAS has been known to charge that the UMNO-led government could not be regarded as Islamic, as it provided no punishment for those who leave Islam, but would fine a citizen heftily just for throwing a cigarette butt on the market floor. PAS, casting itself as the true Islamic party, had already introduced the death penalty for apostasy in its *ḥudūd* law at the state level, while at the federal level its chief ideologue, Hadi Awang, had for years been trying to introduce a private member's bill in Parliament to impose the death penalty for apostasy as a federal law.

Accordingly, in 2000, attempts were made by the government to introduce the Islamic Aqidah (Faith) Protection Bill, which provides for a one-year mandatory detention in a Faith Rehabilitation Centre for those who attempt to leave Islam.[12] If at the end of the detention period, the person still refuses to repent, then the judge will declare that the person is no longer a Muslim and order his release. If he is married, his marriage will be dissolved and the judge will determine his obligations or liabilities under Islamic Family Law. The compromise of one-year mandatory detention instead of death is no concession to freedom of religion: the person's rights and fundamental liberties have been violated. The compromise came in response to the pressure to provide for a specific punishment for apostasy. The pressure came not only from PAS and its supporters, but also from UMNO members and leaders as they found no other answer to the PAS charge.

The tendency to codify the most conservative opinion is all the more present in the area of women's rights. For example, the provision that women cannot be witnesses under the PAS *ḥudūd* law is only a juristic opinion with no explicit support in the Qur'an or Traditions of the Prophet Muhammad. Pregnancy as evidence of *zinā'* is a minority position of the Maliki school. The majority opinion of Islamic legal scholars is that pregnancy is not admissible as proof of *zinā'* because circumstantial evidence cannot be accepted to secure a *ḥudūd* punishment. Yet the PAS ideologues in Malaysia, who belong to the Shafi'i school, chose to ignore the more enlightened Shafi'i opinion and instead codified a harsher Maliki opinion. However, when a Maliki or Hanbali opinion is more advantageous to women, certain jurists would proclaim that this cannot be accepted, with the justification that "We are Shafi'is and we must follow Shafi'i rulings."

Conclusion

If Islam is to be used as a source of law and public policy to govern the public and private lives of citizens, then the question of who decides what is Islamic and what is not is of paramount importance. When only a small, exclusive group of people have the right to interpret the Text and codify it in a manner that very often isolates the Text from the socio-historical context in which it was revealed, isolates classical juristic opinion from the socio-historical context of the lives of the founding jurists of Islam, and isolates both the Text and the juristic heritage from the context of the contemporary society we live in today, the implications for democratic governance are dire.

How can a modernising democratic society search for solutions to the multitude of problems facing the *umma* (community of Muslims) when that search is conducted in ways that are so exclusive, restrictive, intimidating and sometimes even life-threatening? The world is far more complex today than it ever was. No one group can have the exclusive monopoly on knowledge. In a modern democratic nation-state, *ijtihād* must therefore be exercised in concert and through democratic engagement with the *umma*. The experience of others who have traditionally been excluded from the process of interpreting, defining and implementing Islam must be included. The role of women, who constitute half of the *umma*, must be acknowledged and included in this process of dialogue, of policy-making and law-making.

13 The changing concepts of caliphate – Social construction of Shariʿa and the question of ethics

Muhammad Khalid Masud

The emphasis on *khilāfa* or caliphate as the only form of political authority in Islam is contested in modern Muslim political thought. Some Muslim thinkers argue that political authority is essential, but do not necessarily associate it with the institution of caliphate. There are others who insist that politics and political authority are not the essence of Islam as a religion.

Political theories are essentially social constructions which are informed by social perceptions of change and continuity within a community. Some societies value continuity more than change and therefore underplay social change. Consequently, the function of a political theory is to explain changes in such a manner that they are justified in terms of continuity. In such societies it is extremely significant not only to ask what is changeable, but also how something is justified as unchangeable by reference to continuity.

This paper explores this question to study the framework that allows some Muslim thinkers to speak for reform and change, and others to adopt changes and still claim continuity. The paper is divided into four sections. The first section deals with the history of the institution of the caliphate; the second with the political theory of the caliphate, the third with the debate on the caliphate in modern

Muslim political thought and the fourth explores the perceptions of change and continuity in Islamic thought.

History of the institution of the caliphate

Historically, the institution did not exist in pre-Islamic Arabia or during the days of the Prophet, but came to be adopted by the Muslim community after his death. The concept and the form of the institution changed constantly, but the term remained.

The institution of the *khalīfa* or caliph came into existence in 632 with the succession of Abu Bakr, and came to an end in 1924 with the abolition of the Ottoman caliphate. The caliphate as a political authority in Muslim communities began disintegrating during the late ʿAbbasid period. The Fatimid dynasty in Egypt claimed the caliphate in 909, and the Umayyads in Spain claimed it in 928. So would several later dynasties in the Islamic West, like the Hafsids and the Marinids. Muslim rulers in other Muslim lands assumed various titles – Sultan, Amir, Padishah, and so on – and some of them sought legitimacy by requesting investiture from the ruling caliph, but most of them did not regard such investiture as necessary.

The ʿAbbasid caliphate came to an end in 1258 when the Mongols destroyed Baghdad. The Mamluk rulers in Egypt restored the caliphate in 1261 by appointing an ʿAbbasid to the office. This ʿAbbasid caliphate continued until 1517, when the Ottoman Sultan Selim defeated the Mamluks in Egypt and exiled the last ʿAbbasid caliph to Constantinople. Some of the Ottoman sultans and the Mughal rulers sometimes used the title of caliph for themselves, but it was only from the seventeenth century that the Ottomans came to be recognised as caliphs succeeding the ʿAbbasid caliphate.

Under these various dynastic rulers, the institution of the caliphate underwent several changes in form and scope of authority. A brief analytical review of the major changes that took place follows.

Initially there was a wide variety of methods for appointing the caliph. The first caliph was elected in 632 by a group of tribal leaders in Medina; the second was appointed by the first in 634; and the third was elected in 644 by a committee of elders appointed by the second caliph. After a revolt against, and the murder of, the third caliph, the community was divided into two warring factions, one led by the group who appointed ʿAli as caliph and the other led by the rival contender Muʿawiya. The fifth caliph, Hasan, was son of ʿAli; he was appointed by the community. Hasan reunited the community by abdicating in favour of Muʿawiya in 661.

Muʿawiya replaced the principle of election with the principle of hereditary succession within the Umayyad dynasty (Banu Umayya). The practice of *bayʿa* (oath of allegiance) continued, but it was gradually reduced to a mere formality, as the Umayyad caliphs continued to appoint their successors from their own family, until the ʿAbbasids removed the Umayyad dynasty in a bloody revolt, when the ʿAbbasid caliph al-Saffah assumed the caliphate by force in 749. Other ʿAbbasid caliphs came to power under the principle of hereditary succession. Sometimes two successive caliphs were nominated by the ruling caliph. During the ʿAbbasid period the army chiefs gained more power and they assumed the title of Sultan. The later ʿAbbasid caliphs were appointed by these army chiefs. Thus from the tenth century, the method of the appointment of a caliph was based on the principle of hereditary succession, although often imposed by force.

Diversity in the conception of the caliphate is also indicated by the titles chosen by the various caliphs. In the early period, simple titles like "the successor of the Prophet", "the successor of the successor of the Prophet" and the "leader of the faithful" suggested that the position of caliph was simply that of a successor of the Prophet and leader. The Umayyad caliphs began to use titles like "God's caliph", and the ʿAbbasids called themselves "God's authority on the earth" and "Shadow of God", suggesting that their authority was divine. The ʿAbbasid caliphs also used names in a construct form of Allah (e.g. *al-Wāthiq bi-llāh*).

The genealogy of the caliphs also differed. Until the end of the ʿAbbasids, the caliphs belonged to the different clans of the Quraysh. Among the first four caliphs, three belonged to Banu Hashim. ʿUthman and the Umayyad caliphs belonged to Banu Umayya. The ʿAbbasids belonged to Banu Hashim, but the descendants of ʿAli, the fourth caliph, contested their legitimacy, because they descended from the Prophet's uncle, not from the Prophet himself. In Spain, the legitimacy of Banu Nasr, the last Muslim dynasty, was contested because they traced their genealogy to the Ansar of Medina, not to the Quraysh. Similar objections arose against the Ottoman caliphs, who were not descendants of the Quraysh. This aspect of legitimacy will be addressed later.

Early and classical political theories of the caliphate

The concept of the caliphate varies in the early political theories, depending upon the perspective of the writer. Most of the writers support the absolute power of the caliph; most justify it on religious grounds, and some on rational ones. The following are some notable theories.[1]

Ibn al-Muqaffaʿ (d. 756) believed that the legitimacy of political authority is based on the religious conviction held in common by the caliph and his army. Right belief is the cornerstone of his political theory. The caliph's authority is absolute and the caliph unifies the people through unity of belief and law. Ibn al-Muqaffaʿ

advised the caliph to regulate the diverse laws applied by the judges. He recommended, unsuccessfully, that the caliph should create "a code of law based on (i) precedents and usage (*siyar*), (ii) tradition and analogy, and (iii) his own decisions which would in turn be emended by succeeding caliphs".[2]

Abu Yusuf (d. 798) believed that the source of political authority was God's choice, by which the caliph became a vicegerent of God on earth. It is the duty of the subjects to obey their caliph (*imām*), because the caliph is like a shepherd of his people. Abu Yusuf does not mention the principle of election.

Al-Jahiz (d. 868–9) justifies the legitimacy of political authority on a rational basis. He argues that a caliph (*imām*) is needed because humans are by nature predatory and need someone to regulate them. The basis of political authority is therefore the rule of law. It is a duty of Muslims to oppose the transgression of the law – even by the caliph, so the subjects must denounce and depose the caliph who transgresses the law, if they are able to do so.

Abu'l-Hasan ʿAli al-Mawardi (d. 1058) is regarded as the first Muslim jurist to expound a political theory. *Al-Ahkam al-Sultaniyya* is essentially a book dedicated to the details of public administration and rules of government; only a small portion of the work is devoted to political theory. Al-Mawardi certainly benefited from the discussions of previous scholars and was also under their influence. His theory is, however, important because it provided a framework for subsequent political theories in Muslim thought, and his influence remains visible today. The reason for the popularity of his work may also be sought in the fact that it followed a method that assimilated and synthesised change into the heritage in a way that facilitated the assimilation of future change in the same fashion.

A closer examination of his work, though, discloses that al-Mawardi is not a mere recorder of facts handed down to him, but a shrewd statesman and diplomat. There is enough historical data to sanction the view that, on many fundamental questions, al-Mawardi's opinions were dictated by the exigencies of his time and the special circumstances of his life. Seeking to uphold the caliph's authority in theory, though actual power had been usurped by others, he made even the caliph's obligations to uphold the Shariʿa conditional on the possibility of fulfilment.

Without going into the details of al-Mawardi's doctrine, I would like to invite attention particularly to two points: 1) the method of designation of a caliph, and 2) the required qualifications of a caliph. These two points illustrate how al-Mawardi assimilated changing practices into the doctrine to provide a semblance of continuity.

Regarding the method of appointment, al-Mawardi expounds two methods of designating a caliph: 1) election by the group of people who have the political capacity (*ahl al-ḥall wa al-ʿaqd*) and 2) designation by the preceding caliph.[3] It must be noted that at this point al-Mawardi does not refer to the Qur'an or *ḥadīth* or Sunna. Apparently, he has assimilated the historical practice up to his time into his theory. The term *ahl al-ḥall*, as he explains, refers to the people who appointed Abu Bakr and ʿUthman. The nomination by the preceding caliph refers to the caliphate of ʿUmar, who was appointed by Caliph Abu Bakr. It is quite significant that al-Mawardi assimilates the practice of hereditary appointments (*walī al-ʿahd*) in the Umayyad and ʿAbbasid periods as based on a declaration by the preceding caliph.

Regarding the required qualifications, al-Mawardi prescribes seven conditions for the appointment of a caliph. 1) He must be just in all respects. 2) He must be learned enough to have the capacity for *ijtihād* (juristic reasoning). 3) He must not have a physical defect in hearing, sight or speech. 4) He must not have any physical defect in the body affecting his capacity to move. 5) He must be wise in dealing with the subjects and administration. 6) He must be brave. 7) He must belong to the Quraysh.

In actual history, most of these qualifications were disregarded. The majority of the caliphs were not literate, let alone capable of *ijtihād*. Despite the requirement of this capacity, a caliph's right to exercise *ijtihād* was continually disputed. In modern theories (see below), it is no longer considered necessary.

The last qualification, belonging to the tribe of Quraysh, was strictly observed until the sixteenth century. It is particularly significant that al-Mawardi cites two *ḥadīth* of the Prophet saying that the "Quraysh are the leaders" (*al-aʾimmatu min quraysh*) and "Let the Quraysh lead, do not lead them" (*qaddimu qurayshan lā taqaddamūhā*).[4] I have not found these two cited texts in the six collections of *ḥadīth*. Apparently, the condition that the caliph must belong to the Quraysh was not prescriptive in early Islam. The Khawarij who revolted against ʿAli and Muʿawiya did not choose their leaders from the Quraysh, but called them *amīr al-muʾminīn* (commander of the faithful).[5] They cited another *ḥadīth* calling for obedience even to a black African.[6]

Ibn Qutayba (d. 889), almost two centuries before al-Mawardi, does not refer to any *ḥadīth* in this respect. His narrative of the origins of the caliphate reveals that until the ninth century, the concept of the caliphate was not formulated as a Sunna, nor had it any reference to the Qurʾan or *ḥadīth*. It is quite a long narrative. Space does not allow its citation in full, as its historical significance would merit, but the following is a summary.[7]

When the Prophet Muhammad died, several factions formed and contended for the succession to the leadership among the Muslims of Medina, in particular the Muhajirun (immigrants from Mecca) and the Ansar (the tribes from Medina). Each group argued its merits and voiced its concerns, and various power-sharing solutions were proposed, but in the end, the Muhajirun party headed by Abu Bakr and ʿUmar prevailed. Most of the Ansar pledged their oath (*bayʿa*) to Abu Bakr, an outcome that ʿAli contested, on the grounds that the leadership should remain in the house of the Prophet, but was not able to reverse.

The following points in the narrative must be noted, because they are often ignored in later formulations of the political theory.

- The concept of the caliphate is broadly formulated in a non-religious framework of succession. The only religious references are to Abu Bakr's leading prayers on the instructions of the Prophet. They serve as a way of pointing out Abu Bakr's merits, not as a religious justification for the necessity of political authority, nor as the sole reason for his succession.
- Nobody spoke about the necessity of the state or of political authority as an essence of Islam. There were several proposals about succession and forms of government.
- Contrary to the classical theory, reference to the Quraysh is made neither as a religious nor as a necessary qualification for political authority. It is mentioned as a statement of fact that the Meccan Muslim immigrants belonged to this tribe. The superiority of the Meccans on that basis is contested by the tribes in Medina.
- Abu Bakr was not the only contender for the succession.
- The term *khilāfa* or *khalīfa* was mentioned in the ordinary meaning of succession; it was not used in any doctrinal or technical sense. In fact, the term *khalīfa* was not the focal point.
- The plurality and diversity of views was expressed naturally.

Changing conditions of legitimacy

In Ibn Qutayba's narrative, the argument goes as follows: The Quraysh is a powerful tribe and the people would not obey others, so the caliph must be from the Quraysh. In al-Mawardi's doctrine, on the other hand, the position of the Quraysh is supported by a *ḥadīth*. This *ḥadīth* should have been known to the Companions, and no occasion could be more relevant than the one related by Ibn Qutayba to cite that *ḥadīth*. Further, Ibn Qutayba is one of the outstanding supporters of the *ḥadīth* movement. He could not have ignored such an important *ḥadīth*, yet he did not cite it, which suggests that such a *ḥadīth* was not known in Ibn Qutayba's time. The fact that for 800 years, all the political theorists have insisted on the descent from Quraysh as the unchanging requirement for a caliph, has to do with this condition being mentioned as a *ḥadīth*. Reference to a *ḥadīth* provided more legitimacy than Ibn Qutayba's rational argument that the Quraysh were powerful enough to command obedience: 'Abbasid caliphs had virtually no power against the non-Arab military commanders who appointed and deposed these caliphs. The situation changed with the Ottomans. Neither the condition nor the *ḥadīth* is often mentioned in Ottoman political theory. Nor do modern political thinkers regard it as an essential condition (see below).

This is only one example of the changing concept of the caliphate. The concepts had to adjust with history. Debates about the caliphate erupted with some events that challenged the prevailing concepts. After the eventful Rashidun period, great debate arose during the Umayyad period, when the caliphate became hereditary and, later, when more than one caliph claimed authority. The prevailing political theories held that if there were two caliphs, one of them must be killed. However, as we noted earlier, the Fatimids established a separate caliphate in Egypt and part of Africa, and the Umayyads in Spain. During the ʿAbbasid caliphate, there were several independent Muslim kingdoms. Some requested formal recognition from the ʿAbbasid caliph, others did not. A universal caliphate was no longer the norm.

Towards the end of the ʿAbbasid caliphate, a turning point in political theory came when the jurists accepted *de facto* as *de jure*, and legitimised the political authority of the army commanders and their imposed caliphs. Al-Ghazali (1058–1111) recognises the caliph as the symbol of the supremacy of the Shariʿa, and the sultan as the holder of coercive power. He seems to suggest that the sultanate is acquired by force and the caliphate is legitimately bestowed by the sultan's delegation (*tafwīḍ*). The end of the caliphate in Baghdad and the symbolic status of the caliphs in the post-ʿAbbasid period eliminated the distinction between *de facto* and *de jure*. Ibn Jamaʿa (1241–1333), writing after the extinction of the caliphate by the Mongols, not only regarded the seizure of power as a legitimate basis for political authority, but he also attributed to the *de facto* rulers all the constitutional powers that the earlier jurists had expounded. Ibn Taymiyya (1263–1328), "seeking a more radical solution, denied the obligatory nature of the caliphate".[8] He argued that the true caliphate lasted only for 30 years.

Ibn Taymiyya called for governance based on Shariʿa (*al-siyāsa al-sharʿiyya*) – the ruler must abide by the Islamic law. As long as he does so, the people should obey him because, according to Ibn Taymiyya, the political authority has no legitimacy if the ruler does not abide by the divine law. In Ibn Taymiyya's theory, the focus of legitimacy shifts from the emphasis on election, Qurayshi origin, hereditary succession and military power to the Shariʿa. Regardless of the fact that his emphasis on Shariʿa legitimises *de facto* rule by usurpers, Ibn Taymiyya is keen to resolve a dispute on the point that Ibn ʿAqil (d. 1119), another Hanbali jurist, had begun.

Ibn ʿAqil held that governance must be based on justice (*al-siyāsa al-ʿādila*), not on oppression (*al-siyāsa al-ẓālima*). Referring to this dispute, Ibn Qayyim al-Jawziyya (d. 1350) noted that Ibn ʿAqil regarded just governance as Islamic governance. Ibn Taymiyya disagreed: *al-siyāsa al-sharʿiyya* and *al-siyāsa al-ʿādila* are two different concepts. For Ibn Taymiyya, the ideal is the *khilāfa ʿalā minhaj al-nubuwwa* (the caliphate modelled on the Prophethood) and that ideal ended with the first four caliphs. The caliphate after this period is not a true caliphate; it claims legitimacy only in the name of upholding the Shariʿa.

The above summary highlights the diversity and continuous changes in the classical concept and institution of the caliphate. The same diversity is evident in modern Muslim political thought.

The concept of caliphate in modern Muslim political thought

The weakening and the eventual abolition of the Ottoman caliphate in 1924 had a deep impact on the concept of the caliphate in modern times, perhaps more than the destruction of Baghdad.

In the eyes of the Arab nationalists, the Ottoman caliphate was already declining. Nationalist movements in the Middle East had for some time been advocating the transfer of the caliphate to the Arabs. At least three contenders for the caliphate emerged: King Fuad I in Egypt, Sharif Hussein b. ʿAli in Mecca, and the Bey of Tunis. A group of leading Azhar *ʿulamā'* discarded their allegiance to the deposed caliph, and accepted the abolition as a *fait accompli*. These *ʿulamā'* met under the chairmanship of the Shaykh al-Azhar, al-Jizawi, and the President of the Supreme Religious Court, Shaykh al-Maraghi. Apparently this group consisted of the supporters of King Fuad I. Another group of *ʿulamā'* gathered in Al-Aqsa in Palestine and supported the Sharif of Mecca. The groups in Mecca and Tunis both had the backing of the Western powers: the British were behind the Sharif of Mecca and the French were supporting the Bey. There were also other contenders for the caliphate. These competing interests and constituencies surfaced in the Caliphate Conference convened in Cairo in May 1926. They could not agree on a successor to the Ottoman Sultan ʿAbd al-Hamid II. Besides the May conference, two other congresses of the *ʿulamā'* from the Muslim world were held in 1926, one in March in Cairo and the other in July in Mecca. They too failed to agree on a successor caliph, as did a congress in Jerusalem in 1931. The Western powers, though backing rival contenders, did not seem really interested in re-establishing the caliphate either.

The impact of the abolition of the caliphate on Muslims in India was quite different. For Indian Muslims, the Ottoman caliph was the symbol of Islamic political existence. Muslims all over India were deeply shocked. The *ʿulamā'* issued fatwas against Atatürk.[9] A massive agitation, known as the Khilafat Movement (1919–24), called for the restoration of the Ottoman caliph.

The Khilafat Movement had actually started in India in 1919 to protest against the Balkanisation of the Ottoman Caliphate after the First World War. The British had assured the Indian Muslims that the Caliphate would continue: various areas in the Ottoman Empire would be independent on a linguistic basis, but the Empire itself would stay. After the war, when the division of the Ottoman Empire began, Muslims in India were disappointed. In 1919, the All India Muslim Conference held a protest rally in Lucknow and founded the Khilafat Conference. In Delhi the same year, Hindu and Muslim leaders jointly announced the Khilafat Movement. They both declared non-cooperation with the British government. A delegation of Indian Muslims, known as Khilafat Wafd, went to London in 1920 to negotiate the issue of the caliphate with the British government. The British sent the delegation to Turkey, as it would weaken Atatürk's position *vis-à-vis* the caliph, helping to contain his advances in Europe. The Ottoman Caliph received the delegation with pleasure. He hoped that he would continue to enjoy his authority over Muslims in India as their caliph even after the loss of the Empire.

Contrary to the British expectations, Mustafa Kemal gained popularity among the Muslims in India when he began defeating the Greeks. He lost this popularity when, first, in 1922, he abolished the institution of sultan and, then, in 1923, he declared Turkey secular. In March 1924, the Grand National Assembly abolished the caliphate. Consequently, the Khilafat Movement turned into a violent protest against the British as well as against Atatürk. British perception also changed: in their eyes, it was no longer a local Indian movement – it was a pan-Islamic movement for a universal caliphate.[10]

Like popular reactions, intellectual responses were also mixed and diverse; they were informed mostly by local political contexts. Some political thinkers began to review and question the popular concepts of caliphate. In Egypt, Rashid Rida, who proposed the transfer of the caliphate from the Turks to the Arabs, in 1923 restated the classical doctrine of the caliphate in a modern framework in order to bring it closer to a republican form of government. ʿAli ʿAbd al-Raziq in 1925 questioned the need for the institution of the caliphate, because, according to him, political authority was not the mission of the Prophet. In India, Muhammad Iqbal in 1924 welcomed the abolition of the caliphate, as it put an end to autocratic political authority and introduced the republican form of government in Turkey. Even a supporter of the traditional caliphate such as Abu'l Kalam Azad reconsidered tenets of the classical theory such as Qurayshi descent.

Rashid Rida

Rashid Rida[11] (1865–1935) wrote *Al-Khilafa aw al-Imama al-Uzma* (The Caliphate or the Supreme Imamate) in 1923, before the abolition of the caliphate, but after the break-up of the Ottoman Empire, when its demise was imminent. He reformulated the medieval Muslim jurists' doctrine of the caliphate, responding to local political needs. Rida's political theory added the following elements to the classical formulation: 1) the idea of a spiritual caliphate, 2) the need for the political independence of Islam and 3) the promotion of a democratic consultative system of government under a modernised Shariʿa. He argued that an ideal caliphate fulfilling all the classical conditions was not feasible. He revised several of the classical conditions, such as capacity for *ijtihād* and Qurayshi descent; added new concepts, such as the republic; and gave new meanings to classical institutions, such as *shūrā* (consultation) and *ahl al-ḥall wa al-aqd* (those who bind and unbind). The former was reinterpreted to mean a democratic form of government, and the latter to signify limitations on the powers of the caliph and distinguish his rule from monarchy (*mulk*). In Rida's theory, Shariʿa and *ijtihād* bestowed Islamic identity on a modern republican form of government (a rulership with restricted powers).

ʿAli ʿAbd al-Raziq

ʿAli ʿAbd al-Raziq[12] (1888–1966), a teacher and Shariʿa judge, argued that the Caliphate was not essential in Islam, nor, for that matter, was political authority and the state. His main work, *Al-Islam wa Usul al-Hukm* (Islam and the Foundations of Governance), was first published in 1925, soon after the abolition of the Ottoman caliphate. ʿAbd al-Raziq's main argument is that the two main sources of Islamic law (Shariʿa), the Qurʾan and the Sunna, neither demand nor reject the rule of a *khalīfa* (caliphate) or *imām* (imamate). Analysing the role of the Prophet Muhammad, he argued that his was essentially the mission of a prophet, not of a political ruler. "The Prophet's leadership was religious and came as a result of his message and nothing else. His message ended with his death as did his leadership role."[13] The Islamic *umma* is spiritual and bears no relation to politics or forms of government. The Prophet did establish the *umma*, but he never mentioned or proclaimed a specific form of government. Like the Muʿtazila, he regarded the caliphate or political authority as accidental and contingent.

ʿAli ʿAbd al-Raziq's theory triggered a heated intellectual and political debate in Egypt. His thesis was strongly denounced by the Egyptian Higher Council of ʿUlamaʾ, who expelled him from al-Azhar. Several books were written refuting his thesis and insisting on the centrality of the caliphate in Islamic political thought. A more compelling reason for anger against Raziq's theory may have been that, denying the necessity of a caliph in Islam, it undercut King Fuad's claim to the title of caliph, which was endorsed by the leading *ʿulamāʾ* at al-Azhar. Rida's political theory, although proposing republicanism, was not so threatening.

Muhammad Iqbal

Muhammad Iqbal (1876–1938) is one of the few Muslim thinkers who supported the abolition of the caliphate in 1924. He did not join the above-mentioned Khilafat Movement in India. In his long poem *Tulu' Islam* (the rise of Islam), presented at a public meeting in Lahore on 30 March 1923,[14] he welcomed the political changes under Atatürk as a renaissance of Islam. He compared the Ottoman caliph with the stars that had to disappear before the dawn could break. The next year, on 13 December 1924, a few months after the abolition of the caliphate, Iqbal read his paper "al-Ijtihad fi'l-Islam" at a public meeting at the Islamia College Lahore.[15] This paper dealt in detail with the changing concepts of the caliphate. Iqbal discussed three issues relating to the caliphate: 1) the state and the form of government, 2) Islam and nationalism or the nation-state and 3) secularism. He referred to the Turkish Grand Assembly's act of abolishing the caliphate saying,

> Let us see how the Grand National Assembly has exercised this power of Ijtihad in regard to the institution of Khilafat. The first question that arises in this connection is this – Should the Caliphate be vested in a single person? Turkey's Ijtihad is that according to the spirit of Islam the Caliphate or Imamate can be vested in a body of persons, or an elected Assembly.[16]

Iqbal supported this decision, saying,

> Personally I believe that the Turkish view is perfectly sound. It is hardly necessary to argue this point. The republican form of government is not only thoroughly consistent with the spirit of Islam, but has also become a necessity in view of the new forces that are set free in the world of Islam.[17]

Iqbal was convinced that political sovereignty was vested in the Muslim *umma*. The foundation of law-making in Islam was laid down on the principle of *ijmā'*, the consensus of the majority of the *umma*. In the paper "Islam and the Islamic Caliphate" (1908), he argued that political sovereignty belonged to the Muslim people, not to a specific individual.[18] In another paper, "Islam as an Ethical and a Political Ideal", he had concluded, "Democracy, then, was the most important aspect of Islam as a political ideal."[19] His support for Turkish republicanism was the result of a long and sustained deliberation on the issue.

Iqbal believed that the universal caliphate was no longer possible. He developed his argument by analysing Islamic political theories, finding that Muslim thought held four different views on the universal caliphate. The Khawarij did not consider *khilāfa* a universal institution. In fact, they believed that there was no need for such an institution. The Mu'tazila accepted the universal caliphate as a matter of expediency only. The majority of the Sunnis believed that the universal caliphate was a religious necessity. The Shi'a believed in the divine nature of the Imamate.[20] In

Iqbal's view, modern Turkey had shifted to the view of the Mu'tazila.[21] He summed up the Turkish argument as follows:

> [O]ur past political experience [...] points unmistakably to the fact that the idea of Universal Imamate has failed in practice. It was a workable idea when the Empire of Islam was intact. Since the break-up of this Empire independent political units have arisen. The idea has ceased to be operative and cannot work as a living factor in the organisation of modern Islam. Far from serving any useful purpose it has really stood in the way of a reunion of independent Muslim States. [...] And all these ruptures in Islam for the sake of a mere symbol of power which departed long ago.[22]

Iqbal further explained that secularism in Turkey did not mean abandoning Islam. It was so understood because it was seen in the European framework of the separation of church and state. The idea of the separation of church and state is not alien to Islam. The difference between the European and Islamic frameworks of separation is that in Islam it is a division of functions, while in Europe it involved a metaphysical dualism of spirit and matter.[23]

Abu'l Kalam Azad

Abu'l Kalam Azad (1888–1958) was foremost among the leaders of the Khilafat Movement in India. For him, it symbolised a protest movement against the British, who had betrayed the Muslims in weakening the Ottomans. He wrote a small book, *Mas'ala Khilafat*, before the Ottoman caliphate was abolished.[24] Compared with Rashid Rida's work, Azad was not supporting a modern republican system. He formulated his discussion within the framework of classical theory, but since he was supporting the Ottomans, contrary to the Arab nationalists, he developed a thorough critique of that theory, particularly with reference to the qualification of Qurayshi descent. Most of the points in his theory were overtaken by the abolition and there is no need to go into details. However, his critique of the Quraysh requirement is quite interesting on account of his criticism of the classical sources.[25]

Azad explained that the idea of restricting the caliphate to the descent of a particular tribe or family goes against the teachings of Islam. He offers a detailed criticism of the sayings attributed to the Prophet on this point. His main observation is that, even if they are accepted as sound statements, they are not prescriptive. They are either statements of fact or predictions. *Ḥadīth* such as "the masses follow the Quraysh", reported in Bukhari and Muslim, are general statements about the position of the Quraysh among the Arab tribes and do not mention it as a qualification for the caliph. *Ḥadīth* such as "there will be twelve Amirs, all from the Quraysh", reported by Bukhari on the authority of Jabir b. Samra, are simple predictions about the future. They are not prescriptive. Further, such *ḥadīth* as "the Amirs are/will be from the Quraysh", reported by Bukhari, are conditional statements saying that this will continue as long as they abide by the religion of Islam. These *ḥadīth*, according to Azad, clarify that adherence to religion, rather than descent, is the real qualification for political authority. The fact that Muslim jurists and theologians have been defending descent as a qualification for a caliph suggests that this prescription remained disputed.

Azad's position is the one now generally accepted among modern Muslim movements seeking to reestablish the universal caliphate. Not even the radical revivalists of Hizb al-Tahrir, or like-minded thinkers such as Dr Israr Ahmad in Pakistan, consider Qurayshi descent an essential condition.

Hizb al-Tahrir

Taqi al-Din al-Nabhani (1909–77) founded Hizb al-Tahrir, a controversial revolutionary party, in Jerusalem in 1953. Hizb al-Tahrir portrays itself as a political party based on Islamic principles, aiming at the revival of the state of the Islamic caliphate. The following account of the caliphate is drawn from pamphlets published by the party.[26] According to al-Nabhani, the revival of the caliphate is the primary objective, because Muslims are obliged to obey all the Islamic injunctions and they are bound to the authority of divine revelation; this obedience is not possible until an Islamic state is established and there is a caliph who enforces Islam on the people.

The Hizb defines *khilāfa* as a general leadership for the entire Muslim community in the world to establish Islamic law and to carry the call of Islam to the whole world. The establishment of a caliph is a collective duty of all Muslims. The source of this obligation is said to be Sunna and *ijmāʿ*. A caliph is established by a voluntary *bayʿa* (oath of allegiance), but once a caliph is chosen, the others must take another oath to obey him. The first *bayʿa* is the oath of caliphal contract; the second is the oath of obedience. The caliph must be a male, adult, sane, just and free Muslim. In contrast to the classical theory that prescribed the capacity for *ijtihād*, valiance and descent from the Quraysh as essential qualifications for a caliph, the Hizb no longer considers them necessary. Hereditary rule is forbidden. The Hizb is vague about the definition, qualification and composition of the group that elects the caliph, which may consist of as few as three people, and need not conform to the traditional juristic idea of *ahl al-ḥall wa al-ʿaqd*. It neither requires nor rejects modern forms of election and voting.

The Hizb has adopted several modern concepts, such as the political party, revolution and global unity as the meaning of universal caliphate. *Khilāfa*, according to the Hizb, is a political system within the ideological framework of Islam that enshrines: the rule of law, representative government, and accountability to the people through an independent judiciary and the principle of representative consultation.

The highest executive post is that of the *khalīfa*, who appoints ministers without portfolio and governors for the various regions. The legislative sources are the Qur'an and sayings of the Prophet Muhammad; the particular interpretation of these sources adopted by the *khalīfa* must be justified before an independent judiciary, which has the power to remove him from his post should he flagrantly deviate from the boundaries of credible legal interpretation (*ijtihād*). The Hizb al-Tahrir asserts that consultation is one of the pillars of government and is best served by the establishment of representative councils composed of men and women from all religions and ethnic groupings within the state.

Israr Ahmad

Dr Israr Ahmad (1932–) was associated with Jama'at Islami until 1957; in 1975, he founded his own Tanzim Islami in Lahore, Pakistan. He says that he was greatly influenced by Hizb al-Tahrir. He argues that the mission of the Prophet Muhammad was to establish the supremacy of the true religion (*dīn ḥaqq*), and that in history, the real caliphate was that of the Rashidun (the first four caliphs); what we call caliphate in the later periods is in fact monarchy (*mulukiyya*).[27]

Dr Israr describes the following as elements of the concept of *khilāfa*: 1) sovereignty of God, with man as God's deputy on earth; 2) authority of the masses: all mankind is deputy of God, but only Muslims qualify for the caliphate; 3) *khilāfa* is no longer individual and personal, only the prophets were personal deputies. The Qur'an does not provide any political or economic structure; it gives only some principles and some rules.[28] The presidential system is closer to *khilāfa rāshida*;[29] it is better than the parliamentary system. Any political system can be transformed into a caliphate by introducing the following three principles: the sovereignty of God, the prohibition of legislation which is repugnant to the Qur'an and Sunna (a parliament can legislate within these limits) and the negation of mixed nationalism (i.e. the notion that Muslims and Hindus are part of the same nation – for Dr Israr, non-Muslims are a protected minority). A method of voting and election may be adopted:[30]

> The Qur'anic verse prescribes obedience to the executive (*uli'l-amr*) but does not clarify the method of his appointment. The wisdom of this omission is that we can choose the best feasible method in accordance with our cultural conditions and social evolution. However, one thing is made clear: that this person must be from amongst you and not from others. Second, this appointment must be made by consultation.[31]

As the cases of Hizb al-Tahrir and Dr Israr Ahmad suggest, the Islamists exploit the failure of the various political and economic systems to solve society's problems. They simplify the Muslim world's problems into a struggle between religious and secular forces. On this basis some Islamists justify their call for universal *khilāfa* saying that it is an authentic solution against secularism and modernity. It is, however, significant that other Islamist thinkers (e.g. Mawdudi and Qutb) often do not use the term *khilāfa*. They prefer to use other terms, like "Islamic state". They condemn secularism as *lā-dīniyya* (infidelity) and *jāhiliyya* (pre-Islamic ignorance). The Islamic state is defined in modern political language, employing terms such as democracy or theo-democracy, with the stress on two elements: the sovereignty of God instead of the sovereignty of the people, and the supremacy of Shariʿa instead of the mere rule of law.

I need not go into the details of the diverse views and the changes adopted by various modern writers on the caliphate. It is evident that Muslim thought on this subject is neither classical nor monolithic. Quite obviously, contemporary ideas and situations have impacted its formulation. Modern Muslim thought on the caliphate has enabled Muslims to internalise such modern ideas as the state, rule of law, democracy, constitutions, elections and the division of powers between the executive, judiciary and legislature. The interdependence of caliphate and Shariʿa for the justification of political authority in Islam is very basic to Islamist thought. In order to understand what is essential and what is contingent, it is necessary to explore how change and continuity are perceived in Muslim political thought.

Perceptions of change and continuity in Islamic thought

The question of normativity, though common to both law and ethics, was dealt with differently in the two fields. In legal discourse, the normative was essentially related to authority; in ethics, it pertained to justice, reasonableness and acceptability. *Ḥukm*, a key term in early Islamic literature, is common to both law and ethics, but the sense it has of political authority in legal theory and theology differs from its meaning in substantive law. *Ḥukm* in substantive law (*fiqh*) means legal value, the classification of an act in one of five categories, ranging from the obligatory (*wājib*) via the commendable (*mandūb*), indifferent (*mubāḥ*) and reprehensible (*makrūh*), to the forbidden (*ḥarām*). In theology and legal theory, *ḥukm* is perceived as divine and hence indivisible. The jurists' concept of *ḥukm*, on the other hand, is not always divine, because it allows a space for human reason and change. The obligatory and the forbidden are given by divine revelation and therefore unchangeable, but the other three categories are based on human understanding and thus may change.

In substantive law, according to the jurists, change can be introduced by the *ulū al-amr*, a legitimate government that has the authority to raise the *mandūb* to the category of *wājib*, and lower the *makrūh* to *ḥarām*, if circumstances of society and public interest (*maṣlaḥa*) so dictate[32] (the *mubāh* are always liable to change). So, in a wider sense, *aḥkām* (plural of *ḥukm*) are changeable in *fiqh*. In juridical theology and classical political theory, on the other hand, the ruler does not have that authority. But in *uṣūl al-fiqh*, too, *ḥukm* is regarded as changeable: a fatwa based on custom and expediency changes with the change of custom and time.

In the ethical perspective, normativity is socially constructed; change is introduced largely by society. The Shariʿa is generally understood as a religious and sacred law, but, in fact, the Shariʿa developed in history as a discursive tradition. It is evident from the above analysis that it is the social construction of Shariʿa that defines what is normative, because in Islam there is no religious authority to give a final verdict. The debate on the caliphate is also a discourse; it is diversified even on the question of what constitutes the caliphate. It is through a public discourse that a consensus on normativity is developed on all matters, be they legal, ethical or political.

Normativity in Islamic political theories appears to be justified in at least three ways: first, with reference to revelation; second, to the Sunna; and third, to universality. This leads to the core issue of permanence and continuity. Muslim theologians have discussed incessantly the question of normativity with reference to revelation and reason – in particular, which of these two is normative or a source for norms. Their arguments link normativity to permanence as follows. God is permanent and unchangeable and therefore His Revelation is also unchangeable. Humans are not permanent, and so reason, being human, is not permanent either. It follows, therefore, that the Qur'an, being revelation, is unchangeable, and that its teachings are not subject to reform. Muslim jurists do not usually contest this position, but rather use the difference between reason and revelation to distinguish *fiqh* (doctrines of Muslim jurists) from Sharīʿa (the revealed laws). They argue that *fiqh* is the product of human reason and therefore cannot be permanent.

In the medieval ethical tradition, the authentic normative was defined as *kullī*, or a metaphysical universal, which does not change. Today the emphasis is not on metaphysical universality, but rather on acceptability and globalism. Today "universal" does not mean "unchangeable": what is globally accepted is universal.

I want to emphasise that in Islamic thought, there has been more emphasis on continuity than on change. In medieval ethics, change is considered something defective. Because of that, all the changes were absorbed as if everything was continuous. I have argued how diverse practices in the appointment of a caliph came to be accepted as continuity, and how a continuous practice came to be regarded as unchangeable Sunna.

In the juridical theology formulated by Imam Shafiʿi, this continuity was achieved through the concept of Sunna; the unchangeable was defined as the Sunna, which conforms to the Qurʾanic text, the Sunna of the Prophet especially. For juridical theology, changeable matters were controlled by the methods of *qiyās* (analogy) and *ijmāʿ* (consensus), which connected them to, and lent them continuity with, the Qurʾan and Sunna. So if anything is derived through *qiyās* or accepted through *ijmāʿ*, it becomes unchangeable, because it is connected with the text. Thus normativity in juridical thought was defined as connectivity and continuity with the scriptural text. Juridical thought nevertheless recognises the possibility of change by taking into account social acceptability through *ijmāʿ* and the exercise of human reason through *qiyās*. *Uṣūl al-fiqh* also recognised the ethical perspectives of *maʿrūf* (what is reasonable and customary) and *maṣlaḥa* (public interest).

Unlike the above, the method of *maqāṣid al-sharīʿa* (the intention of law), which became popular in the fourteenth century and later, does not focus on the text, *qiyās* and *ijmāʿ*, but rather stresses the notion of acceptability and universality. The significance of this method has become clear to modern Muftis who deal with the problems of changeability. Abu Ishaq al-Shatibi (d. 1388), who systematised this theory, talks about *maqāṣid* which are universal, he states that they are "recognised by all people" (*muraʿan fī kullī milla*). This goes beyond Islamic tradition, which does not recognise the practices of non-Muslim societies as normative. Acceptance by society, not only by the *ʿulamāʾ*, becomes central. That is why he talks about custom (*ʿāda*, *ʿurf*) and *maṣlaḥa*.

Shatibi defines *maṣlaḥa* as "that which concerns the subsistence of human life, human livelihood, and that which emotional and intellectual faculties require of human beings in an absolute sense".[33] Shatibi's definition clearly defines *maṣlaḥa* as an individual self-interest. Communicative action can easily turn this individual interest into a "common good", because *maṣlaḥa* is a commonly shared self-interest, and individuals can easily develop an overlapping consensus by discussing these interests among themselves.

Shatibi explained that *ʿādāt* (social customs and practices) defined what was good and evil in human experience, and that the Shariʿa endorsed that social understanding. He elaborated that *maṣlaḥa* did not exist in a pure and absolute form; it was always found mixed with discomfort, hardship or other painful aspects, because the world of existence is created as a combination of opposites. Human experience determines what is good or bad in view of what is predominant in a given matter or situation. If the good elements are overwhelming, it is called good. The Shariʿa endorses these criteria and confirms the findings of human reason.[34] Shatibi argued that the five basic values or norms of the Shariʿa (i.e. protection of religion, life, reproduction, property and reason) were universally recognised among all other nations.[35] Shatibi divides the Shariʿa laws into *ʿibādāt* and *ʿādāt*.

The *ʿibādāt* or ritual obligations protect religious interests, and they are beyond human reason because their goodness cannot be adjudicated by human experience. The *ʿādāt*, which represent most of the Shariʿa laws, are within the scope of human reason. Restricting the religious matters to those that cannot be rationalised by the human mind, Shatibi linked the development of law in general to the principle of *maṣlaḥa*. He entered into controversy with his contemporary fellow jurists when he supported the imposition of a tax by the Nasrid sultan in order to build a protective wall around the city of Granada. He justified this tax on the basis of the principle of *maṣlaḥa*, namely the security of the people. Other jurists opposed this tax and Shatibi's reasoning, saying that such a tax was not prescribed in the authoritative texts.[36]

Shatibi's conception, that the Shariʿa was revealed for the benefit of mankind, was an argument against those who denied any causality or any rationalisation of divine revelation; it was against the creed that good and bad stem solely from an omnipotent will. Waliullah (d. 1762) also refutes the conception of Shariʿa as the commands of a master intending only to test his slave's loyalty and sense of obedience. He argued that the Shariʿa laws were issued not merely for the sake of obedience, but have human welfare as their inherent goal.[37] He explained prophecy and the revelation of divine laws as a process of reform. The prophets examined the laws in practice. They retained most of them and reformed only those that no longer contributed to human welfare due to changes in social practice. Discussing the Islamic laws of marriage, Shah Waliullah explained that the Prophet Muhammad retained most of the pre-Islamic Arab practices such as engagement before the wedding, dower and the wedding feast. Similarly, the Prophet confirmed the pre-Islamic penal practices, which the Muslim jurists assimilated into Islamic law under the heading of *ḥudūd*.[38] Shah Waliullah stated very clearly that customs constituted the major material source of the Shariʿa. He clarified in particular the pre-Islamic Arab bases of the Qur'anic laws.

The above two examples explain the pivotal significance for the question of normativity, of understanding the Shariʿa as socially or discursively constructed. The interpretation of the Shariʿa must take into consideration the changing social norms, because the laws based on such norms must also change. Further, the new interpretations must be grounded in already accepted social norms.

Conclusion

To sum up the above discussion, the abolition of the caliphate was not as shocking to the Arab world as it was in India. There were rival contenders for the caliphate in the Arab world. In India Muslims agitated against the British because, for them, *khilāfa* symbolised Muslim unity and political power. This agitation came to an end, but the idea of *khilāfa* as a universal symbol of Muslim unity continued. However, the concept underwent several changes, and, even for those who still use this term and call for a universal Islamic caliphate, the classical formulation of this concept is no longer relevant. Several modern Muslim scholars have in fact challenged some of the elements in the classical doctrine of the caliphate.

The question of changeable and unchangeable in Islamic political thought may perhaps be better understood in terms of the social construction of the Shari'a. Communicative action or social discourse introduces self-reflection, internal criticism and external challenges, and through discussion and debate a consensus develops on the normativity, rationality and acceptability of concepts and institutions. Once something is accepted as rational and normative, it assumes the status of something permanent and unchangeable pending further consensus.

Part Four

Dialogue on New Directions

14 Can the state enforce Shari'a? – A discussion in Yogyakarta

Kari Vogt, Lena Larsen and Christian Moe

Should the state enforce the Shari'a? Whose understanding of Shari'a? Can the state enforce one law on Muslims and another on non-Muslims? More fundamentally, is it by definition even possible for the state to enforce the Shari'a?

At our workshop in Yogyakarta, Indonesia, this question kept coming up over three days of discussions, particularly between two scholars of Islamic law, Abdullahi An-Na'im and Fikret Karčić. At issue was An-Na'im's thesis (see chapter 10) that the Shari'a ceases to be Shari'a when enacted by the state. The debate was closely informed by the experiences of four different countries: Bosnia-Herzegovina, Sudan, Malaysia and Iran.[1]

Karčić, as a legal historian, related how the abolition of Shari'a courts in Bosnia (1946) had posed the question of the continuing relevance of Islamic law. The answer, he explained, was sought, first, in a differentiation between the religious, ethical and strictly legal aspects of Shari'a norms and, second, in an emphasis on the objectives and principles of the Shari'a, rather than the particular rules and sanctions. The next speaker, a Malaysian politician, effectively presented the platform of the Malaysian PAS party in her discussion of eleven principles for an Islamic government. A very different Malaysian point of view was presented by Zainah Anwar, who detailed the deleterious practical consequences for Muslim women, minorities and democratic governance of such law-making in the name of Islam as already takes place in Malaysia (see chapter 12). One participant then posed the question of whether there could be room for a plurality of laws, including an option for Muslims to live by Islamic law. Ziba Mir-Hosseini went on to note a contradiction in the PAS principles between supremacy of Shariʿa law and international standards:

Ziba Mir-Hosseini: ... The experience of democratic government originated from the West. This does not mean that we can not have our own notion of democracy, but we cannot have any form of democracy or equality before the law when pre-modern Islamic law and patriarchal and absolutist interpretations of the Shariʿa are applied. Consider what has happened in Iran. Many Islamists, who in 1979 wanted to create an Islamic utopia, by the beginning of the 1990s came to realise that this project led to *estebdad-e dini*, a religious despotism. (Mehdi Bazargan – a prominent Islamic ideologue in pre-revolutionary Iran, who became Prime Minister in the first government after the Revolution – termed this the worst kind of dictatorship, much more pernicious than secular despotism.) The main dilemma that these Iranian Islamists had to face was the contradiction that emerged when a pre-modern interpretation of Shariʿa became the law of the land. (By the mid-1990s this led to a critique of the Islamic state from within, among a number of dissident clerics and Muslim intellectuals who came to be known as New Religious Thinkers – *now-andishan-e dini.*) They came to the conclusion that once you have Islam as a political ideology, you produce a class of official interpreters of ideology, an official Shariʿa married to power, which allows no room for practising your faith in accordance with your conscience and belief.

... They argued that democracy should come first; once democratic structures are in place, then we can discuss what the Shariʿa commands us to do and what form of government is compatible with the normative values of the Shariʿa. ...

Fikret Karčić: ... We should keep in mind that Shariʿa includes the totality of God's commands related to both religion, ethics and the legal field. It cannot be reduced to a legal system, as in the positivist understanding, of norms sanctioned by state. There are some Shariʿa norms that are not enforceable by the state at all. The addressee of the Shariʿa norms are individuals, society and sometimes, in certain matters, states.

… About plurality in the realm of law, … whether, in one country, with a Muslim population or a mixed population, there should be one uniform system, or several parallel systems. This question is related to the concept of the nation-state – in the nation-state there is a tendency to have uniform law.

In the Ottoman State, there was uniform application of law in the public sphere, and there was plurality in the private sphere. … Importantly, what was applied in the public sphere was not only Shari'a but *qānūn* as well, that is, the secular or political legislation of Muslim rulers. … For instance, some Ottoman sultans introduced fines for adultery in the form of *qānūn* and this applied to all citizens. In the form of Shari'a they could not have done so, but that was meant as a solution acceptable to both the Muslim and the non-Muslim population. … The whole concept of the *millet* system as developed in the Ottoman State was based on the legal and judicial autonomy of the non-Muslim population. … The well-known Ottoman codification of Hanafi Shari'a rules, the Mecelle, interestingly, was enforced in Palestine not only during Ottoman and British times, but also in Israel until 1972. … [T]hey simply considered it as the law of the land, even though most of the regulations were Hanafi *fiqh*. Obviously that was in accordance with the legal consciousness of the Jewish population of Israel as well.

Zainah Anwar: … The issue we are dealing with is the role of the state. In order to bring about a moral society, should the state turn sins into crimes against the state? That is what the new Shari'a criminal laws drawn up in the state of Terengganu under PAS rule have done. Indecent behaviour, indecent dress, all kinds of behaviour is regarded as an offence … If you are not doing your five daily prayers, that is an offence. A virgin woman who absconds, whatever that means, from the custody of her guardian, without a legitimate Shari'a reason, commits a criminal offence. Laws are being made in the name of Islam without considering the implications and consequences if they are implemented.

The implementation of a law on offences against the precepts of religion leads to selective prosecution, to discrimination. Who is arrested for indecent dress? Not the children of the powerful people in their spaghetti straps, but the factory girls, the young girls coming from the rural areas …

Such morality laws are just unenforceable within a framework where everyone is equal before the law and within the framework of a multicultural society: non-Muslim couples are being arrested for holding hands and are very angry that Muslims are imposing their value system and morality on them. PAS and other Islamic groups who want an Islamic state say … the laws will not affect non-Muslims. But in fact they do, because you create a whole mindset and culture …

This has already been seen in the civil judiciary, where some senior judges are scared to handle constitutional issues that could lead to conflict with Shariʿa law, the issue of freedom of religion especially. In the 1970s the Malaysian judiciary came up with decisions that basically favoured the constitutional guarantee of freedom of religion. The trend in interpretation now is that freedom of religion is a Shariʿa issue and should be dealt with under the jurisdiction of the Shariʿa court, not the civil court, even though it is guaranteed by federal law. The judges are scared, some because they do not want to be accused of allowing apostasy among Muslims, others because of fear and lack of knowledge on issues of rights in Islam …, so instead of dealing with the challenges they just throw it out and say it is under the jurisdiction of the Shariʿa court.

The issue of plurality is also problematic. We have a dual legal system in Malaysia. … When you have a plurality of laws, and one law is in the name of religion, the question is: Who decides this is what Islamic law should be? Who decides which opinion should be codified into law? …

If you have laws that do not reflect the public sense of justice, of what's right, what's fair, then these laws are not enforceable and, eventually, as in Iran, there will simply be escalating protest. In the end, if you govern in the name of Islam, then the failure of your government to deliver on the wishes of the people will be seen as the failure of Islam, of God, of Shariʿa. People are not going to draw the distinction.

Fikret Karčić: I would like to add two points. We have mentioned several times the issue of codification of Shariʿa. It is important to note that, before Muslim countries go for codification, it is necessary first to go for the reformulation of *fiqh*. Otherwise, many problems will be created. In many cases existing codifications are codifications of traditional or pre-modern *fiqh*. So reformulation or new *ijtihād* should precede codification.

Second, I don't consider the question of the authority to interpret Shariʿa a big problem, or a big question. Actually, it is the same question as in other legal systems. In English law, also, judges interpret law, not the public. The public is involved through the democratic procedure in formulating law, but, when law is formulated, experts should interpret it. I think something like that should be accepted for Muslims as well: a role for the public in formulating law, in the law-making process, but not in its interpretation and application.

Abdullahi An-Naʿim: I am from Sudan. We have been through this experience. In fact, Sudan has had a more complex experience with the Islamic state idea than Iran has. That idea has been tried and has failed, and has been seen to have failed … My position is that Shariʿa is too important to be entrusted to the state. The nature of the post-colonial, present-day state is such that it is unavoidably corrupted by and corrupting of Shari'a, when it seeks to apply it as a state instrument, a state institution.

Regarding Fikret's remark that codification can happen after reformulation of *fiqh*, I say: codification – never! Shari'a ceases to be Shari'a by the very act of enacting it as law, because it becomes the political will of the state and not the religious law of Islam. Any codification, even after a reformulation of *fiqh*, is going to be selective. The nature of *fiqh* is the diversity of opinion. A tremendous advantage of Shari'a is that it gives Muslim believers choices. You follow your conscience and you are responsible for the choices you make, but when you enact it as law to enforce it by the coercive power of the state, you are denying Muslims freedom of choice among competing opinions. …

… Law is to be enacted as public law based on public reason, reason to which all citizens can subscribe, or contest and challenge, without charges of heresy and apostasy. I have to be able to challenge a law as bad law, without that challenge reflecting on my religious belief. Otherwise you intimidate me by creating a law that I cannot resist, because of the risk of apostasy.

Fikret Karčić: … You said that Muslims should be given the possibility to choose. … Even in the past, in situations where the law was not codified, there was no such absolute freedom. You will remember that in every *fiqh* manual, the discussion always ended: "But the predominant opinion is such and such", or, "the opinion on which a fatwa will be given is such and such".

Simply, codification could mean that for a certain period of time, certain countries, upon public acceptance, may codify the predominant opinion. It doesn't mean that it is forever and cannot change. I admire the work of the Egyptian lawyer Sanhuri (1895–1971) on codification. I agree with you that public acceptance is the foundation of law … If the majority of the population opts for Shari'a, if they don't want a secular, neutral state, is it democratic to accept that?

… You said it will be difficult to define who is Muslim. Yes, that will be difficult. In Pakistan there was a famous inquiry: Who is Muslim? But the same goes for others: Who is a Jew in Israel, for the purpose of the Law of Return? Who is a Sikh in England, for the purpose of the Racial Discrimination Act? And so on. Other laws based on religion and personal application face the same problem, not only Islamic law.

The following day, in a discussion on how the Islamic Republic had imposed *ḥijāb* but had failed to inculcate it as an ideal, Mir-Hosseini again brought up An-Naim's argument that when Shari'a is applied by the state, it ceases to be Shari'a, prompting the following discussion.

Fikret Karčić: It was said that when Shariʿa is applied by state, it ceases to be Shariʿa. That is one view, but there are other views as well. I would translate Shariʿa as the Islamic normative system, a system of norms, which is related to *ʿibādāt* (rituals), to ethics and to social affairs. This system of norms is addressed to at least three categories: individuals, collectives and states or governments. We know that certain duties only individuals can perform. Even in the Islamic Republic, the government cannot go instead of individuals to the mosque and pray. Even in the Islamic Republic or any other established Islamic regime, there is still the collective duty of neighbourliness, and the collective duty to seek knowledge, what we call *kifāya* duties. Finally, no country or society can survive without organised authority, so there is a governmental responsibility …

… When talking about the application and enforcement of Shariʿa by the state, we can talk about Shariʿa being a main source or the main source of legislation. Some of the constitutions of today's Muslim countries use similar expressions, like the Egyptian one: "Islamic Shariʿa is a main source of legislation." There was discussion on whether it was the main source. So we can find different degrees of the enforcement of Shariʿa in the politico-legal system, and Shariʿa as a source of law, rather than the totality of Shariʿa being applied or imposed by the state. We know that in a number of Muslim countries, the terms *sharīʿa* and *qānūn* were always mentioned together.

… [W]hat would be the possible role of Shariʿa in Muslim society? First, legally speaking, it could be a source of legislation, and that is nothing exceptional; canon law was and still is a source of legislation in a number of Christian countries. Second, the Shariʿa also plays a role in politics, and it has a psychological significance. I think that Shariʿa could play a role in Muslim societies equivalent to that of natural law in Western societies, as a source of positive law and also a criterion for the evaluation of positive law.

Of course, the question will be what constitutes Shariʿa, what is changeable and what is unchangeable in Shariʿa; but that is another, and a very long, story.

Ziba Mir-Hosseini: I think we are talking about two different things. I am talking about the modern nation-state, a new invention. This nation-state has the power to define and implement the law, thus it can monopolise and appropriate Islamic law, Shariʿa, or whatever we call Islamic law. I see Islamic law as having developed separately from the state. *Fiqh* books and fatwas are the work of jurists, who have no power of enforcement. … Unlike Abdullahi, I do make a distinction between Shariʿa, which in Muslim belief is divine, and *fiqh*, which is the work of jurists, created in debate, and represents their attempts to interpret the Shariʿa and their understanding of the ideals. Once you cease to problematise these matters, you end up having Islamic law appropriated by the state …

Abdullahi An-Na'im: ... My proposition is not to say that we don't need the state, or that the state does not have to protect property and life and so on. The question is about the relationship between the state as an institution and Shari'a, as you correctly defined it, as the normative system of Islam. ... Whatever is enforced by the institution of the state is enforced by virtue of its political will, not by virtue of being the normative system of Islam.

Ziba's point, that the nature of the state in the post-colonial era is drastically different, it is critical, and it is well taken. However, even in the so-called classical period, and at any given point in time since Abu Bakr, it was the state that decided what law applied, not some sort of autonomous or abstract entity called Islam. Abu Bakr, against the opinions of all the other Companions, decided to fight the *murtaddūn* who refused to pay the *jizya*, as it was derived from the political will of the state. The Companions who disagreed with Abu Bakr followed him into battle because they abided by the political will of the state, not because they were required to as a matter of Shari'a. That was not the opinion of any of the *ṣaḥāba* except Abu Bakr ... but when Abu Bakr as the *khalīfa* decided to go out and fight, the others followed because they followed the Caliph, they did not want *fitna*.

The debate naturally carried over into the Public Forum held on the last day of the meeting, where Abdullahi An-Na'im and Fikret Karčić were scheduled to speak on "Shari'a, state and society", and Ziba Mir-Hosseini and Zainah Anwar on "gender issues".

Abdullahi An-Na'im: ... My point is that the state cannot, and has never been able to, enforce Shari'a. The idea of an Islamic state is incoherent, it is a contradiction in terms. A state does not have a conscience and does not believe ...

... There is some argument about the distinction between Shari'a and *fiqh*. ... Any understanding of Shari'a or any understanding of *fiqh* is a product of human interpretation. Whether it is *fiqh* or Shari'a, it is a product of human agency, of human thinking, interpretation, practice and experience ... Not only our understanding of Shari'a is human and our understanding of *fiqh* is human, but the boundary made between the two is also human. Any claim that "this is the boundary between Shari'a and *fiqh*" or that Shari'a is permanent and *fiqh* temporary, itself is a product of human thinking, and as such it can be challenged. ... For me, therefore, the question has to be how to keep the conditions where persons can challenge opposing views of Shari'a or *fiqh* without suffering negative consequences ... [W]hether it is Shari'a or *fiqh*, it cannot be enacted and remain the same. Once you enact it as positive law, ... [i]t is the political will of the state, that is, of those who control the state ...

The process of state policy formulation and legal enactment in the modern post-colonial state has to be selective, so you have to choose among competing views of Muslim scholars on what Shari'a is, or what the *fiqh* elaboration is on any given issue. We know that for every single conceivable question, Muslim scholars have disagreed fundamentally – I am talking about *mu'āmalāt*, not doctrine, though even in *'ibādāt* and doctrine there are differences. ... A recent example from Nigeria is the question of accepting pregnancy as proof of *zinā'* (adultery). That type of proof is accepted by the Maliki school in Nigeria, but not by any of the other Sunni schools.

... Our understanding of Islam, whatever it is, wherever we are, is absolutely central to the core of our identity as Muslims. It will be extremely important in our public policy, in our legal and ethical reflection. The point is simply that the state has no business enforcing any human understanding of Islam as positive law, but the community has every right to live by it in its own institutions away from the state. (However, community compliance cannot be allowed to violate the fundamental rights of any person, whether a member of that community or not. There is no right to violate the rights of others. That is why I insist on the supremacy of the constitution and requirement of public reason for any rule or policy that is enforced by state institutions, or allowed by the state to be "enforced" by community institutions.)

The nature of our tradition is that it defies centralisation and institutionalisation. How Shari'a evolved, and how *fiqh* evolved was a spontaneous, consensus-based, intergenerational process. We do not have a Vatican *al-ḥamdu li'llāh* (thanks be to God). ... I say that Islamic jurisprudence is radically democratic, because it does not permit the possibility of anyone interfering between the believer and the Qur'anic or *ḥadīth* text, nor between the experience and choice of that believer ...

Fikret Karčić: ... Abdullahi An-Na'im has said that throughout history, Muslim scholars have disagreed on every single issue. Now you may see an example of that.

First, I wish to clarify some terms. I would go for differentiation between Shari'a and *fiqh*. I understand Shari'a as divine law, God's law ... *Fiqh* is understanding, the human understanding of Shari'a. I go for a difference between Shari'a and *fiqh* even though, sometimes, borders are not clear. In other laws, too, we have similar differences ... For example, in Roman law, there is a very clear difference between *lex*, which is law, and *iuris prudentia*, which is the science of law, the study of law, or the understanding of law ...

Second, I agree that Shari'a has a future. As my colleague said, the future of Shari'a will be to be linked with the community, not with the state; it will be kept – guarded – by the community. If that is the future, I come from the future, because in Bosnia we have such a situation. In Bosnia there are no Shariʿa courts, the state does not enforce Shariʿa, but there is an organised Muslim community, we call it the Islamic Community. … We have discussed the issue of what the Shariʿa means to us for the last 50 years. We say that for us, the Shariʿa is a religious and ethical code. That is the situation we have in my homeland, but I will not exclude, in the future, other possibilities as well, because we can never exclude something happening in the future.

Also, there was a thesis which challenged enforcement of Shariʿa by the state. My colleague is talking from the viewpoint of a visionary, a reformist. By education, I am a historian of law. … I cannot deny the enforcement of Shariʿa by the state in the past, because I went to archives, I studied *sijills* (registers of the Shariʿa courts) and I found hundreds of them. So Shariʿa was applied by the state.

What do we mean by application of the Shariʿa? Very often we use the term very narrowly. The term *tatbīq*, application, has at least three meanings. First, it is behaviour according to a rule. Shariʿa was not revealed to make punishments for people but to direct people to the right path. When we behave according to a *ḥukm sharʿī*, we apply Shariʿa … The second meaning of 'application' is to apply a general rule to a specific case, to relate law to a specific case. The third meaning is the application of sanctions by some authority. Today when people talk about application of Shariʿa, very often they mean only application of sanctions, of punishments, but that is not true – that is a very reductionist approach.

… Even in a state where Islam is enforced, each of us as a Muslim will be obliged to go to pray, to fast, to give *ṣadaqa*, to go for *hajj*; the state cannot do that instead of us. But what the state can do is to ensure conditions for performing religious duties, to have conditions, to have freedoms, to have justice, to have economic opportunities to work and to live as Muslims. That is the function of the state. And the most important function of the state, as far I understand it, is to ensure justice. …

Also, I agree with what my colleague Abdullahi said, that each society chooses its own model. That is true, and that should remain true. In the Muslim world today we have different models of relations between the Shariʿa and the state. We have models where Shariʿa is proclaimed as the only source of law, in some cases as one of the sources of law, or in some cases there is no connection with law or the state at all.

Here I would like to relate what happened to me in 1990, when the Communist government fell in Bosnia. We had a meeting like this, and there was a Franciscan scholar sitting in the room and discussing with us, and he asked me a question, since I was a lecturer in the history of Islamic law: "If you Muslims obtain a majority of the population, will you ask for an Islamic state?" My answer was, "We will ask for a just state, for a state where justice will prevail." Later on, Alija Izetbegović, former President of Bosnia, but more importantly, a Muslim intellectual, wrote, "we don't want an Islamic state, we need a state where Islam will be respected." So we don't want to enforce something, but we also don't want to be suppressed. We want to be free and to have freedom of choice and freedom to exercise our religion.

Is it correct that … Shariʿa is no longer Shariʿa when applied by the state? Let me ask the question: When Roman law was applied by the Roman state, did it cease to be Roman law? When English law is applied by the English state, does it cease to be English law? It is the same question in every other legal system.

Similarly, when we talk about Shariʿa and *fiqh*, this difference is important. It is important to know what is unchangeable in Islamic law, in the Islamic normative system, and what is changeable. *Fiqh* refers to what is changeable. … It is not just Muslims who differentiate in this sense. In Jewish law there is Torah and there is *halakha*, which is understanding of Torah. In French law there is the difference between *donné* and *construit*, what is given and what is interpreted. What is given is unchangeable, what is interpreted is changeable and should be changeable …

I completely agree that the evolution of *fiqh*, the development of *fiqh*, was a spontaneous, intergenerational process. Historical reports prove that. *Fiqh* was developed by scholars, individual scholars or groups of scholars, divorced from the state power … So it is true, really, that Islamic jurisprudence is radically democratic, and it possesses its own internal mechanism for finding out what is truth and what is not. When we deal with normative disciplines, … there is only one way to know what is the true interpretation and what is not, and that is consensus … The only way is to have competent scholars, coming from different parts of the world or areas, and if they agree that a certain interpretation is correct, then we accept that as correct. We know that in Islam, the result of each *ijtihād* was *ẓannī*, probable, but when *ijmāʿ* was achieved, it became *qaṭʿī*, even though that could later be revisited.

Abdullahi An-Naʿim: My brother Fikret asked: Does Roman law cease to be Roman law, does English law cease to be English law when enforced by the state? The point is that Roman law and English law are secular laws. Roman law is made by people, and if enforced by people, it is the same law. But we claim that Shariʿa is divine, and if the state enforces it, it is no longer the divine law. It becomes human understanding of the divine law. So there is a difference between Roman and English law and all of these other laws, and Shariʿa …

When it is proposed to enact a principle of Shariʿa as law, we do not call it Shariʿa, we call it law. Naming it makes a difference. If we call it law, then I can change it and challenge it, just like Roman law and English law, without being called a heretic. But if we call it Shari'a, it becomes difficult, if not impossible, for a Muslim to challenge.

Fikret Karčić: … The Ottomans found the following solution: the draft *qānūn* (legislation of the ruler) would sent to the Shaykh al-Islam, the Mufti in Istanbul, who would approve it, usually with the formulation "in accordance with the noble Shari'a". This was not always functional, because you can imagine that the Shaykh al-Islam would need a lot of personal courage and integrity to tell the powerful Grand Vizier his draft was not in accordance with Shari'a. This is what is problematic about Islamic institutions when they are linked to the state. The question is, who controls whom? In rare cases we had situations where *'ulamā'* control the government. Usually, politicians control *'ulamā'*.

The point was made that, even if we say Shari'a is divine law, we have access only through human agency. I think there is no contradiction there. Shari'a is divine law which is meant to regulate human affairs, so it is meant for us, for human beings. It is given in a language which we know, in a logic which we use, – which is accessible to us – and we have scholars who have developed tools of linguistic and logical interpretation. If we rely upon those tools we can probably be sure we have discovered the true meaning. But the whole of *fiqh* is what Bernard Weiss called "the search for God's law".[2]

Contributors

Khaled Abou El Fadl is Professor of Law at the UCLA School of Law. He has previously taught Islamic law at the University of Texas at Austin Law School, Yale Law School and Princeton University. He holds degrees from Yale University (BA), University of Pennsylvania Law School (JD) and Princeton University (MA/PhD), and also received formal training in Islamic jurisprudence in Egypt and Kuwait. Abou El Fadl serves on the Advisory Board of Middle East Watch. Previously he was on the Board of Directors of Human Rights Watch, and was appointed to the US Commission on International Religious Freedom. His most recent work focuses on issues of authority, terrorism, tolerance, Islam and Islamic law. He is the author of ten books and over 50 articles on Islamic law and Islam. His recent books include: *The Search for Beauty in Islam: A Conference of the Books* (2006), *The Great Theft: Wrestling Islam from the Extremists* (2005), *Islam and the Challenge of Democracy* (2004), *The Place of Tolerance in Islam* (2002), *Speaking in God's Name: Islamic Law, Authority and Women* (2001) and *Rebellion and Violence in Islamic Law* (2001).

Kecia Ali has a PhD in Religion from Duke University and is Assistant Professor of Religion at Boston University, where she teaches classes that explore the diversity and complexity of Muslim experience in both classical and modern periods. Her research interests centre on Islamic religious texts, especially jurisprudence and women in both historical and contemporary Muslim discourses. She is the author of *Sexual Ethics and Islam: Feminist Reflections on Qur'an, Hadith, and Jurisprudence* (2006), the co-author with Oliver Leaman of *Islam: The Key Concepts* (2007), and is completing a book on marriage and spousal rights in ninth-century jurisprudence. She is also working on a biography of the jurist al-Shafi'i. Before beginning her current appointment at Boston University, Ali was a research associate in the Women's Studies in Religion Program at Harvard Divinity School and held a Florence Levy Kay Postdoctoral Fellowship at Brandeis University.

Abdullahi An-Na'im is Charles Howard Candler Professor of Law at Emory University, Atlanta, USA. He is the author of *Islam and the Secular State: Negotiating the Future of Shari'a* (2008), *African Constitutionalism and the Contingent Role of Islam* (2006) and *Toward an Islamic Reformation: Civil Liberties, Human Rights and International Law* (1990). His edited publications include *Human Rights under African Constitutions* (2003), *Islamic Family Law in a Changing World: A Global Resource Book* (2002) and *Human Rights in Cross-Cultural Perspectives: Quest for Consensus* (1992). He has also published more than 50 articles and book chapters on human rights, constitutionalism, Islamic law and politics. Translations of his more recent book manuscript, "Islam and the Secular State", into eight languages of Islamic societies can be downloaded from the website http://www.law.emory.edu/fs.

Zainah Anwar was the Executive Director of Sisters in Islam (SIS), a nongovernmental organisation working on the rights of Muslim women within the framework of Islam. She now serves on the SIS Board of Directors and is Project Director of Musawah, a global initiative for equality and justice in the Muslim family. Sisters in Islam, founded in 1987, is at the forefront of the women's movement which seeks to end discrimination against women in the name of religion, carrying out activities in research, legal services and advocacy, public education and capacity-building at the national and international levels. Her other work experience includes: Chief Programme Officer, Political Affairs Division, at the Commonwealth Secretariat, London; Senior Analyst in the Institute of Strategic and International Studies, Kuala Lumpur; Political and Diplomatic Writer for *The New Straits Times*, Kuala Lumpur; Member of Human Rights Commission of Malaysia and as a freelance writer. Her book *Islamic Revivalism in Malaysia: Dakwah Among the Students* has become a standard reference in the study of Islam in Malaysia. She was educated at the Fletcher School of Law and Diplomacy, Boston University and the MARA Institute of Technology, Malaysia, in the fields of international relations and journalism.

Asma Barlas is a Professor of Politics and Director of the Center for the Study of Culture, Race, and Ethnicity at Ithaca College, New York. She has a PhD in International Studies (University of Denver), an MA in Journalism (University of the Punjab, Pakistan) and a BA in English Literature and Philosophy (Kinnaird College for Women, Pakistan). Her recent research has focused on Islam and, in particular, on how Muslims interpret and live it. In "Believing Women" in Islam: Unreading Patriarchal Interpretations of the Qur'an (2002), she proposed a Qur'anic hermeneutic that allows Muslims to argue on behalf of sexual equality and against patriarchy from within an Islamic framework. Her other publications include Islam, Muslims, and the U.S.: Essays on Religion and Politics (2004) and Democracy, Nationalism, and Communalism: The Colonial Legacy in South Asia (1995). She is currently studying Christian–Muslim encounters from a theological and a historical perspective with a view to analysing their views on difference (Otherness).

Aïcha El Hajjami holds a doctorate in Public Law (doctorat de troisième cycle) from the Paris II Faculty of Law. She taught at the Public Law departments of the Law faculties of Fès and Marrakech (1978–2005), and is the author of numerous studies in the field of women's political and legal rights. She is a founding member of the Centre d'Etudes et de Recherche sur la Femme et la Famille at the Faculty of Law in Marrakech, and is a consultant to various national and international bodies.

Mohsen Kadivar, a leading intellectual of the Islamic reform movement in Iran, was born in 1959. He obtained the degree of Ijtihad (the highest level in Islamic Studies) from Grand Ayatollah H. A. Montazeri in Qom Seminary in 1997, and a PhD in Islamic Philosophy and Theology from Tarbiat-e Modarres University (Tehran) in 1999. He was sentenced by the Special Court for Clergy to 18 months in prison because of his political criticism of the Islamic Republic, and was released in July 2000. In 2007, he was forced to leave his post as Associate Professor at the Department of Philosophy and Wisdom in Tarbiat Modarres University and then took a position at the Research Center of the Iranian Institute of Philosophy. Kadivar has published 13 books and more than 100 papers on Islamic philosophy, theology, law and political thought.

Mohammad Hashim Kamali is the founding Chairman and CEO of the International Institute of Advanced Islamic Studies (IAIS). He studied in England from 1969 to 1976 and obtained an LLM and a PhD in Law from the University of London. Kamali was Professor of Islamic Jurisprudence at the International Islamic University Malaysia, and also Dean of ISTAC from 1985 to 2007. He was previously Assistant Professor at the Institute of Islamic Studies, McGill

University in Canada; he was a Visiting Professor at the Capital University, Ohio and also at the Institute for Advanced Study (Wissenschaftskolleg) of Berlin. He was a member of the Constitution Review Commission of Afghanistan (2003). He served as a UN expert on constitutional reform in the Maldives (2004). He advised on the new constitution of Iraq (2004-5) and is currently on the UN Alliance of Civilisations Global Experts panel. He now serves on the boards of 13 local and international academic journals. Kamali has addressed over 130 national and international conferences, and he has published 17 books and over 140 academic articles.

Lena Larsen is a Research Fellow at the Norwegian Center for Human Rights, University of Oslo, studying the development of Islamic legal thought in Western Europe. She has been Co-ordinator of the Oslo Coalition, associate editor of *Facilitating Freedom of Religion or Belief: A Deskbook* (2004) and a former Chair of the Islamic Council in Norway.

Muhammad Khalid Masud holds a PhD in Islamic Studies from McGill University, 1973) is the Chairman of the Council of Islamic Ideology, Islamabad; and formerly Professor and Academic Director of the International Institute for the Study of Islam in the Modern World (ISIM), Leiden, The Netherlands. He has published extensively on Islamic law, contemporary issues and trends in Muslim societies. His publications include *Shatibi's Philosophy of Islamic Law* (1995) and *Iqbal's Reconstruction of Ijtihad* (1995); he has edited *Islamic Laws and Women in the Modern World* (1996) and *Travelers in Faith: Studies on Tablighi Jama'at* (2000), co-edited *Islamic Legal Interpretation: The Muftis and their Fatwas* with Brinkley Messick and David Powers (1996) and *Dispensing Justice in Islam: Qadis and their Judgments* with David S. Powers and Ruud Peters (2006) and translated into Urdu T. Izutsu's *Ethical Terms in the Qur'an* (2005).

Ziba Mir-Hosseini is an independent consultant, researcher and writer on Middle Eastern issues, specialising in gender, family relations, Islamic law and development. A Senior Research Associate at the London Middle Eastern Institute, SOAS, University of London, she obtained her BA in Sociology from Tehran University (1974) and her PhD in Social Anthropology from the University of Cambridge (1980). She has held numerous research fellowships and visiting professorships, most recently: Fellow at the Wissenschaftskolleg zu Berlin (2004–5) and Hauser Global Law Visiting Professor at the School of Law, New York University (alternate years since 2002). Her publications include *Marriage on Trial: A Study of Islamic Family Law in Iran and Morocco* (1993, 2002), *Islam and Gender: The Religious Debate in Contemporary Iran* (1999, 2000) and with Richard Tapper *Islam and*

Democracy in Iran: Eshkevari and the Quest for Reform (2006). She has also directed with Kim Longinotto two award-winning feature-length documentary films on contemporary issues in Iran: *Divorce Iranian Style* (1998) and *Runaway* (2001).

Christian Moe is an independent researcher based in Slovenia. He writes on Islam, human rights and religious affairs in the Balkans.

Tariq Ramadan is Professor of Islamic Studies. He holds an MA in Philosophy and French Literature and a PhD in Arabic and Islamic Studies from the University of Geneva, and has trained in classic Islamic scholarship under al-Azhar University scholars. He is currently Research Fellow at St Antony's College (Oxford), Doshisha University (Kyoto, Japan) and at the Lokahi Foundation (London) and is Visiting Professor of Identity and Citizenship at Erasmus University (Holland), as well as President of the European think-tank European Muslim Network (EMN) in Brussels. He is active both at the academic and grassroots levels, lecturing extensively throughout the world on social justice and dialogue between civilisations. His recent publications include *In the Footsteps of The Prophet: Lessons from the Life of Muhammad* (2007), *Les Musulmans d'Occident et l'Avenir de l'Islam* (2003), in English as *Western Muslims and The Future of Islam* (2004), *Peut-on vivre avec l'islam ? Entretien avec Jacques Neirynck* (2004) and *Globalisation: Muslim Resistances* (2003). His *To be a European Muslim* (1999) has been translated into 14 languages.

Nazife Şişman gained her BA degree in Economics from Bosphorus University and did postgraduate studies in Sociology. She works as a freelance writer, translator and social worker. Her writing interests centre on women's issues in the Muslim experience of the modern period. Her recent work *Günün Kısa Tarihi (Short History of the Present)* (2008) deals with the question of practising faith in a secular world. She is completing a book on the socio-politics of the headscarf issue in Turkey. Her publications include: *Global Konferanslarda Kadın Politikaları (Women's Politics in Global Conferences)* (1996), *Emanet'ten Mülk'e: Kadın, Beden, Siyaset (Women, Body and Politics]* (2003), *Küreselleşmenin Pençesi İslam'ın Peçesi (Pawn of Globalisation, Veil of Islam)* (2005). Her translations from English to Turkish include Martin Lings' *The Life of the Prophet*, Seyyid Hossein Nasr's *An Introduction to Islamic Cosmological Doctrines*, Mawdudi's *Tefhim'ül Qur'an*, Amina Wadud's *Qur'an and Woman* and Sachico Murata's *The Tao of Islam* (soon to be published).

Abdolkarim Soroush was born in Tehran in 1945. He obtained degrees in pharmacy and analytical chemistry, before going on to study the history and philosophy of science at Chelsea College, London. After the Islamic Revolution, Soroush returned to Iran, where he was appointed by Ayatollah Khomeini to the Advisory Council on Cultural Revolution, charged with re-opening the universities and restructuring the syllabi. He resigned from the Council in 1983, and has since held no official position in Iran, but has been a Researcher at the Institute for Cultural Research and Studies. Dr Soroush emerged in the 1990s as one of the most prominent religious intellectuals critical of the political role played by the Iranian clergy. He co-founded the monthly *Kiyan* and his speeches circulate widely on audio tape. Harassed and censored, his lectures disrupted by hardline protesters, he lost his job. Since 2000, Abdolkarim Soroush has been a Visiting Professor at Harvard University, a scholar in residence in Yale University, and a visiting scholar at the Wissenschaftkolleg in Berlin (2003–4) and at ISIM in Leiden (2007). He also taught at Princeton University (2002–3). A selection of his writings have been published as *Reason, Freedom, and Democracy in Islam* (2000).

Kari Vogt is Associate Professor at the Department of Cultural Studies and Oriental Languages at the University of Oslo, Norway. She has published widely on Islamic and Middle East issues.

Notes

Introduction

1 Mehran Kamrava, "Introduction: Reformist Islam in Comparative Perspective", in Mehran Kamrava (ed.), *The New Voices of Islam: Reforming Politics and Modernity – A Reader* (London and New York: I.B.Tauris, 2006), pp. 1–27 at pp. 22–4.

2 For more information see the Oslo Coalition website (http://www.oslocoalition.org).

Chapter 2

1 The title borrows from 7:145. The translation of A. Yusuf Ali, *The Holy Qur'an* (New York: Tehrike Tarsile Qur'an, 1988), has been used throughout.

2 See Paul Ricoeur (John B. Thompson, trans. and ed.), *Hermeneutics and the Human Sciences* (Cambridge: Cambridge University Press, 1981), p. 145.

3 There are several Qur'anic references to time. Sura 103, entitled Time, begins: "By (the token of) Time (through the Ages)" (103:1–2).

4 For why Muslims need to historicise the Qur'an, see Fazlur Rahman, *Major Themes of the Qur'an* (Minneapolis: Bibliotheca Islamica, 1980); Asma Barlas, *"Believing Women" in Islam: Unreading Patriarchal Interpretations of the Qur'an*

(Texas: University of Texas Press, 2002), pp. 58–62.

5 Kenneth Cragg, *The Event of the Qur'an* (Oxford: Oneworld, 1994), p. 114; his emphasis.

6 Of course, as Cragg points out, content and context possess one another in the Qur'an; even so, one can historicise the Qur'an without undermining its universal nature. See Barlas, *op. cit.*

7 Amina Wadud, *Qur'an and Woman: Rereading the Sacred Text from a Woman's Perspective* (Oxford: Oxford University Press, 1999).

8 Barlas, *op. cit.*, especially chapter 2.

9 To say this is not to say that revelation is the Prophet's speech, however; rather, it remains divine discourse. See Abdullah Saeed, "Rethinking 'Revelation' as a Precondition for Reinterpreting the Qur'an", *Journal of Qur'anic Studies* 1, no. 1 (1999), pp. 93–114.

10 See the discussion below.

11 By patriarchy I mean a politics of sexual differentiation that privileges males. For a fuller description and why I define it in this way, see Barlas, *op. cit*, chapter 1.

12 Such a position assumes, of course, that there is authorial intent in the discourse.

13 This is Toshihiko Izutsu's understanding of the term *ẓulm*. Izutsu, *The Structure of Ethical Terms in the Qur'an* (Tokyo: Keio Institute of Philological Studies, 1959), p. 152.

14 See Barlas, *op. cit.*, for a full exposition.

15 I am grateful to Ulises Ali Mejias for this insight and wording.

16 See Asma Barlas, "Women's and Feminist Readings of the Qur'an", in Jane McAuliffe (ed.), *The Cambridge Companion to the Qur'an* (Cambridge: Cambridge University Press, 2006), pp. 255–71.

17 I borrow this phrase from Paulo Freire, *Pedagogy of the Oppressed* (New York: Continuum, 2000).

Chapter 3

1 Cf. Muʿtaz al-Khatib, "al-Wazifa al-Maqasadiyya: Mashruʿiyatuha wa Ghayatuha", in IIUM, *Maqasid al-Shariʿa wa Subul Tahqiqiha* (Conference Proceedings, Kuala Lumpur: International Islamic University Malaysia, 2006/1427), vol. 1, p. 99.

2 *Ibid.*

3 Muhammad Rashid Rida, *Tafsir al-Qurʿan al-Hakim*, 2nd ed. (Cairo: Mutbaʿat al-Manar, 1367/1956), vol. 3, p. 30.

4 Cf. ʿUbayd Allah Sindhi as quoted in Mazharuddin Siddiqi, *Modern Reformist Thought in Muslim World* (Islamabad: Islamic Research Institute, 1402/1982), pp. 78–9.

5 "Al-Murad bi-maqasid al-ghayat minha wa'al-asrar al-lati wada'aha al-shari

'inda kulli hukm min ahkamiha". 'Allal al-Fasi. *Maqasid al-Shari'a al-Islamiyya wa Makarimuha* (Casablanca: Maktabat al-Wahda al-'Arabiyya, n.d.), p. 3.

6 Muhammad Tahir Ibn 'Ashur, *Maqasid al-Shari'a al-Islamiyya* (Tunis: al-Sharikat al-Tunisiyya, 1993), p. 52. Ibn 'Ashur has replaced al-Shatibi's phrase of *al-thubūt min ghayr zawāl* with the word *al-inḍibāṭ* (constancy).

7 Ahmad al-Raysuni, *Nazariyyat al-Maqasid 'ind al-Imam al-Shatibi* (Rabat: Matba'a al-Najah, 1411/1991), p. 7: "Maqasid al-Shari'a hiya al-ghiyat al-lati wudi'at al- Shari'a li-ajli tahqiqhali-maslahat al-'ibad". Cf. the recent English translation: Ahmad al-Raysuni (Nancy Roberts, trans.), *Imam al-Shatibi's Theory of the Higher Objectives and Intents of Islamic Law* (Herndon, VA: International Institute of Islamic Thought, 2005), p. xxiii.

8 'Iwad bin Muhammad al-Qarni, *al-Mukhtasar al-Wajiz fi Maqasid al-Tashri'* (Jeddah: Dar al-Andalus al-Khudra', 1419/1998), p. 18.

9 Khalid bin Mansur al-Daris, "Athar al-Maqasid al-Shari'a fi Fahm Hadith al-Nabawi 'ind al-Imam Ibn Taymiyya", in IIUM, *Maqasid al-Shariah*, vol. 2, p. 420.

10 Al-Raysuni, *op. cit.*, p. 149.

11 Imam al-Haramayn al-Juwayni, *al-Burhan fi Usul al-Fiqh* (Abd al-'Azim al-Dib, ed.) (Doha, Qatar: Shaykh Khalifah b. Hamad al-Thani, 1399/1980), vol. 2, p. 518.

12 Abu Hamid Muhammad al-Ghazali, *al-Mustasfa min 'Ilm al-Usul* (Cairo: al-Maktabat al-Tijariyya, 1356/1957), vol. 1, p. 287. Note that al-Ghazali places religion first, but I submit that life comes first.

13 Yusuf al-Qaradawi, *Madkhal li-Dirasat al-Shari'a al-Islamiyya* (Cairo: Maktaba Wahba, 1411/1990), p. 73.

14 'Izz al-Din 'Abd al-Salam al-Sulami, *Qawa'id al-Ahkam Fi Masalih al-Anam* (Beirut: Mu'assasat al-Rayyan li'l-Taba'a wa'l-Nash, 1410/1990), vol. 1, p. 8.

15 Taqi al-Din Ahmad Ibn Taymiyya ('Abd al-Rahman b. al-Qasimi, comp.), *Majmu' Fatawa Shaykh al-Islam Ibn Taymiyya* (Beirut: Mu'assasat al-Risala, 1398/1988), vol. 32, p. 134.

16 Muhammad 'Abid al-Jabiri, *al-Din wa al-Dawla wa Tatbiq al-Shari'a* (Beirut: Markaz al-Dirasat al-Wahda al-'Arabiyya, 1996), p. 190.

17 Al-Qaradawi, *op. cit.*, p. 73.

18 Jamal al-Din 'Atiyya, *Nahw Taf'il Maqasid al-Shari'a* (Damascus: Dar al-Fikr and the International Insitute of Islamic Thought, 1422/2001).

19 Abu Ishaq Ibrahim al-Shatibi (Shaykh 'Abd Allah Diraz, ed.), *al-Muwafaqat fi Usul al-Shari'a* (Cairo: al-Maktabat al-Tijariyyat al-Kuba, n.d), vol. 2, p. 293.

20 *Ibid.*, vol. 3, p. 394.

21 *Ibid.*, vol. 2, p. 6; al-Qaradawi, *op. cit.*, p. 58; al-Jabiri, *op. cit.*, p. 173.

22 Al-Shatibi, *op. cit.*, vol. 1, p. 2453; al-Qaradawi, *op. cit*, pp. 64–5.

23 Abu Hamid Muhammad al-Ghazali, *Shifa' al-Ghalil fi Bayan al-Shubh wa'l*

Makil wa Masalik al-Ta'lil (Baghdad: Matba'at al-Irshad, 1970), p. 195.

24 Al-Shatibi, *op. cit.*, vol. 2, p. 5 and vol. 2, p. 223; see also Nur al-Din al-Khadimi, *'Ilm al-Maqasid al-Shari'a al-Islamiyyah* (Riyad: Maktabat al-'Abikan, 2001), pp. 71f.

25 'Atiyya, *op. cit.*, pp. 33f; Mohamed al-Tahir al-Messawi, "Maqasid al-Shariah: An Usuli Doctrine or Independent Discipline: A Study of Ibn 'Ashur's Project", in IIUM, *Maqasid al-Shari'a and its Realization in Contemporary Societies* (IIUM Proceedings, English volume, Kuala Lumpur: International Islamic University of Malaysia, 2006), p. 100.

26 Al-Shatibi, *op. cit.*, vol. 2, p. 400; see also al-Khadimi, *op. cit.*, p. 155.

27 Al-Shatibi, *op. cit.*, vol. 4, p. 179.

28 For details on *ḥiyal*, see M. H. Kamali, "Shariah as Understood by the Classical Jurists", *IIUM Law Journal* 6, no. 1–2 (1998), pp. 65f.

29 Cf. Riyad Mansur al-Khalifi, "Al-Maqasid al-shar'iyya wa atharuha fi al-fiqh al-mu'amalat al-maliyya", *Majalla Jami'a al-Malik 'Abdulaziz al-Iqtisad al-Islami* 17, no. 1 (1425/2004), pp. 3–48 at p. 14.

30 Al-Shatibi, *op. cit.*, vol. 2, pp. 13–14; see also al-Khalifi, *op. cit.*, p. 16.

31 See for details M. H. Kamali, *Freedom, Equality and Justice in Islam* (Cambridge: The Islamic Texts Society, 2002), chapter 4 ("Justice").

32 Cf. Wahbah al-Zuhayli, *Nazariyyat al-Darurat al-Shar'iyya*, 4th ed. (Beirut: Mu'assasat al-Risala, 1405/1985), pp. 70–1.

33 Toshihiko Izutsu, *Ethico-Religious Concepts in the Qur'an* (Montreal: McGill University Press, 1966).

34 Daud Rahbar, *God of Justice: A Study of the Ethical Doctrines of the Qur'an* (Leiden: E.J. Brill, 1960).

35 Fazlur Rahman, *Major Themes of the Qur'an* (Minneapolis and Chicago: Bibliotheca Islamica, 1980).

36 George Hourani, "Ethical Presuppositons of the Qur'an", *The Muslim World* 70, no. 1 (January 1980), pp. 1–28.

37 Cf. Toshihiko Izutsu, *God in the Qur'an: Semantics of the Qur'anic Weltanschauung* (Tokyo: Keio Institute of Cultural and Linguistic Studies, 1964), chapter 8 ("Jahiliyya and Islam").

38 Ibn 'Ashur, *op. cit.*, p. 51.

39 Cf. al-Shatibi, *op. cit.*, vol. 1, p. 29; al-Khatib, *op. cit.*, pp. 96, 98.

40 Cf. al-Khatib, *op. cit.*, pp. 91–2, 96.

41 Cf. Hasan al-Turabi, *Qadaya al-Tajdid: Nahw Minhaj Usuli* (Beirut: Dar al-Hadi, 2000), p. 158; al-Khatib, *op. cit.*, p. 96.

42 Ibn 'Ashur, *op. cit.*, p. 331.

43 For details on these, see M. H. Kamali, *Principles of Islamic Jurisprudence*, 3rd ed. (Cambridge: Islamic Texts Society, 2003), chapter 3 ("Rules of Interpretation").

44 Cf. 'Abd al-Majid al-Najjar, "Taf'il al-Maqasid al-Shari'a fi Mu'alajat al-Qadaya

al-Mu'asira li'l-Umma", in IIUM, *Maqasid al-Shari'a*, vol. 1, p. 24.

45 I.e. the *wājib* (obligatory), *mandūb* (recommended), *makrūh* (reprehensible), *mubāḥ* (permissible) and *ḥarām* (forbidden).

46 *Cf.* M. H. Kamali, *Punishment in Islamic Law: An Enquiry into the Hudud Bill of Kelantan* (Kuala Lumpur: Ilmiah Publishers, 2000), pp. 41–2.

47 Al-Najjar, *op. cit.*, p. 26.

48 Cf. *ibid.*, pp. 26–7.

49 For details, see Kamali, *Jurisprudence*, chapter 17 ("*Ḥukm Shar'ī*: Law or Value of *Shari'ah*").

50 The Qur'anic verses of direct relevance to equality include 2:229, 3:195, 4:12–13, 4:32, 4:34, 4:58, 16:97, 17:70, 33:55, 49:13, and 52:21.

51 There is a section on the status of women in Kamali, *Freedom, Equality and Justice in Islam*, pp. 61–78, where I have discussed the basic evidence in the text, the main juristic positions of the schools, as well as modern developments on the subject. See also M. H. Kamali, *The Dignity of Man: an Islamic Perspective* (Cambridge: Islamic Texts Society, 2002), which contains brief presentations on the commitment to essential human dignity, equality and freedom in Islam. In my latest book, *An Introduction to Shari'ah* (Kuala Lumpur: Ilmiah Publishers, 2006), revised ed., *Shari'ah Law: An Introduction*, (Oxford: Oneworld, 2008), I have presented my own views on gender equality and justice in a section of chapter 13 ("Reflection on Some Challenging Issues").

52 Further details on mid-twentieth-century family law reforms in Muslim countries can be found in M. H. Kamali, *Law in Afghanistan: A Study of the Constitution, Matrimonial Law and the Judiciary* (Leiden: E.J. Brill, 1985), pp. 154f and pp. 189f.

53 To give another example, the text prohibits usury (*ribā*) in respect of only six specified commodities, but the governing idea and purpose is to prevent exploitation, and the prohibition of *ribā* has consequently been extended to other commodities and financial instruments that are covered by that purpose. See for details on this and other examples Muhammad Baqir al-Sadr (Sa'ib 'Abd al-Hamid, ed.), *Takamul al-Mashru' al-Fikri wa al-Hadari* (Qum: Maktabat al-Sadr; Baghdad: Dar al-Kitab al-'Arabi, 1422/2002), pp. 64, 107.

54 Sherman A. Jackson, "Concretising the Maqasid: Islam in the Modern World", in IIUM, *Maqasid al-Shari'ah* (English vol.), vol. 3, p. 1.

Chapter 4

1 Mohsen Kadivar, "Hoghoogh-e Bashar va Roshanfekri-e Dini", *Aftab* 3, no. 27 (August 2003), pp. 54–9, and no. 28 (September 2003), pp. 106–15. The original was structured as an interview.

2 What I mean by the notion of human rights is the system of rights that has been set out in the Universal Declaration of Human Rights (1948), the Interna-

tional Covenant on Economic, Social and Cultural Rights and the International Covenant on Civil and Political Rights (1966). What I mean by historical Islam or the traditional reading of Islam is the Islam that is mainly represented by the al-Azhar community for Sunnis and the Al-Najaf and Qom seminaries for Shiʿis; an Islam that has produced the *Tawzih al-Masaʾil* treatises and books such as *Al-ʿUrwa al-Wuthqa*, *Tahrir al-Wasila* and *Minhaj al-Salihin* in fatwa-based *fiqh* (Islamic jurisprudence) or *Jawahir al-Kalam*, *al-Makasib*, Sarakhsi's *al-Mabsut*, Ibn Qudama's *al-Mughni* and Shawkani's *Nayl al-Awtar* in demonstrative *fiqh*.

3 In the introductory note of this article.

4 Mohsen Kadivar, "Freedom of Religion and Belief in Islam", in Mehran Kamrava (ed.), *The New Voices of Islam: Reforming Politics and Modernity – A Reader*, (London: I.B.Tauris, 2006), pp. 119–42.

Chapter 5

1 There is a growing literature on Islamic feminism; for a discussion of the literature, see Ziba Mir-Hosseini, "Muslim Women's Quest for Equality: Between Islamic Law and Feminism", *Critical Inquiry* 32 no. 1 (2006), pp. 629–45.

2 For instance, see Kecia Ali, "Money, Sex and Power: The Contractual Nature of Marriage in Islamic Jurisprudence of the Formative Period" (PhD dissertation, Duke University, 2002); Ali, "Progressive Muslims and Islamic Jurisprudence: The Necessity for Critical Engagement with Marriage and Divorce Law", in Omid Safi (ed.), *Progressive Muslims: On Justice, Gender, and Pluralism* (Oxford: Oneworld, 2003); Ali, *Sexual Ethics and Islam: Feminist Reflections on Qur'an, Hadith, and Jurisprudence* (Oxford: Oneworld, 2006); Asma Barlas, *"Believing Women" in Islam: Unreading Patriarchal Interpretations of the Qur'an* (Austin: Texas University Press, 2002); Nimat Hafez Barazangi, *Women's Identity in the Qur'an: A New Reading* (Gainesville: University of Florida Press, 2004); Riffat Hassan, "Equal Before Allah? Woman–Man Equality in the Islamic Tradition", *Harvard Divinity Bulletin* 7, no. 2 (Jan–May 1987) (also "Women Living Under Muslim Laws" in her *Selected Articles*, [n.d], pp. 26–9); Hassan, "Feminist Theology: Challenges for Muslim Women", *Critique: Journal for Critical Studies of the Middle East* 9 (1996), pp. 53–65; Hassan, "Feminism in Islam", in A. Sharma and K. Young (eds.), *Feminism and World Religions* (Albany: SUNY Press, 1999); Aziza al-Hibri, "Islam, Law and Custom: Redefining Muslim Women's Rights", *American University Journal of International Law and Policy* 12 (1997), pp. 1–44; al-Hibri, "An Introduction to Muslim Women's Rights", in Gisela Webb (ed.), *Windows of Faith: Muslim Women Scholar-Activists in North America* (Syracuse, NY: Syracuse University Press, 2000); al-Hibri, "Muslim Women's Rights in the Global Village: Challenges and Opportunities", *Journal of Law and Religion* 15, nos. 1–2 (2001), pp. 37–66; Haifaa Jawad, *The*

Rights of Women in Islam: An Authentic Approach (London: Macmillan, 1998); Fatima Mernissi (Mary Jo Lakeland, trans.), *Women and Islam: An Historical and Theological Enquiry* (Oxford: Blackwell, 1991); Saʿdiyya Shaikh, "Exegetical Violence: Nushuz in Qur'anic Gender Ideology", *Journal for Islamic Studies* 17 (1997), pp. 49–73; Amina Wadud, *Qur'an and Woman: Rereading the Sacred Text from a Woman's Perspective* (New York: Oxford University Press, 1999); Wadud, "Qur'an, Gender and Interpretive Possibilities", *Hawwa: Journal of Women of the Middle East and the Islamic World* 2, no. 3 (2004), pp. 317–36; Wadud, *Inside the Gender Jihad: Women's Reform in Islam* (Oxford: Oneworld, 2006).

3 A clear statement of position is important, as the literature on Islam and women is replete with polemic in the guise of scholarship, see Ziba Mir-Hosseini, *Islam and Gender: The Religious Debate in Contemporary Iran* (Princeton: Princeton University Press, 1999), pp. 3–6.

4 Among current scholars of Islamic law, Kamali and Abou El Fadl use this distinction; An-Naʿim does not. Muhammad Hashim Kamali, "Sources, Nature and Objectives of Shariʿah", *Islamic Quarterly* 33 (1989), pp. 215–35 at p. 216; Khaled Abou El Fadl, *Speaking in God's Name: Islamic Law, Authority and Women* (Oxford: Oneworld, 2001), pp. 32–5; Abdullahi An-Naʿim, "Islamic Foundation for Women's Human Rights", in Zainah Anwar and Rashidah Abdullah (eds.), *Islam, Reproductive Health and Women's Rights* (Kuala Lumpur: Sisters in Islam, 2000).

5 For a discussion of conceptions of justice in Islamic texts, see Majid Khadduri, *The Islamic Conception of Justice* (Baltimore: Johns Hopkins University Press, 1984). In brief, there are two main schools of theological thought. The prevailing Ashʿari school holds that our notion of justice is contingent on religious texts: whatever they say is just and not open to question. The Muʿtazili school, on the other hand, argues that the value of justice exists independent of religious texts; our sense and definition of justice are shaped by sources outside religion, are innate and have a rational basis. For a discussion of the absence of these debates in the work of contemporary jurists, see also Khaled Abou El Fadl, "The Place of Ethical Obligations in Islamic Law", *UCLA Journal of Islamic and Near Eastern Law* 4, no. 1 (2004–5), pp. 1–40. I adhere to the second position, as developed by Abdolkarim Soroush, the Iranian reformist philosopher, and Khaled Abou El Fadl, the reformist theologian and jurist. According to Soroush, we accept religion because it is just; any religious texts or laws that defy our contemporary sense of justice or its definition should be reinterpreted in the light of an ethical critique of their religious roots. In other words, religion and the interpretation of religious texts are not above justice and ethics. In summer 2004, Soroush expounded his argument in a series of four lectures on "Religious Society, Ethical Society", delivered in Amir-Kabir University, Tehran

(not yet available in print but available as audio cassettes (Tehran: Sarat)).

6 Mohammad Hashim Kamali, "Methodology in Islamic Jurisprudence", *Arab Law Quarterly* (1996), pp. 3–33 at p. 21.

7 Space does not allow me to elaborate on these differences, and the discussion below is intended merely to outline the salient features of the marriage contract; for differences between *fiqh* schools, see Muhammad Jawad Maghniyyah, *Marriage According to Five Schools of Islamic Law*, (Tehran: Department of Translation and Publication, Islamic Culture and Relations Organization, 1997), vol. 5; for a discussion of the relevance and importance of differences among the Sunni schools and their impact on the conception of gender rights, see Ali, "Money, Sex and Power".

8 Imam Abu Hamid al-Ghazali (Muhtar Holland, trans.), *The Proper Conduct of Marriage in Islam* (Adab an-Nikah), *Book Twelve of Ihya 'Ulum ad-Din (Revival of Religious Sciences)*, (Hollywood, FL: Al-Baz, 1998), p. 89. For another rendering of this passage, see Madelain Farah, *Marriage and Sexuality in Islam: A Translation of Al-Ghazali's Book on the Etiquette of Marriage from the Ihya* (Salt Lake City: University of Utah Press, 1984), p. 120.

9 Muhaqqiq Hilli (Persian trans. by A. A. Yazdi, Muhammad Taqi Danish-Pazhuh comp.), *Sharayiʿ al-Islam* (Tehran: Tehran University Press, 1985), vol. 2, p. 428.

10 This Latin phrase – literally translated as "woman's pasture" – is Ruxton's prudish rendering of the Arabic word *buzʿ* as used by Hilli, quoted above.

11 F. H. Ruxton, *Maliki Law: A Summary from French Translations of Mukhtasar Sidi Khalil* (London: Luzac, 1916), p. 106. Jorjani, another Maliki jurist, defines marriage in the following terms: "a contract through which the husband acquires exclusive rights over the sexual organs of woman" (quoted by Octave Pesle, *Le Mariage chez les Malekites de l'Afrique du Nord* (Rabat: Moncho, 1936)), p. 20.

12 For similarities in the juristic conceptions of slavery and marriage, see Shaun E. Marmon, "Domestic Slavery in the Mamluk Empire: A Preliminary Sketch", in Shaun E. Marmon (ed.), *Slavery in the Islamic Middle East* (Princeton: Department of Near Eastern Studies, 1999); Ralph Willis, "The Ideology of Enslavement in Islam: Introduction", in John Ralph Willis (ed.), *Slaves and Slavery in Muslim Africa*, vol. 1, *Islam and the Ideology of Slavery* (London: Frank Cass, 1985).

13 For these disagreements see Ali, "Progressive Muslims and Islamic Jurisprudence", pp. 70–82; for the impact of these disagreements on rulings related to *mahr* and the ways in which classical jurists discussed them, see Ibn Rushd (Imran Ahsan Khan Nyazee, trans.), *The Distinguished Jurist's Primer* (Bidayat al-Mujtahid wa Nihayat al-Muqtasid). (Reading: Garnet Publishing Ltd, 1996), vol. 2, pp. 31–3.

14 For differentiation by Hanafi jurists between social and commercial exchange,

and the valorisation of the human body, see Baber Johansen, "Commercial Exchange and Social Order in Hanafite Law", in Christopher Poll and Jakob Skovgaard-Petersen (eds.), *Law and the Islamic World: Past and Present* (Copenhagen: Royal Danish Academy of Sciences and Letters, 1995); Baber Johansen, "Valorization of the Human Body in Muslim Sunni Law", in Devin J. Stewart, Baber Johansen and Amy Singer (eds.), *Law and Society in Islam* (Princeton: Markus Wiener, 1996).

15 For a discussion, see Hammudah ʿAbd Al ʿAti, *The Family Structure in Islam* (Indianapolis: American Trust Publications, 1997); the last purpose, preservation of morality, takes the prime place in the writings of radical Islamists such as Maududi (Abul A'ala Maududi, *Laws of Marriage and Divorce in Islam* (Kuwait: Islamic Book Publishers, 1983); *Purdah and the Status of Women in Islam*, 16th ed. (Lahore: Islamic Publication (PVT) Ltd, 1998)).

16 In Shiʿi law a man may contract as many temporary marriages (*mutʿa*) as he desires or can afford. For this form of marriage, see Shahla Haeri, *Law of Desire: Temporary Marriage in Iran* (London: I.B.Tauris, 1989).

17 Many terms commonly used today in different countries for "the veil", such as *ḥijāb*, *parda* ("purdah"), *chador*, *burqa*, are not found in classical *fiqh* texts. For a discussion of *ḥijāb* in *fiqh* texts, see Murtaza Mutahhari (Laleh Bakhtiar, trans.), *The Islamic Modest Dress*, 3rd ed. (Chicago: Kazi Publications, 1992).

18 For a critical discussion of these two assumptions, see Abou El Fadl, *Speaking in God's Name*, pp. 239–247.

19 Some argue that the advent of Islam weakened the patriarchal structures of Arabian society. Abd Al ʿAti, *Family Structure in Islam*; John L. Esposito, *Women in Muslim Family Law* (Syracuse: Syracuse University Press, 1982). Others argue that it reinforced them: Leila Ahmed, *Women and Gender in Islam: Historical Roots of a Modern Debate* (New Haven: Yale University Press, 1992); Mernissi, *Women and Islam*. The latter also maintain that, before the advent of Islam, society was undergoing a transition from matrilineal to patrilineal descent, that Islam facilitated this by giving patriarchy the seal of approval, and that the Qur'anic injunctions on marriage, divorce, inheritance, and whatever relates to women both reflect and affirm such a transition. Both base their conclusions on the work of William Robertson Smith. For concise accounts of the debate, see Jane Smith, "Women, Religion and Social Change in Early Islam", in Yvonne Yazbeck Haddad and Ellison Banks Findly (eds.), *Women, Religion, and Social Change* (Albany: SUNY Press, 1985); Denise Spellberg, "Political Action and Public Example: A'isha and the Battle of the Camel", in Beth Baron and Nikki Keddie (eds.), *Women in Middle Eastern History: Shifting Boundaries in Sex and Gender* (New Haven: Yale University Press, 1991).

20 Of more than six thousand verses in the Qur'an, only a few treat men and women differently; four of these (2:222, 228 and 4:3, 34) are frequently cited as justi-

fications for unequal gender rights in marriage. For a discussion, see Shaheen Sardar Ali, "Women's Human Rights in Islam: Towards a Theoretical Framework", *Yearbook of Islamic and Middle Eastern Law* 4 (1997–8), pp. 117–52; Kh. Husein Muhammad, Faqihuddin Abdul Kodir, Lies Marcoes Natsir and Marzuki Wahid, *Dawrah Fiqh Concerning Women: Manual for a Course on Islam and Gender* (Cirebon, Indonesia: Fahmina Institute, 2006). For egalitarian interpretations of these verses, see Barlas, *"Believing Women" in Islam*; Jolanda Guardi, "Women Reading the Qur'an: Religious Discourse in Islam", *Hawwa: Journal of Women of the Middle East and the Islamic World* 2, no. 3 (2004): pp. 301–15; Muhammad et al., *Dawrah Fiqh*; Hadia Mubarak, "Breaking the Interpretive Monopoly: Re-examination of Verse 4:34", *Hawwa* 2, no. 3 (2004), pp. 290–300; Nasruddin Umar, "Gender Biases in Qur'anic Exegesis: A Study of Scriptural Interpretation from a Gender Perspective", *Hawwa* 2, no. 3 (2004), pp. 337–63; Wadud, *Qur'an and Woman*; Wadud, "Interpretive Possibilities". For Qur'anic verses denoting gender equality, see Muhammad et al., *Dawrah Fiqh*, pp. 72–5; salient among them are: 2:187, 233; 4:1; 9:71; 16:97; 30:21; 33:35; 49:13.

21 For differences among classical schools on the issue of matrimonial guardianship or *wilāya*, see Muhammad Jawad Maghniyyah, *Marriage According to Five Schools*, vol. 5, pp. 47–53.

22 See Mernissi, *Women and Islam*; Fadwa El Guindi, *Veil: Modesty, Privacy and Resistance* (Oxford: Berg, 1999), pp. 152–7; Barbara Stowasser, "The Hijab: How a Curtain Became an Institution and a Cultural Symbol", in Asma Afsaruddin and A.H. Mathias Zahniser (eds.), *Humanism, Culture, and Language in the Near East: Studies in Honor of Georg Krotkoff* (Indiana: Eisenbrauns, 1997).

23 There are two important recent studies of this, both published in Sajida Sultana Alvi, Homa Hoodfar and Sheila McDonough (eds.), *The Muslim Veil in North America: Issues and Debates* (Toronto: Women's Press, 2003). Soraya Hajjaji-Jarrah, "Women in Qur'anic Commentaries", shows the influence of social forces on the way in which the *ḥijāb* verses were understood in the works of two commentators (al-Tabari and al-Razi). Linda Clark, "Hejab According to Hadith: Text and Interpretation", shows the lack of concern with women's covering in the *ḥadīth* literature, and the lack of explicit reference to the covering of hair; there are more *ḥadīth* on men's dress and covering their *ʿawra* than on women's dress.

24 As Abou-Bakr shows, women remained active in transmitting religious knowledge, but their activities were limited to the informal arena of homes and mosques and their status as jurists was not officially recognised. Omaima Abou-Bakr, "Teaching the Words of the Prophet: Women Instructors of the Hadith (Fourteenth and Fifteenth Centuries)", *Hawwa* 1, no. 3 (2003), pp. 306–28.

25 For a critique of faith-based assumptions demeaning to women, see Abou El Fadl, *Speaking in God's Name*, pp. 207–63.

26 See Barlas, *"Believing Women" in Islam*; Hassan, "Equal Before Allah?"; Hassan, "Feminist Theology"; Mernissi, *Women and Islam*; Wadud, *Qur'an and Woman*; Wadud, "Interpretive Possibilities"; Wadud, *Inside the Gender Jihad.*

27 See Fatima Mernissi, *Beyond the Veil: Male–Female Dynamics in Muslim Society*, rev. ed. (London: Al Saqi, 1985); Mir-Hosseini, "Sexuality, Rights and Islam: Competing Gender Discourses in Post-Revolutionary Iran", in Guity Nashat and Lois Beck (eds.), *Women in Iran from 1800 to the Islamic Republic* (Urbana and Chicago: University of Illinois Press, 2004); Fatna Sabbah, *Woman in the Muslim Unconscious* (New York: Pergamon, 1984).

28 This rationale is found in many contemporary texts on women in Islam; an explicit example is Maududi, *Purdah.*

29 See, for instance, Yossef Rapoport, *Marriage, Money and Divorce in Medieval Islamic Society* (Cambridge: Cambridge University Press, 2005); Amira El Azhary Sonbol, *Women, Family and Divorce Laws in Islamic History* (Syracuse, NY: Syracuse University Press, 1996); Sonbol, "Women in Shariah Courts: A Historical and Methodological Discussion", *Fordham International Law Journal* 27 (2003–4), pp. 225–53; Judith Tucker, *In the House of Law: Gender and Islamic Law in Ottoman Syria and Palestine* (Berkeley and Los Angles: University of California Press, 2000).

30 Ali, "Progressive Muslims and Islamic Jurisprudence", p. 183.

Chapter 6

1 Muslim scholars have long pondered the exact nature of the Qur'an's origins and its precise relationship to the Divine. Early philosophers and theologians considered whether God created the Qur'an in history or whether it has always existed, co-eternal with God. The closest thing to an inquisition that Muslim civilisation ever experienced was over the "createdness" or "uncreatedness" of the Qur'anic text: what was the relationship between the heavenly archetype of the Qur'an, the "preserved tablet", and the text revealed to Muhammad in seventh-century Arabia? See Richard C. Martin (Jane Dammen MacAuliffe, ed.), "Createdness of the Qur'an", in *Encyclopaedia of the Qur'an*, (Leiden: Brill, 2001), vol. 1, pp. 467–71.

2 See Kecia Ali, *Sexual Ethics and Islam: Feminist Reflections on Qur'an, Hadith, and Jurisprudence* (Oxford: Oneworld, 2006), pp. 6–13.

3 With the possible exception of the discussions of punishment for sexual transgressions. As other scholars have argued with regard to corporal punishments such as amputation and stoning (as recorded in Sunna), one must understand these punishments as unoriginal in their ancient Near Eastern context. On punishment for illicit sex, see, e.g. 4:15–16 and 24:2–3.

4 Fazlur Rahman, *Major Themes of the Qur'an* (Minneapolis: Biblioteca Islamica, 1980), p. 47.

5 On feminist reluctance to engage with *ḥadīth*, see Linda Clarke, "Hijab according to the Hadith: Text and Interpretation", in Sajida Alvi, Homa Hoodfar and Sheila McDonough (eds.), *The Muslim Veil in North America: Issues and Debates* (Toronto: Women's Press, 2003), pp. 214–86; also Kecia Ali, "'A Beautiful Example': The Prophet Muhammad as a Model for Muslim Husbands", *Islamic Studies* 43, no. 2 (Summer 2004), pp. 273–91.

6 For an overview of the development of legal methodologies, see Wael B. Hallaq, *A History of Islamic Legal Theories: An Introduction to Sunni Usul al-Fiqh* (Cambridge: Cambridge University Press, 1999).

7 Amira Sonbol has made this argument persuasively in the introduction to her edited volume *Women, the Family, and Divorce Laws in Islamic History* (Syracuse, NY: Syracuse University Press, 1996).

8 These contradictions, however, may be of more concern for scholars concerned with theoretical consistency than for activists who focus on practical outcomes. See Kecia Ali, "Progressive Muslims and Islamic Jurisprudence: The Necessity for Critical Engagement with Marriage and Divorce Law", in Omid Safi (ed.), *Progressive Muslims: On Justice, Gender, and Pluralism* (Oxford: Oneworld, 2003), pp. 163–89; Ali, *Sexual Ethics and Islam*, chapter 6.

9 See, for instance, Mohammed Hashim Kamali's work on the *maqāṣid* or objectives of Shariʿa in this volume. With regard to gender issues specifically, see Ziba Mir-Hosseini, "Muslim Women's Quest for Equality: Between Islamic Law and Feminism", *Critical Inquiry* 32 (Summer 2006), pp. 629–45. Mir-Hosseini critiques certain "inequalities embedded in current interpretations of shariʿa" (*ibid.*, p. 644) and argues for the need to "engage with Islam's sacred texts and its legal tradition" in order to "bring change from within" (*ibid.*, p. 644). *Fiqh*, which "is nothing more than the human understanding of the divine will", must be distinguished from Shariʿa, which "is the transcendental ideal that embodies the justice of Islam and the spirit of the Koranic revelations". Further, "This transcendental ideal, which condemns all relations of exploitation and domination, underpins Muslim women's quest and the critique of patriarchal constructions of gender relation, which are to be found not only in the vast corpus of jurisprudential texts but also in the positive laws that are claimed to be rooted in the sacred texts" (*ibid.*, p. 633). The critique is deserved, yet key questions remain to be asked, including: how do verses that seemingly endorse hierarchy relate to this "transcendental ideal" of justice? While I accept the notion that "the inequalities embedded in *fiqh* are … human constructions"; and that particular doctrines, such as those governing *ṭalāq*, are not necessary interpretations of the Qur'anic text, I find unconvincing the much larger claim that "such unequal constructions contradict the very essence of divine justice as revealed in the Koran" (*ibid.*, p. 642). Although the Qur'an undoubtedly establishes justice as vital (e.g. 57:25), it does not always or fully define the content of that justice (e.g.

with regard to justice between wives in 4:129, something the jurists discussed more extensively). Insofar as the Qu'ran discusses justice, it does not explicitly define it as the same or equal treatment for each individual regardless of freedom or gender.

10 Mahmoud Mohamed Taha (Abdullahi A. An-Na'im, trans. and intro.), *The Second Message of Islam* (Syracuse, NY: Syracuse University Press, 1996). I would like to thank Lena Larsen for pointing out that the distinction between Meccan/universal and Medinan/particular verses can be referred back to al-Shatibi (on whose work see Muhammad Khalid Masud, *Shatibi's Philosophy of Islamic Law* (Delhi: Kitab Bhavan, 1997)).

11 Rahman, *op. cit.*, pp. 46–51.

12 See Tamara Sonn, "Fazlur Rahman and Islamic Feminism", in Earle H. Waugh and Frederick M. Denny (eds.), *The Shaping of an American Islamic Discourse: A Memorial to Fazlur Rahman* (Atlanta: Scholars Press, 1998), pp. 123–45.

13 Kecia Ali, "Money, Sex, and Power: The Contractual Nature of Marriage" in "Islamic Jurisprudence of the Formative Period" (PhD dissertation, Duke University, 2002); Ali, "Progressive Muslims and Islamic Jurisprudence"; Ali, *Sexual Ethics and Islam*, chapter 9.

14 The *ḥadīth* sources do present female desire and acknowledge the importance of female satisfaction, but also reproduce certain presumptions about women's acquiescence to male desire. For a preliminary investigation of some relevant texts, see Ali, *Sexual Ethics and Islam*, chapter 1.

15 See Ali, "Money, Sex, and Power"; Ali, "Progressive Muslims and Islamic Jurisprudence".

16 *Zinā'*, the major sexual crime detailed in the Qur'an, is a subset of *fāḥisha*. On this point in relation to same-sex acts and the Qur'anic story of Lot, see Scott Siraj al-Haqq Kugle, "Sexuality, Diversity, and Ethics in the Agenda of Progressive Muslims", in Safi, *Progressive Muslims*, pp. 190–234. See also the brief discussion of Lot's townsfolk, below.

17 Verse 4:34's reference to "those (fem. pl.) who guard the unseen" is also often interpreted to refer to a wife's sexual continence in her husband's absence. See the entries on morality and *'awra* in Kecia Ali and Oliver Leaman, *Islam: The Key Concepts* (London: Routledge, 2008).

18 See also 70:29–31. The text sometimes refers to "their/your spouses, *azwāj*, and what their/your right hands possess" and sometimes uses the slightly different phrase "their/your women, *nisā'*, and what their/your right hands possess". Exegetes have generally not distinguished between these uses but seen *azwāj* and *nisā'* as synonymous, meaning wives, and it is thus that both phrases have been repeatedly translated into English. *Azwāj* is a masculine/inclusive plural. In some of its Qur'anic uses it presumably refers to mates of both sexes, but it also appears referring to female spouses – as with the phrase, "*azwāj* of the Prophet". (For basic discussions of grammatical gender and Qur'anic address, see Ali,

Sexual Ethics and Islam, chapter 7, and the sources cited there.) According to traditional understandings, then, men are the only ones addressed by these verses, which permit them lawful sexual access to both their wives and those female captives or slaves whom "their right hands own".

19 The phrase "what your right hands own" (*mā malakat aymānukum*) appears in the Qur'an on a number of occasions as a euphemism for slaves or war captives, and does not always refer just to females. See 4:3, 24–5, 36; 16:71; 23:6; 24:31, 33, 58; 30:28; 33:50, 52, 55; 70:30. Some of these references use the phrase in the second-person singular or third-person plural, or specific to the Prophet (e.g. 33:50). As to the scope of the term, Ingrid Mattson suggests that the Qur'anic verses may make a distinction between permissible sex with war captives and (impermissible) sex with female slaves obtained in another fashion. Mattson, "A Believing Slave is Better Than an Unbeliever: Status and Community in Early Islamic Society and Law" (PhD dissertation, University of Chicago, 1999), pp. 131–41.

20 Few discussed the possibility of women having sexual access to their male slaves, or, for that matter, either male or female owners having sexual access to same-gender slaves. Traditionally, the Qur'anic passages that mention sexual access to "what your right hands own" have been uniformly understood to mean that only male owners had sexual rights over their female slaves. In an article in progress, I analyse two ninth-century texts that consider a woman taking her male slave as a sexual partner.

21 Ali, *Sexual Ethics and Islam*, chapter 3.

22 The only discussion of compulsion to sex is 24:33: "Do not compel your slave girls (*fatayāt*, a term also used in 4:25) to whoredom (*bighā'*)." The other sex-related uses of the concept of "whoredom" are both denials of the status of being "a whore", *baghī*, perhaps more idiomatically rendered "a slut" or, more diplomatically, "unchaste". One is Mary's own denial that she is "a *baghī*" (19:20) and another is an imputation that the term applies to her (as an unwed mother) when her own "mother was not a *baghī*" (19:28). The term is also used near "indecency" in 16:90; although the context is not overtly sexual, the joining of these terms may be significant.

23 Verse 4:24 seems to present a possible exception, but it was almost universally held by interpreters not to permit sexual access to married female captives/slaves but rather to dissolve their marriages, thus rendering them sexually lawful exclusively to their masters.

24 Ali, *Sexual Ethics and Islam*, pp. 82–3.

25 This does not mean that one cannot argue that these factors should override other considerations in defining (morally) good sex, merely that one ought to be cautious about rooting such claims in shallow scriptural ground.

26 See A. Kevin Reinhart, "Islamic Law as Islamic Ethics", *Religious Ethics* 11, no.

2 (Fall 1983), pp. 186–203; and Jonathan E. Brockopp, "Taking Life and Saving Life", in Jonathan E. Brockopp (ed.), *Islamic Ethics of Life: Abortion, War, and Euthanasia* (Columbia: University of South Carolina Press, 2003), pp. 1–19.

27 Notably, the rules presented in this verse for observing the fast are understood to apply to women as well as to the men to whom they are explicitly addressed. Interpreters have also applied different interpretive techniques to portions of the same verse or verse cluster in 5:5–6. I have addressed this point in a preliminary fashion in "Maleness and Embodiment in the Qur'an: Thoughts on Gendered Interpretation" (paper presented at the workshop "Reconsidering 'Islamic Feminism': Deconstruction or the Quest of Authenticity?", Wissenschaftskolleg, Berlin, April 2007).

28 Ali, *Sexual Ethics and Islam*, chapter 7.

29 The Qur'an does not portray female sexuality as purely passive, at least not in the story of Joseph and the ʿAziz's wife (12). The substantial interpretive literature produced on this story is central to the juristic construction of dangerous female sexuality, although not all readings are misogynistic.

30 Broadly on the historical production of sexuality, see David Halperin, *How to Do the History of Homosexuality* (Chicago: University of Chicago Press, 2002); Jeffrey Weeks, "The Rights and Wrongs of Sexuality", in Belinda Brooks-Gordon et al. (eds.), *Sexuality Repositioned: Diversity and the Law* (Portland, OR: Hart 2004), pp. 20–37; and Jeffrey Weeks, *Invented Moralities: Sexual Values in an Age of Uncertainty* (New York: Columbia University Press, 1995).

Chapter 7

1 The Personal Status Code, commonly known as the Mudawwana, was enacted in the wake of independence in 1958 as part of the Moroccanisation of the Moroccan legal system. It was prepared by a committee appointed by the late Mohammed V, composed solely of *ʿulamāʾ*, lawyers specialising in theology, including the great Salafi reformist ʿAllal al-Fasi (1910–74). The six books of the Code were drafted in five months, which hardly left time for thorough reflection on the adaptation of the legal rules of the Maliki school, on which it draws, to twentieth-century Moroccan reality. The first reform of the Personal Status Code took place in 1993 and, although deemed insufficient, received credit for desacralising the text of the Mudawwana.

2 On the subject of ambivalence over the frame of reference and its implications in Morocco, see Aïcha El Hajjami, "La problématique de la réforme du statut juridique de la femme au Maroc: entre référentiel et procédure" (The problem of reforming the legal status of women in Morocco: between frame of reference and procedure), *Revue de Droit et d'Economie* 19, no. 2 (2002), pp. 33–53 (published by the Faculty of Law of Fez).

3 The basic problems raised by the issue of women nowadays are the same in all

Muslim countries. Nevertheless, the Moroccan process in this area has been influenced by the specific political and social context of this country, which since the 1970s has experienced both a truly dynamic civil society and a real political will for change at this level.

4 Principally those introduced by the Union de l'Action Féminine (Union for Women's Action) (UAF) in a 7 March 1992 press release demanding equality between the two sexes, especially with regard to inheritance, published in the newspaper, *8 Mars* 57 (March 1992). This demand had already featured in an article signed "Souad" and published by the periodical *Démocratie*, the organ of the Democratic Independence Party, of Mohamed Ben Lhassan Ouazzani, on 4 February 1957, cited in *Monde arabe: Maghreb–Machreq*, 145 (July–September 1994), pp. 3–4.

5 On 14 March 1998 the left-wing opposition parties came to power for the first time, as part of an alternating government, following a consensus reached with the monarchy.

6 Featuring among the innovative fatwas within the sphere of women's rights is the concept of *al-kadd wa al-siʿāya*, which consists of awarding the divorced wife or widow a share of the wealth accumulated by the couple during the marriage. This concept inspired Article 49 of the new Family Code, as it had served previously as an argument put forward by the authors of the draft Action Plan in their clash with the opponents to their proposals. Consult the compendium of these fatwas compiled by Professor Mohammed El Habti El Mawahibi, *Fatawa Tatahada al-Ihmal: Fi Shafshawan wa ma Hawlaha min al-Jibal* (Ministère des Affaires Islamiques, 1998). See also: Milki Husayn, *Nizam al-Kadd wa al-Siʿaya*, 2 vols. (Rabat: Dar al-Salam, 2001).

7 Joining forces in opposition to the draft Action Plan were the *ʿulamā'*, the Islamist Party of Justice and Development, and the traditionalist Istiqlal Party, together with some members of the government, including the Minister for Islamic Affairs.

8 Two petitions for and against the Plan were circulated on this occasion. The polarisation of the conflict reached its climax on 12 March 2000, with two large rallies organised by the opposing forces, the one in Rabat by the modernists, and the one in Casablanca by the Islamists and their sympathisers, which included some persons politically affiliated with the former clan.

9 Aïcha El Hajjami, "La philosophie générale du Code de la Famille", *La revue du Forum de la Recherche Juridique* 5 (2005).

10 The stance of the two movements with regard to the two frames of reference was not as marked as one might be led to believe from the public declarations and slogans bandied about by the two movements during the debate on the draft Action Plan. An in-depth analysis of the different positions clearly shows the presence of convergences and crossovers between the two movements. It is also

worth noting that the initially radical views softened over the years under pressure from the political and social context, before ending in a consensus which allowed the adoption of the new Code. For further details on this subject, see Aïcha El Hajjami, "La problématique de la réforme".

11 Islam is rarely referred to in the literature of this movement; one speaks instead of cultural identity, heritage, or the nation. See the draft National Action Plan for the Integration of Women in Development, Arabic version (booklet of the Secrétariat d'Etat chargé de la Protection Sociale, de la Famille et de l'Enfance, 1999), p. 23. See also the two open letters sent by the Union for Women's Action (UAF) to human rights organisations in Morocco and to the Chamber of Representatives. It refers solely to international conventions. Both letters are published in *8 Mars* 57 (March 1992).

12 The position of the Islamist movement Al-Tawhid wa al-Islah published in *Mawqifuna min al-Khutta al-Maz'uma li-Idmaji al-Mar'a fi al-Tanmiya* (Our Position on the So-called Plan for the Integration of Women in Development) (Rabat: Top Presse, 2000), pp. 6, 8–17. See also the position of the dissident Islamist movement Al-ʿAdl wa al-Ihsan (Justice and Charity) in *Risalat al-Futuwwa* 14 (22 March 2000), p. 5.

13 See the "Communiqué" of the movement Al-Tawhid wa al-Islah, dated 1 January 2000, published in *Al-Tajdid* 53 (26 January 2000), p. 24.

14 See on this subject the manifesto sent by a group of *ʿulamāʾ* to the Prime Minister and to the President of the Chamber of Representatives, following publication of the press release by the UAF which demanded equality between the two sexes in family law, on 8 March 1992, in Al-Raya 25 (6 July 1992), pp. 8–10. The manifesto announced that all reforms of the Personal Status Code constituted a direct attack on the Shariʿa. Accordingly, the first reform of this Code in 1993 was greeted as the desacralisation of the Mudawwana.

15 Al-ʿIzz ibn ʿAbd al-Salam, *Qawaʿid al-Ahkam fi Masalih al-Anam*, 2nd ed. (Beirut: Dar al-Jabal, 1980), vol. 1, p. 43; Ibn al-Qayyim al-Jawziyya, *Iʿlam al-Muwaqqiʿin* (Beirut: Dar al-Fikr, n. d.), vol. 1, p. 241.

16 Al-Shatibi, *Muwafaqat*, 2nd ed. (Beirut: Dar al-Maʿrifa, 1975), vol. 4, pp. 165–7. Al-Shatibi is the first to require as a condition expert understanding of the *maqāṣid* by the *mujtahid*. *Muwafaqat*, vol. 4, pp. 105–6.

17 Muhammad Tahir ibn ʿAshur, *Maqasid al-Shariʿa al-Islamiyya* (Amman: Dar al-Nafa'is, 2001), pp. 330f; quoted from the English translation: Ibn Ashur (El-Mesawi, trans.), *Treatise on Maqasid al-Shariʿah* (London and Washington: International Institute of Islamic Thought, 2006), pp. 150–1.

18 Two other great reformers of the twentieth century adopt the same attitude with regard to the restriction on the right to equality for women, once again legitimised by reference to a woman's "nature". They are Muhammad ʿAbduh and Rashid Rida. It is true that Tahir Ibn ʿAshur relativises his judgement at

the end of the chapter on equality by specifying that the permanence of certain natural/innate impediments may be reconsidered by the *fuqahā'* or political figures.

19 See Aïcha El Hajjami, "L'option de l'ijtihâd dans la réforme de la condition juridique de la femme au Maroc" (The option of *ijtihād* in the reform of the legal status of women in Morocco), in Christiane Veauvy, Marguerite Rollinde and Mireille Azzoug (eds.), *Les femmes entre violences et stratégies de liberté: Maghreb et Europe du Sud* (Women between violence and strategies for freedom: Maghreb and Southern Europe) (Paris: Bouchene, 2004), pp. 85–6. See also Zaïd Boucha'ra, "Al-Ijtihād ma'a Wujud al-Nass" (*Ijtihād* in the Presence of the Text), *Al-Tajdid* 39 (20 October 1999), pp. 10–11.

20 On the application of the new Family Code in the courts, see the recent field study by a team under the direction of Aïcha El Hajjami, *Le Code de la Famille à l'épreuve de la pratique judiciaire* (Marrakech: Editions El Watania, October 2008).

Chapter 8

1 Lila Abu-Lughod, *Remaking Women* (Princeton: Princeton University Press, 1998), p. 7.

2 *Ala turka* and *ala franga* are two terms that were used in Turkish modernisation to denote the degree of acceptance of the Western life style. In different periods, the two terms were used with different connotations; sometimes they were used in a pejorative sense in order to criticise the opponents.

3 Seyla Benhabib, *The Claims of Culture: Equality and Diversity in the Global Era* (Princeton and Oxford: Princeton University Press, 2002), p. 84.

4 For a detailed analysis of the Young Ottomans see Şerif Mardin, *The Genesis of Young Ottoman Thought: A Study in the Modernization of Turkish Political Ideas* (Princeton: Princeton University Press, 1962).

5 *Tanzimat* means reorganisation. It was a period of reform in the Ottoman Empire from 1839 to 1876.

6 Şerif Mardin, "Yeni Osmanlı Düşüncesi" (Young Ottoman Thought), in Murat Gültekingil and Tanıl Bora (eds), *Modern Türkiye'de Siyasi Düşünce*, 5th ed., vol. 1, Mehmet Ö. Alkan (ed.), *Tanzimat ve Meşrutiyet'in Birikimi*, (Istanbul: İletişim publications, 2003), p. 44.

7 Leila Ahmed, *Women and Gender in Islam: Historical Roots of a Modern Debate* (New York: Yale University Press, 1992), p. 149.

8 *Ibid.*, pp. 151–2.

9 Chandra Talpade Mohanty, "Under Western Eyes: Feminist Scholarship and Colonial Discourses", in A. McClintock, A. Mufti and E. Shohat (eds.), *Dangerous Liaisons: Gender, Nation and Postcolonial Perspectives*, 3rd printing, (Minneapolis and London: University of Minnesota Press, 2002).

10 Marnia Lazreg, "Feminism and Difference: The Perils of Writing as a Woman

on Women in Algeria", in M. Hirsch and E. Fox Keller (eds.), *Conflicts in Feminism* (New York: Routledge, 1990).

11 Western scholarship tends to see Third World women as a homogeneous group, and to hold a homogenous notion of oppression, mostly associated with veiling. Mohanty refers to this phenomenon as methodological universalism. Its reasoning goes as follows: the greater the number of women who wear the veil, the more universal is the sexual segregation and control of women, i.e. the more women are victimised. This leads to an image of the "average Third World woman". This representation of average Muslim women in turn leads implicitly to the self-representation of Western women as modern, as having control over their own bodies and sexualities, and the freedom to make their own decisions. The relationship turns out to be between a privileged group that constitutes the norm or the referent and the "other". Mohanty, *op. cit.*, p. 258.

12 Ahmet Mithat was a prolific writer and publisher. He can be counted as one of the first proponents of the "new woman" who is not only defined by her chastity, but also by her education and success. He showed his eagerness in this cause by supporting the first female Turkish novelist, Fatma Aliye, and the particular occasion on which he wished Muslim women to be unveiled was a controversy concerning her. When she wrote her first novel, most people thought that her father (Cevdet Paşa, a prominent lawyer and minister of the time), or her teacher Ahmet Mithat should have helped her to write. His expression in the letter shows that Ahmet Mithat might have felt that if Fatma Aliye had not been veiled, he would not have been in the position of defending himself against this criticism. For the letter see *Atatürk Kitaplığı Fatma Aliye Hanım Evrakı*, File no: 14. For a portrait of Mithat, see Carter V. Findley, "An Ottoman Occidentalist in Europe: Ahmed Midhat Meets Madame Gülnar, 1889", *American Historical Review* 103, no. 1 (February 1998), pp. 15–49.

13 For instance Namık Kemal, "*Aile*", *İbret* 56 (1288 H); Namık Kemal, "Terbiye-i Nisvan Hakkında bir Layiha", *Tasvir-i Efkar* 467 (1283 H); Ahmet Mithat, *Felsefe-i Zenan* (Istanbul, 1287 H); Celal Nuri İleri, *Kadınlarımız* (Our Women) (Istanbul: İçtihat matbaası, 1331/1915); Şemseddin Sami, *Kadınlar* (Istanbul, 1311/1896); Fatma Aliye, "*Kadın Nedir?*" *Yeni Mecmua* 1, no. 21 (29 Aralık 1917), pp. 415–17; Fatma Aliye, *Nisvan-ı İslam* (Istanbul, 1309/1894); Rıza Tevfik, "*Kadın Meselesi Etrafında*", *İçtihad* 4, no. 94 (20 Şubat 1319/5 March 1913), pp. 2097–101.

14 Selim Deringil, *İktidarın Sembolleri ve İdeoloji: II. Abdülhamid Dönemi, 1876–1909* (Istanbul: YKY Publications, 2002), pp. 157–71. Originally published in English as Deringil, *The Well-Protected Domains: Ideology and the Legitimation of Power in the Ottoman Empire, 1876–1909* (London: I.B.Tauris, 1999).

15 "The worlding of a world … inscribed what was presumed to be uninscribed. Now this worlding actually is also a texting, textualising, a making into art, a

making into an object to be understood". Gayatri Spivak, "Criticism, Feminism, and the Institution", in Sarah Harasym (ed.), *The Post-colonial Critic: Interviews, Strategies, Dialogues* (New York and London: Routledge, 1990), p. 1.

16 İsmail Kara, *Din ile Modernleşme Arasında: Çağdaş Türk Düşüncesinin Meseleleri* (Istanbul: Dergah Publications, 2003), p. 29.

17 *Ibid.*, pp. 41–6.

18 *Ibid.*, pp. 54–9.

19 Egyptian reformist Qasim Amin in 1899 wrote *Tahrir al-Mar'a* (The Liberation of Woman), in which he argued on Islamic grounds for a complete transformation in practices related to women.

20 Selahattin Asım wrote a book called *Türk Kadınlığının Tereddisi yahut Karılaşmak* (The Degeneration of Turkish Womanhood) (Istanbul: Resimli Kitab Matbaası, n.d.). He explicitly addresses the question of unequal share in inheritance, and argues that women should be treated equally in this respect; otherwise, their economic dependence on men would cause them to be treated as sexual objects, not as persons.

21 Nuri İleri, *Kadınlarımız* (Istanbul: Içtihat Matbaası, 1331/1915).

22 Halil Hamit, *İslamiyette Feminizim yahut Alemi Nisvanda Müsavaat-ı Tamme* (Feminism in Islam or Full Equality in the World of Women) (Istanbul : Leon Lütfi, 1328/1912).

23 Ahmet Cevat, *Bizde Kadın* (Istanbul: "Kadĭr" Matbaasĭ, 1328/1912).

24 Fatma Aliye Hanım, "İlim ve Cehl" (Knowledge and Ignorance), *Inkılab* 7 (4 September 1909), pp. 1–2.

25 For a brief history of women's movements in Ottoman times see Serpil Çakır, *Osmanlı Kadın Hareketi* (Women's Movement in Ottoman Times) (Istanbul: Metis publications, 1994).

26 Deniz Kandiyoti, "End of Empire: Islam, Nationalism and Women in Turkey", in Deniz Kandiyoti (ed.), *Women, Islam and the State* (Philadelphia: Temple University Press, 1991), p. 23.

27 Ayşe Durakbaşa, "Cumhuriyet Döneminde Modern Kadın ve Erkek Kimliklerinin Oluşumu: Kemalist Kadın Kimliği ve 'Münevver Erkekler'" (The Formation of Modern Man and Woman Identities in the Republican Period: Kemalist Woman Identity and "Enlightened Men"), in Ayşe Berktay Mirzaoğlu (ed.), *75 Yılda Kadınlar ve Erkekler* (Istanbul: TVY Publications, 1998).

28 Mustafa Kemal Atatürk, Türkan Arıkan (ed.), *Atatürk'ün Türk Kadını Hakkındaki Görüşlerinden Bir Demet* (Ankara: TBMM Publications, 1984), p. 2.

29 Etyen Mahçupyan, "Osmanlı'dan Günümüze Parçalı Kamusal Alan ve Siyaset", *Doğu ve Batı* 5 (November–January 1998–9), p. 23.

30 Abu'l Ala al-Mawdudi, Muhammad Qutb, Hüseyin Hatemi, Abdurrahman Dilipak and Bekir Topaloğlu were among the writers of "women and Islam" books.

31 *Zaman Gazetesi* was founded by a religious group in 1986. It has since been acquired by another group, affiliated to the Fethullah Gülen community (Nur Cemaati), but that happened after the aforementioned debates took place. The owners and publishing team were a somewhat autonomous group.
32 Ali Bulaç, "Feminist Bayanların Kısa Aklı", *Zaman* (17 March 1987).
33 Mualla Gülnaz, "Ali Bulaç'ın Düşündürdükleri", *Zaman* (1 September 1987); Tuba Tuncer, "*Kimin Aklı Kısa?*" *Zaman* (1 September 1987); Elif H. Toros, "Feminist Kime Derler?" *Zaman* (15 September 1987); Yıldız Kavuncu, "İslam'da Kadın ya da İpekböceği", *Zaman* (29 September 1987).
34 Yeşim Arat, "1980'ler Türkiye'sinde Kadın Hareketi: Liberal Kemalizm'in Radikal Uzantısı", in Necla Arat (ed.), *Türkiye'de Kadın Olgusu* (Istanbul: Say Publications, 1992), p. 90.
35 Nilüfer Göle, *The Forbidden Modern: Civilization and Veiling* (Ann Arbor, MI: University of Michigan Press, 1997). Originally published as *Modern Mahrem: Medeniyet ve Örtünme* (Metis, 1991).
36 "Türbanlı Feministler", *Nokta* 50 (1987).
37 Ruşen Çakır, *Direniş ve İtaat: İki İktidar Arasında İslamcı Kadın* (Resistance and Obedience: Islamist Women between Two Powers) (Istanbul: Metis Publications, 2000).
38 Hidayet Şefkatli Tuksal, Cihan Aktaş, Yıldız Ramazanoğlu, Sibel Eraslan and Mualla Gülnaz are among the writers who use feminist terminology in their writings.

Chapter 9

1 In this context, I take note of the tradition attributed to the Prophet that states: "Defer to your heart even if others advise you, advise you and advise you."
2 On the authenticity of this report, see Ibn Qayyim al-Jawziyya (ʿAbd al-Rahman Muhammad ʿUthman, ed.), *ʿAwn al-Maʿbud Sharh Sunan Abi Dawud,* 2nd ed. (Medina: al-Maktaba al-Salafiyya, 1968/1969), vol. 6, pp. 177–8.
3 Ibn Hajar al-ʿAsqalani, *Fath al-Bari: Sharh Sahih al-Bukhari* (Beirut: Dar al-Maʿrifa, n.d.), vol. 9, p. 294.
4 Ibn Qayyim al-Jawziyya, *op. cit.*, vol. 6, p. 179.
5 Al-Mubarakfuri, *Tuhfat al-Ahwadhi bi Sharh Jamiʿ al-Tirmidhi* (Beirut: Dar al-Kutub al-ʿIlmiyya, n.d.), vol. 4, pp. 283–4.
6 Ibn Fawzan (ʿAdil b. ʿAli b. Ahmad al-Faridan, ed.) *Al-Muntaqa min Fatawa Fadilat al-Shaykh Salih b. Fawzan b. ʿAbd Allah Ibn Fawzan,* 2nd ed. (Medina: Maktabat al-Ghurban al-Athariyya, 1997), vol. 3, pp. 14–15, 40, 56, 294, 300, 307, 308, 309–10, vol. 5, pp. 123–35; al-ʿUthaymin (Ashraf b. ʿAbd al-Maqsud ʿAbd al-Rahim, ed.), *Fatawa al-Shaykh Muhammad al-Saliḥ al-ʿUthaymin* (Riyad: Dar ʿAlam al-Kutub, 1991), vol. 1, pp 352–3, 362–3, vol. 2, pp. 825–8; Ibn Baz et al. (Qasim al-Shamaʿi al-Rifaʿi, ed.), *Fatawa Islamiyya* (Beirut: Dar

al-Qalam, 1988), vol. 3, pp. 182, 183–4, 189, 204–5; Ibn Baz, (Muhammad b. Sa'd al-Shawi', ed.), *Majmu' Fatawa wa Maqalat Mutanawwi'a* (Cairo: Maktabat Ibn Taymiyya, 1990), vol. 2, pp. 84–5, 173, 189–91, vol. 4, pp. 242–4, 254–8; Ahmad b. 'Abd al-Razzaq al-Dawish (ed.), *Fatawa al-Lajnah al-Da'ima li al-Buhuh al-'Ilmiyya wa al-Ifta'* (Riyad: Dar 'Alam al-Kutub, 1991), vol. 4, pp. 126–7.

7 Abu Zakariyya Muhyi al-Din b. Sharaf al-Nawawi, *Sharh Sahih Muslim al-Musamma al-Minhaj Sharh Sahih Muslim b. Hajjaj* (Beirut: Dar al-Ma'rifa, 1996), pp. 17–18:57–8; al-Mubarakfuri, *op. cit.*, vol. 6, p. 356–9; Isma'il b. Muhammad al-'Ajluni al-Jirahi, *Kashf al-Khafa' wa Muzil al-Ilbas 'an ma Ishtahar min al-Ahadith 'ala Alsinat al-Nas*, 2nd ed. (Beirut: Dar Ihya' al-Turath al-'Arabi, 1968), p. 39.

8 Ibn Hajar al-'Asqalani, *op. cit.*, vol. 9, p. 137; al-Mubarakfuri, *op. cit.*, vol. 8, p. 53; al-Nawawi, *op. cit.*, 17–18:57; Ibn Jar Allah al-Yamani (Muhammad 'Abd al-Qadir Ahmad 'Ata, ed.), *al-Nawafih al-'Atira fi al-Ahadith al-Mushtahira* (Beirut: Mu'assasat al-Kutub al-Thaqafiyya, 1992), p. 306; al-Jirahi, *op. cit.*, p. 183; al-Sakhawi (Muhammad 'Uthman al-Khasht, ed.), *al-Maqasid al-Hasana fi Bayan Kathir min al-Ahadith al-Mushtahira 'ala al-Alsina*, 2nd ed. (Beirut: Dar al-Kitab al-'Arabi, 1994), p. 428; al-Shaybani, *Kitab Taymiz al-Ṭayyib min al-Khabith fi ma yadur 'ala Alsinat al-Nas min al-Hadith* (Beirut: Dar al-Kitab al-'Arabi, n.d.), p. 144.

9 Al-Jirahi, *op. cit.*, pp. 315–6; al-Shaybani, *op. cit.*, p. 183.

10 Al-Mubarakfuri, *op. cit.*, vol. 4, p. 283.

11 This version is considered to be of weak transmission. Another version asserts that women have two sources of effective protection, a husband and the grave. See Abu Hamid al-Ghazali, *Ihya' 'Ulum al-Din* (Beirut: Dar al-Ma'rifa, n.d.), vol. 2, p. 58. At the symbolic level, this tradition is consistent with reports that assert that a woman, in total, is a *'awra*. See Abu al-Sa'adat al-Mubarak b. Muhammad Ibn al-Athir al-Jazri (Abu 'Abd al-Rahman b. 'Uwida, ed.), *al-Nihaya fi Gharib al-Hadith wa al-Athar* (Beirut: Dar al-Kutub al-'Ilmiyya, 1997), vol. 3, p. 288.

12 Al-Nawawi, *op. cit.*, pp. 9–10, 181.

13 Qur'an 6:164, 17:15, 35:18, 39:7, 53:38, 24:11, 2:286, 4:32, 33:58.

14 Reportedly, these verses were revealed in response to several incidents in which the hypocrites of Medina harassed and molested Muslim women. Fakhr al-Din Muhammad b. 'Umar b. al-Husayn al-Razi, *al-Tafsir al-Kabir li al-Imam Fakhr al-Din al-Razi*, 3rd ed. (Beirut: Dar Ihya' al-Turath al-'Arabi, 1999), vol. 9, pp. 183–4; Abu Ja'far Muhammad b. Jarir al-Tabari (Bashshar 'Awwad Ma'ruf and 'Isam Faris al-Harastani, eds.), *Tafsir al-Tabari min Kitabihi Jami' al-Bayan 'an Ta'wil Ayat al-Qur'an* (Beirut: Mu'assasat al-Risala, 1994), vol. 6, pp. 199–200; Abu 'Abd Allah Muhammad b. Ahmad al-Ansari al-Qurtubi, *al-Jami'*

li Ahkam al-Qur'an (Beirut: Dar al-Kutub al-'Ilmiyya, 1993), vol. 14, pp. 157–8; 'Imad al-Din Abu al-Fida' b. 'Umar Ibn Kathir (Muhammad 'Ali al-Sabuni, ed.), *Mukhtaṣar Tafsir ibn Kathir*, 7th ed. (Beirut: al-Qur'an al-Karim, 1981), vol. 3, pp. 114–15.

15 See for such reports 'Abd al-Halim Abu Shuqqa, *Tahrir al-Mar'a fi 'Asr al-Risala* (Kuwait: Dar al-Qalam, 1990), vol. 2, pp. 174–348.

16 Ibn Kathir, *op. cit.*, vol. 3, pp. 108–9; al-Qurtubi, *op. cit.*, vol. 14, pp. 143–8; al-Tabari, *op. cit.*, vol. 6, pp. 195–6; al-Razi, *op. cit.*, vol. 9, pp. 178–80.

17 Abu Ja'far Muhammad b. Jarir al-Ṭabari, *Jami' al-Bayan fi Tafsir al-Qur'an* (Beirut: Dar al-Ma'rifa, 1989), vol. 18, pp. 93–5, vol. 22, pp. 33–4; Abu al-Barakat 'Abd Allah b. Ahmad b. Mahmud Hafiz al-Din al-Nasafi, *Tafsir al-Nasafi* (Cairo: Dar Ihya' al-Kutub al-'Arabiyya, n. d.), vol. 3, pp. 140, 313; Abu Bakr Ahmad b. 'Ali al-Razi al-Jassas, *Ahkam al-Qur'an* (Beirut: Dar al-Kitab al-'Arabi, 1986), vol. 3, pp 409–10, 486; 'Imad al-Din b. Muhammad al-Kiyya al-Harrasi (Musa Muhammad 'Ali and 'Izzat 'Ali 'Id 'atiyya, eds.), *Ahkam al-Qur'an*, (Cairo: Dar al-Kutub al-Haditha, 1974), vol. 4, pp. 288, 354; Abu Bakr Muhammad b. 'Abd Allah Ibn al-'Arabi ('Ali Muhammad al-Bajawi, ed.), *Ahkam al-Qur'an* (Beirut: Dar al-Ma'rifa, n.d.), vol. 3, pp. 1368–78, 1586–87; al-Qurtubi, *op. cit.*, vol. 12, pp. 152–3, 157, vol. 14, pp. 156–7; Ibn Kathir, *op. cit.*, vol. 2, p. 600, vol. 3, pp. 114–15; Muhammad b. Yusuf Abu Hayyan al-Andalusi ('Adil 'Abd al-Mawjud and 'Ali Muhammad Mu'awwad, eds.), *Tafsir al-Bahr al-Muhit* (Beirut: Dar al-Kutub al-'Ilmiyya, 1993), vol. 6, p. 412, vol. 7, pp. 240–1; Abu al-Qasim Jar Allah Mahmud b. 'Umar al-Zamakhshari, *al-Kashshaf 'an Haqa'iq al-Tanzil wa 'Uyun al-Aqawil fi Wujuh al-Ta'wil* (Beirut: Dar al-Fikr, n.d.), vol. 3, pp. 60–2, 274; Abu al-Faraj 'Abd al-Rahman b. 'Ali b. Muhammad Ibn al-Jawzi (Ahmad Shams al-Din, ed.), *Zad al-Masir fi 'Ilm al-Tafsir* (Beirut: Dar al-Kutub al-'Ilmiyya, 1994), vol. 5, pp. 377–8; vol. 6, p. 224; Abu al-Hasan 'Ali b. Muhammad b. Habib al-Mawardi (al-Sayyid b. 'Abd al-Maqsud b. 'Abd al-Rahim, ed.), *al-Nukat wa al-'Uyun* (Beirut: Dar al-Kutub al-'Ilmiyya, 1992), vol. 4, pp. 90–3, 424–5; Muhammad al-Amin b. Muhammad al-Mukhtar al-Shinqiti, *Adwa' al-Bayan fi Idah al-Qur'an bi al-Qur'an* (Beirut: 'Alam al-Kutub, n.d.), vol. 6, pp. 192–203, 586–600; Taqi al-Din Ahmad b. 'Abd al-Halim Ibn Taymiyya ('Abd al-Rahman 'Umira, ed.), *al-Tafsir al-Kabir* (Beirut: Dar al-Kutub al-'Ilmiyya, n.d.), vol. 6, p. 23; al-Razi, *al-Tafsir al-Kabir*, vol. 23, pp. 176–9, vol. 25, pp. 198–9; Abu Muhammad 'Abd al-Haqq b. Ghalib al-Andalusi Ibn 'Atiyya ('Abd al-Salam 'Abd al-Shafi, ed.), *al-Muharrar al-Wajiz fi Tafsir al-Kitab al-'Aziz* (Beirut: Dar al-Kutub al-'Ilmiyya, 1993), vol. 4, p. 178, 399; Jalal al-Din 'Abd al-Rahman b. Abi Bakr al-Suyuti, *al-Durr al-Manthur fi al-Tafsir bi al-Ma'thur* (Cairo: Matba'at al-Anwar al-Muhammadiyya, n.d.), vol. 5, pp. 45–6, 239–41; Isma'il Haqqi al-Burusi (Muhammad 'Ali al-Sabuni, ed.), *Tanwir al-Adhhan min Tafsir Ruh al-Bayan* (Damascus: Dar al-Qalam,

1989), vol. 3, pp. 57–9, 254–5; Abu Hafs ʿUmar b. ʿAli bin ʿAdil al-Dimashqi, ʿAdil Ahmad ʿAbd al-Mawjud and ʿAli Muhammad Muʿawwad (eds.), *al-Lubab fi ʿUlum al-Kitab* (Beirut: Dar al-Kutub al-ʿIlmiyya, 1998), vol. 14, pp. 355–8, vol. 15, pp. 588–90; Abu al-Fadl Shihab al-Din al-Sayyid Mahmud al-Alusi, *Ruh al-Maʿani fi Tafsir al-Qurʾan al-ʿAzim wa al-Sabʿ al-Mathani* (Beirut: Dar Ihyaʾ al-Turath al-ʿArabi, 1985), vol. 18, pp. 140–2, vol. 22, p. 89; Ahmad b. Muhammad al-Sawi, *Hashiyat al-ʿAllama al-Sawi ʿala Tafsir al-Jalalayn* (Beirut: Dar Ihyaʾ al-Turath al-ʿArabi, n.d.), vol. 3, pp. 136–7, 288–9.

18 Ibn Qayyim al-Jawziyya, *op. cit.*, vol. 2, p. 277; Ibn Hajar al-ʿAsqalani, *op. cit.*, vol. 2, p. 350; ʿAlaʾ al-Din ʿAli al-Muttaqi b. Husam al-Din al-Burhan Fawzi al-Hindi, *Kanz al-ʿUmmal fi Sunan al-Aqwal wa al-Afʿal* (Beirut: Mu'assasat al-Risala, 1985), vol. 16, pp. 413–14.

19 Sahnun b. Saʿid al-Tanukhi, *Al-Mudawwana al-Kubra* (Beirut: Dar al-Kutub al-ʿIlmiyya, 1994), vol. 1, p. 195; Abu Muhammad ʿAbd Allah b. Abi Zayd al-Qayrawani (ʿAbd al-Fattah al-Hilw, ed.), *al-Nawadir wa al-Ziyadat* (Beirut: Dar al-Gharb al-Islami, 1999), vol. 1, p. 296; Abu Muhammad ʿAbd Allah b. Ahmad b. Muhammad Ibn Qudama, *al-Mughni* (Beirut: Dar Ihyaʾ al-Turath al-ʿArabi, n.d.), vol. 2, p. 44; Abu Shuqqa, *op. cit.*, vol. 2, pp. 195–202.

20 Ibn Hajar al-ʿAsqalani, *op. cit.*, vol. 2, pp. 101–2; Abu Shuqqa, *op. cit.*, vol. 2, pp. 181–94.

21 Al-Mubarakfuri, *op. cit.*, vol. 1, p. 402; al-Nawawi, *op. cit.*, pp. 5–6, 145–6; Ibn Hajar al-ʿAsqalani, *op. cit.*, vol. 2, pp. 54, 55, 351.

22 Shams al-Din Muhammad b. Ahmad b. ʿUthman al-Dhahabi, *Siyar Aʿlam al-Nubalaʾ*, 4th ed. (Beirut: Mu'assasat al-Risala, 1986), vol. 3, p. 172.

23 For a review of such authors, see Wael Hallaq, *A History of Islamic Legal Theories: An Introduction to Sunni Uṣūl al-Fiqh* (Cambridge: Cambridge University Press, 1997), pp. 207–54. Fazlur Rahman arguably relies on a similar process in his book on the Qur'an. However, he does not address law, and in fact considers the positive legal tradition and its institutions partly to blame for moral stagnancy. Fazlur Rahman, *Major Themes of the Qur'an*, 2nd ed. (Minneapolis: Bibliotheca Islamica, 1994), pp. 47–8. See also Abdolkarim Soroush, Mahmoud Sadri and Ahmad Sadri (trans.), *Reason, Freedom, and Democracy in Islam: Essential Writings of Abdolkarim Soroush* (New York: Oxford University Press, 2000).

24 Rahman, *op. cit.*, pp. 42–3, 46–51; Toshihiko Izutsu, *Ethico-Religious Concepts in the Qur'an* (Montreal: McGill University Press, 1966), pp. 209–11.

25 Emphases added.

Chapter 10

1 This argument is presented in detail in *Islam and the Secular State: Negotiating the Future of Shariʿa* (Cambridge, MA: Harvard University Press, 2008). The manuscript of this book in several languages of Islamic societies can be down-

loaded from the website: http://www.law.emory.edu/fs.

2 John Rawls, *Political Liberalism* (New York: Columbia University Press, 2003), p. 442.

3 *Ibid.*, pp. 442–3.

4 Jürgen Habermas, "Reconciliation Through the Public Use of Reason: Remarks on John Rawls' Political Liberalism", *Journal of Philosophy* 92, no. 3 (March 1995), pp. 109–31 at pp. 118–19, 129.

5 See, generally, Wael B. Hallaq, *The Origins and Evolution of Islamic Law* (Cambridge: Cambridge University Press, 2005).

6 Essam Fawzy, "Muslim Personal Status Law in Egypt: The Current Situation and Possibilities of Reform Through Internal Initiatives", in Lynn Welchman (ed.), *Women's Rights and Islamic Family Law: Perspectives on Reform* (London: Zed Books, 2004) pp. 15–94.

7 Mahmoud Mohamed Taha, *The Second Message of Islam* (Syracuse, NY: Syracuse University Press, 1987); and Abdullahi Ahmed An-Na'im, *Toward an Islamic Reformation: Civil Liberties, Human Rights and International Law* (Syracuse, NY: Syracuse University Press, 1990).

Chapter 11

1 "An International call for Moratorium on corporal punishment, stoning and the death penalty in the Islamic World", http://www.tariqramadan.com/article.php3?id_article=264&lang=en.

2 In some Arab and African countries countries the death penalty or the corporal punishments are not directly implemented in the name of Islam, but the societies accept it in silence because the common understanding is that such laws are legitimated by the Islamic teachings, and therefore *per se* cannot be opposed.

3 "An Impotent Call", *Islamonline.net*, 19 April 2005, http://www.islamonline.net/english/In_Depth/ShariahAndHumanity/Articles/2005-04/08.shtml.

4 Taha Jabir al-'Alawani, "Unacceptable Allegation", *IslamOnline.net*, 19 April 2005, http://www.islamonline.net/english/In_Depth/ShariahAndHumanity/Articles/2005-04/09.shtml.

5 Dr Muzzamil H. Siddiqi, "Response on Dr Tariq Ramadan's Call for Moratorium on the Hudud Law of Islam", *IslamOnline.net*, 19 April 2005, http://www.islamonline.net/english/In_Depth/ShariahAndHumanity/Articles/2005-04/06.shtml.

6 The Arabic statement may be found attached to my response at http://oumma.com/Reponse-au-communique-de-la.

7 Dr Jum'a's response and my reply are available in English at http://www.tariqramadan.com/article.php3?id_article=323&lang=en. The Arabic text of his response first appeared at http://www.islamonline.net/Arabic/news/2005-03/30/article09a.shtml.

8 In the United States, where an African-American is far more likely to be executed than a White, opposition to the death penalty appears to me to be the only position in conformity with the message of Islam.

9 A sampling of these reactions can be found on my website, http://www.tariqramadan.com. There have also been several good discussions in French on the *Oumma.com* website, http://www.oumma.com.

10 Al-Qaradawi said he had been told that I was rejecting the clear-cut texts of the Qur'an and speaking against the Shari'a, but now that my position had become clearer to him, he wanted to study the text of the Call. I have since seen him answer an online query to the effect that, if what the Call means is that we have to start by implementing justice, that is right.

11 Dina Abdel-Mageed, "Tariq Ramadan's Call for a Moratorium: Storm in a Teacup", *IslamOnline.net*, 18 April 2005, quoting Sano Koutoub Mustapha, a scholar of the Islamic Fiqh Academy of the Organization of the Islamic Conference (OIC) (http://www.islamonline.net/English/Views/2005/04/article01.SHTML).

12 Cf. Aziz Zemouri, *Faut-il faire taire Tariq Ramadan*? (Paris: L'Archipel, 2005). This is a long dialogue with a journalist addressing sensitive legal, social and political issues.

13 My book *Radical Reform: Ethics and Liberation* (forthcoming) tackles the issue of "ethics" and "objectives" for our time and proposes a new way to think about it. I also address the moratorium debate and its scope.

Chapter 12

1 Some of the pivotal scholarship that has assisted women's groups in their work for reform includes: Khaled Abou El Fadl, *Speaking in God's Name: Islamic Law, Authority and Women* (Oxford: Oneworld, 2001); Leila Ahmed, *Women and Gender in Islam: Historical Roots of a Modern Debate* (New Haven: Yale University Press, 1992); Asghar Ali Engineer, *The Qur'an, Women and Modern Society* (New Delhi: Sterling Publishers Private Limited, 1999); Abdullahi Ahmed An-Na'im, *Towards an Islamic Reformation: Civil Liberties, Human Rights and International Law* (Syracuse, NY: Syracuse University Press, 1990); Asma Barlas, *"Believing Women" in Islam: Unreading Patriarchal Interpretations of the Qur'an* (Austin: University of Texas Press, 2002); Farid Esack, *Qur'an, Liberation and Pluralism: An Islamic Perspective of Interreligious Solidarity against Oppression* (Oxford: Oneworld, 1997); Muhammad Hashim Kamali, *Freedom of Expression in Islam* (Kuala Lumpur: Ilmiah Publishers, 1998); Ziba Mir Hosseini, *Islam and Gender: The Religious Debate in Contemporary Iran* (London and New York: I.B.Tauris, 2000); Fatih Osman, *Concept of the Qur'an: A Topical Reading* (Kuala Lumpur: ABIM, 2000); Fatih Osman, *Muslim Women in the Family and Society* (Kuala Lumpur: Sisters in Islam, 1996); Abdolkarim Soroush (Mahmoud Sadri and Ahmad Sadri, trans.), *Reason, Freedom and Democracy*

in Islam (Oxford: Oxford University Press, 2000); Barbara Stowasser, *Women in the Qur'an, Traditions and Interpretation* (Oxford: Oxford University Press, 1994); Amina Wadud, *Qur'an and Woman: Rereading the Sacred Text from a Woman's Perspective* (New York: Oxford University Press, 1999).

2 Malaysia has a plural legal system for Muslims and non-Muslims with regard to personal laws, charitable endowments, bequests, inheritance and offences that are not governed by federal law; the latter include matrimonial offences, *khalwat* (close proximity), and offences against the precepts of Islam. The "Islamic" laws apply only to Muslims, who cannot opt out of them and use civil laws instead.

3 Islamic Family Law (Federal Territories) Act 1984 [Act 303], amended in 1994 by the Islamic Family Law (Federal Territories) (Amendment) Act 1994 [Act A902] and in 2006 by the Islamic Family Law (Federal Territories) (Amendment) Act 2006 [Act A1261], which was enacted by Parliament in December 2005, with Royal Assent granted by the Yang di-Pertuan Agong (King) in January 2006.

4 Syariah Criminal Offences (Federal Territories) Act 1997 [Act 559].

5 In principle, a *fatwa* is a non-binding legal opinion issued in response to a legal problem by a qualified scholar, the Mufti. In the Malaysian legal system, however, the Mufti is a state-appointed official whose fatwas are gazetted as public documents.

6 Administration of Islamic Law (Federal Territories) Act 1993 [Act 505], Articles 34–6; Syariah Criminal Offences (Federal Territories) Act 1997 [Act 559], Articles 9, 12, and 13. Most state legislatures passed corresponding laws in the same time period.

7 Syariah Criminal Code (II) 1993 State of Kelantan, passed 25 November 1993; Syariah Criminal Offences (Hudud and Qisas) (Terengganu) Enactment 2003, passed 8 July 2002, gazetted 27 October 2003. These laws have not yet been implemented.

8 Islamic Family Law (Federal Territories) (Amendment) Act 2006 [Act A1261], which is not yet in force as of 1 November 2007.

9 Article 160 of the Federal Constitution of Malaysia defines Malays as Muslims. The religion of Malaysians of Chinese and Indian descent is not defined.

10 See Kamali, *op. cit.*; S. A. Rahman, *Punishment of Apostasy in Islam* (New Delhi: Kitab Bhavan, 1996).

11 http://www.sunnah.org/history/Scholars/mashaykh_azhar.htm; cf. Abdullah Saeed and Hassan Saeed, *Freedom of Religion, Apostasy and Islam* (Aldershot: Ashgate, 2004), p. 139.

12 The state of Perlis passed the Islamic Aqidah Protection (Perlis) Bill in April 2000. It was based on the model statute drafted by the federal authorities. In the face of public opposition, the federal bill has never been tabled in the Federal Parliament.

Chapter 13

1 The following brief survey is largely based on D. Sourdel, “Khalifa”, and A. K. S. Lambton, “Khalifa in Political Theory”, in *Encyclopedia of Islam*, new ed. (Leiden: E. J. Brill, 1978), vol. 4, pp. 937–50.
2 Lambton, *op. cit.*, p. 948.
3 Abu al-Hasan al-Mawardi, *al-Ahkam al-Sultaniyya* (Cairo: Halabi, 1973), p. 6.
4 *Ibid.*
5 G. Levi della Vida, “Kharijites”, in *Encyclopedia of Islam*, vol. 4, p. 1133.
6 Muḥammad ibn Isma‘īl Bukhārī, *Sahih* (Riyadh: Dar al-Salam li al-nashr wa al-tawzi‘, 1997), *ḥadīth* no. 693, 697 (chapter “Adhan”), p. 140.
7 Ibn Qutayba, *al-Imama wa al-Siyasa* (Cairo: Mu’assat al-Halabi, n.d.), pp. 12–19.
8 Lambton, *op. cit.*, p. 949.
9 Iqbal said that to his knowledge no scholar in India or Egypt had opposed this view. Mu‘in al-Din Aqil states that the *‘ulamā’* of al-Azhar issued a fatwa against Atatürk, but he has not reproduced a text. Aqil, *Iqbal awr Jadid Dunyai Islam* (Lahore: Maktaba Ta‘mir Insaniyat, 1986), p. 231. It is, however, immaterial whether a fatwa was actually issued. The question that Iqbal raised, namely, whether the caliphate could be transformed into a representative institution rather than being vested in an individual, was not under consideration. In fact it still is not so.
10 M. Naeem Qureshi has studied the Khilafat Movement in depth in *Pan-Islam in British Indian Politics: A Study of the Khilafat Movement 1918–1924* (Leiden: Brill, 1999).
11 Emad Eldin Shahin, “Muhammad Rashid Rida”, in *The Oxford Encyclopedia of the Modern Islamic World* (Oxford: Oxford University Press, 1995), vol. 3, pp. 410–12.
12 Eric Davis, “Ali Abd al-Raziq”, in *The Oxford Encyclopedia of the Modern Islamic World*, vol. 3, pp. 5–7.
13 *Ibid.*, citing ‘Ali ‘Abd al-Raziq, *Al-Islam wa Usul al-Hukm: Bahth fi al-Khilafa wa al-Hukuma* (Cairo: Ratba’ sarika mahima miṣriya, 1925), p. 90.
14 Iqbal read this poem at an annual meeting of the Anjuman Himayat Islam, Lahore. The poem struck a very emotional popular response. See Jawed Iqbal, *Zinda Rud* (Lahore: Shaykh Ghulam Ali, 1983), p. 277. The poem is included in Iqbal, *Bangi Dara: Kulliyati Iqbal* (Lahore: Shaykh Ghulam Ali, 1975).
15 This lecture formed a part of a series of lectures later delivered in Madras and Aligarh during 1928–30. These lectures were published by the Oxford University Press in 1934 with the title *The Reconstruction of Religious Thought in Islam*. The lecture “al-Ijtihad fi’l-Islam” constitutes the sixth chapter entitled “The Principle of Movement in the Structure of Islam”. This paper refers to the following edition: Muhammad Iqbal (M. Saeed Sheikh, ed.), *The Reconstruc-*

tion of Religious Thought in Islam (Lahore: Institute of Islamic Culture, 1986).

16 *Ibid.*, p. 124.

17 *Ibid.*, pp. 124–5.

18 Muhammad Iqbal (Chaudhari Muhammad Husayn, Urdu trans.), "Khilafat Islamiyya", in Sayyid Abdul Wahid Mu'ìni (ed. and coll.), *Maqalat Iqbal* (Lahore: Sh. Muhammad Ashraf, 1963), pp. 85–112 at p. 88.

19 Muhammad Iqbal (S. Y. Hashimi, ed.), *Islam as an Ethical and a Political Ideal* (Lahore: Islamic Book Service, 1977), p. 103.

20 Iqbal, *Reconstruction*, p. 125.

21 *Ibid.*, p. 125.

22 *Ibid.*, p. 125.

23 Muhammad Iqbal, *Islam and Ahmadism* (Lahore: Sheikh Muhammad Ashraf, 1976), pp. 47–8.

24 This book is based on the presidential address delivered in Calcutta at the Khilafat Conference in 1920. It was published the same year by the newly founded Urdu type printing press in Calcutta in 1920 with the title *Mas'ala Khilafat awr Jazirat al-'Arab*. See Khaliq Anjum, *Mawlana Abul Kalam Azad: Shakhsiyyat awr Karname* (Lahore: Tayyib Publishers, 2005), pp. 41, 395.

25 See Abu'l Kalam Azad, *Mas'ala Khilafat* (Lahore: Khayaban Irfan, n.d.), pp. 89–111.

26 The pamphlets *Hizb al-Tahrir* (1985) and *al-Khilafa* (n.d.).

27 Israr Ahmad, *Khutbat i khilafat* (Lahore: Markazi Anjuman Khuddam al-Qur'an, 1996).

28 *Ibid.*, p. 84.

29 *Ibid.*, p. 88.

30 *Ibid.*, p. 98.

31 *Ibid.*, p. 97.

32 *Cf.* Mohammad Hashim Kamali, *Principles of Islamic Jurisprudence*, rev. ed. (Cambridge: Islamic Texts Society, 1991), p. 34.

33 Abu Ishaq al-Shatibi, *Al-Muwafaqat fi Usul al-Shari'a* (Beirut: Dar al-Ma'rifa, 1975), vol. 2, p. 25; see also Muhammad Khalid Masud, *Shatibi's Philosophy of Islamic Law* (Kuala Lumpur: Islamic Book Trust, 2000), p. 152.

34 Shatibi, *Muwafaqat*, p. 307.

35 *Ibid.*, pp. 2–10.

36 Masud, *op. cit.*, p. 94.

37 Shah Waliullah, *Hujjat Allah al-Baligha* (Lahore: al-Maktaba al-Salafiyya, n.d. (Cairo: Bulaq, 1878)), vol. 1, p. 4.

38 *Ibid.*, vol. 1, p. 124.

Chapter 14

1 This is not a verbatim record of the debate. It has been edited for brevity, clarity and style. The participants have had the opportunity to revise their own words; only those revisions that have added substantial new points are marked with brackets.

2 Bernard G. Weiss, *The Search for God's Law: Islamic Jurisprudence in the Writings of Sayf al-Din al-Amidi* (Salt Lake City: University of Utah Press, 1992).

Index